Psychotropic Drugs
and Popular Culture

Psychotropic Drugs and Popular Culture

*Essays on Medicine,
Mental Health and the Media*

Edited by LAWRENCE C. RUBIN

McFarland & Company, Inc., Publishers
Jefferson, North Carolina, and London

ISBN 0-7864-2513-X (softcover : 50# alkaline paper)

Library of Congress control number 2006014346

LIBRARY OF CONGRESS CATALOGUING DATA ARE AVAILABLE

British Library cataloguing data are available

Cover art ©2006 Super Stock Images

Manufactured in the United States of America

*McFarland & Company, Inc., Publishers
Box 611, Jefferson, North Carolina 28640
www.mcfarlandpub.com*

For Randi, Zach and Becca

Acknowledgments

The idea for this volume originated during a brief moment of clinical downtime at a colleague's practice. Waiting for my next client, I wandered through the empty offices, which in a few short hours would become centers of bustling psychiatric and psychotherapeutic activity. I was immediately struck by a plastic handlotion dispenser, emblazoned with the Prozac logo. Antidepressant skin care! Was this possible? As I read the contents of the bottle, I was soon informed that "This product contains no Fluoxetine," which is the active ingredient in Prozac.

While I had been to this office many times in the past, and mused with my colleague about the lavish lunches the pharmaceutical reps supplied to entice and remind, I suddenly became aware of the myriad office supplies, trinkets, and toys that virtually littered the offices ... each brandishing the logo of one of many pharmaceutical companies and their psychotropic offerings. There were notepads, sticky pads, clip boards, paper clip holders, wall clocks, desk clocks, tissue boxes, computer mice, mousepads, telephone shoulder rests, plastic bag dispensers, coffee mugs, cups and of course pens, pencils and markers ... and numerous professional journals and popular magazines peppered with psychotropic drug ads. I was fascinated!

My burgeoning fascination took me to the Internet, which I realized was an outlet for a veritable cornucopia of (psycho-) pharmaceutical merchandise, Prozac earrings included. Subsequent eBay searches using psychotropic keywords took me to the Web sites of pharmaceutical giants, where once again I was reminded of the plethora of drugs designed to treat anxiety, depression and psychosis. And soon, it was the magazine ads, prime time commercials, television and movie dialogue and song lyrics containing references to Prozac, lithium, Valium and Thorazine that peaked my interest, which had started during my graduate studies in clinical psychology over two decades before.

This "merchandising of madness," as I came to call it, was a tailor made outlet for the expression and integration of my varying research interests, which encompassed popular culture, cultural studies, advertising, collecting and medical sociology. More than anything else, it reinforced and gave voice to my passion for thinking outside of the box. And it is this particular passion that I am grateful to my wife Randi for nurturing, to my children Zachary and Rebecca for tolerating, and to my parents, Esther and Herbert, for recognizing many years before. I thank my brother Ken, whose own psychiatric professionalism has provided a healthy tension for the ideas found in this book, his wife Deborah, who satisfied my appetite for psychotropic merchandise and my oldest brother Stephen, whose intellectual curiosity and cool savvy have been an inspiration. I thank all of the essayists in this book who gave of their time and creative energies. And finally, thanks to Ben Mirtenbaum for lending me his bottle of Prozac hand lotion. I promise to return it.

Table of Contents

Introduction

Marx said that religion is the opiate of the people. In the United
States today, opiates are the religion of the people.[1]
                                                    — Thomas Szasz

The content of the medium is like the juicy piece of meat carried by the burglar to distract the watchdog of the mind.[2]
                                                    —Marshall McLuhan

In 1961, sociologist Erving Goffman[3] focused national attention on the
dehumanizing conditions of psychiatric institutions, or as he referred to
them, asylums. This attention, along with the advent of psychotropic medication, was one of several factors contributing to the subsequently debated
deinstitutionalization of the mentally ill. Now, over four decades later, while
this debate continues, the use of psychotropic medication for both serious
and benign symptomatology has become endemic to our culture. This proliferation is due in large part to the simultaneous success of the advertising and media industries at reinstitutionalizing our society into a
modern-day psychotropic drug culture. This "Psychotropia" has become
the new asylum, and we its inmates.

When Goffman wrote his landmark exposé, he sought to demonstrate
how psychiatric hospitals, like monasteries, prisons and the military, were
"total institutions," which systematically medicalized, homogenized and
dehumanized their occupants. The inmate began to participate as, and was
seen as, a "third person" in their own life. While discharge from the formal
bounds of the institution ended the inpatient phase of their indoctrination,
their life was transformed. They no longer needed to be surrounded by
institutional walls (prison, military, religious or psychiatric) in order
to identify themselves as a member of the asylum. In Goffman's view,
their autonomy, self-sufficiency and identity became forever shaped by

membership in the asylum, regardless of whether they happened to be residing within or beyond its walls.

Goffman's work was groundbreaking. It was among several confluent social, economic and political forces that would ultimately bring about a sweeping change. In place of the fortresses that once dominated the psychiatric landscape of the first half of the nineteenth century was erected a loosely constructed network of care for those who once inhabited them. More germane, however, is how the line that once so neatly divided the mentally ill from the mentally healthy evolved into a circle enveloping them both. The argument here being proposed is that the boundary delineating these two societal factions has, with the proliferation of psychotropic medication, been blurred to the point that with the exception of the floridly mentally ill, it has become difficult to know where mental health ends and mental illness begins. Without such a boundary, the whole of society becomes a potential community of deviance — a global asylum, and all its citizens, residents. Deviant behavior is measured against prevailing standards of normalcy and then categorized according to those standards (diagnostic criteria). Consumers are socialized through the process of medication management into the sick role, provided with a medicalized re-interpretation of their suffering and along with their intimates, begin to view the events in their lives through the lens of pathology — their route to mental health depending largely on compliance with their medication regimen.

The infusion of psychotropic drugs into the consummate body politic of American culture has forever transformed our society into a wall-less asylum — a Psychotropia. The communal need, whether real or manufactured, for psychotropic drugs derives from our culture's perception of itself as psychologically damaged or disturbed. The more disturbed it perceives itself to be, the greater its need for relief from that disturbance. The greater the need for relief from that disturbance, the more openly it embraces a cure for it. Clearly tautological, this argument nevertheless leads us to reflect on the relationship between illness, cure and culture. More specifically, it requires us to ask how we have been sold on the ubiquity of mental illness to the point that we readily walk through the gates of Psychotropia, diagnosis in hand, heads bowed, and mouths open in eager anticipation of the host of psychotropic salvation.

This selling of psychiatric salvation has gone by several names: commodification, disease mongering and medicalization, the mention of which reveals the postmodern constructivist bias of the essays in this volume. Inherent in each of the terms is the notion that there is a fundamental difference between disease and illness. They all resonate with the argument that a disease is an objective and objectifiable entity, while an illness is a subjective experience, which may or may not have an organic or bodily basis.

In this regard, the American public has, through massive and brilliantly crafted advertising campaigns, been targeted by psychotropic drug manufacturers. Our health-fixated culture has by virtue of mass communication and the media been overwhelmed by a hyped-up reality of images, and given a vision of a hyper-reality[4] of psychiatric well-being. Movies and television shows carry dialogue referencing psychotropic drugs by their brand names, and the music industry is replete with lyrical references to antidepressants, anxiolytics, sedatives and stimulants.

In 1961, social critic Marshall McLuhan urged a public awakening to an electronic revolution to avoid the message in the medium, as it was merely the juicy meat carried by the burglar to distract the watchdog of the mind. The implication of this metaphor was that if we could tame and utilize our media to extend our psychic and physical abilities rather than be seduced by their content, we could thrive in the postmodern era and not be imprisoned by its illusions. With regard to the marketing of psychotropic drugs through the media, McLuhan's fateful warning has apparently gone unheeded. We have become so accustomed to the power of psychotropic drugs (McLuhan's juicy meat), that our otherwise vigilant watchdogs of self control and autonomy have been exchanged at the gates of the asylum for a prescription to psychotropic well-being.

* * *

In Chapter 1, "The Asylum: Its Construction and Deconstruction," William Wingfield traces the origins of the brick and mortar asylum through a sociohistorical discussion of mental illness that takes us across continents and time. Through a poignant analysis of the social, political, medical and cultural forces that shaped our perception and treatment of the mentally ill, Wingfield shows us how the psychotropic revolution was a historical inevitability, which with the advent of mass media, television in particular, brought us to the doorstep of the virtual asylum.

Chapter 2, "Hollywood Rx" by Meredith Kneavel and Ann Kneavel, will addresses the place and implication of psychotropic drug references in movies, both past and present, cutting across film genres, e.g., comedy, drama, fantasy and musical. In doing so, they reveal the perceived role that psychotropics play in the lives of the protagonists, and the cultural implications.

In Chapter 3, which is titled "Cheerful Robots in Cyberspace: Prozac, Postmodernism, and Politics," Simon Gottschalk moves from a discussion of the ideological aspects of psychiatric discourse and the contextual aspects of psychotropic drugs to a conversation about the self in Interaction Theory. A sampling of psychotropic ads on the internet are embedded in an interpretation of psychiatric illness and of the distortion of social relations and the (re)construction of the self in cyberspace.

In Chapter 4, "Advertising Madness," I focus on the proliferation of print advertisement for psychotropic medicines in professional and popular magazines. I focus on the cultural and historical forces that have shaped this proliferation: decontextualization (the reduction of problems in living to mental illness), commodification (the creation of mental illness to sell cures), marginalization (reducing the physician's role to that of pill dispenser) and gender issues, as they have been affected by this movement.

Chapter 5, "Psychotropics, It's What's for Dinner! Technologies of Sex, Gender, the Body and Mind in the Medicalization of Food" by Phillip Vannini, discusses how a psychotropic society is a synoptic one, in which the presentation of a deviant self is punished through the disciplining of one's eating. The deviant and abnormal — arguably all of us — are persuaded to eat psychotropic foods that are marketed as powerful antidepressive and anti-anxiety agents, hallucinogens, antipsychotics, and tranquilizers. Such "psychotropization" of food turns eating into a medicalized practice responsible for curing shortcomings in sexual and gender performances.

In Chapter 6, "Rappers, Ravers, and Rock Stars: The Deviantizing Hand of Music in Psychotropia," Robert Keller argues that music is one of the strongest, if not the strongest forms of media through which to communicate with the masses. Its role in our self-imposed asylum is both complex and unique. This chapter explores the direct and indirect references to psychotropic and psychoactive drugs in various popular music venues, e.g., rock, hip-hop, club music and rap. In this way, it is argued that the music and pharmaceutical industries work hand in hand to maintain the demand for psychotropics that they have created, thus oiling the machinery of Psychotropia.

In Chapter 7, "From Playground to Pharmacy: Medicating Childhood" by Michael Brody, M.D., the marketing of psychotropic drugs to children and the psychiatric medicalization of childhood is addressed. It focuses on the rise of biological psychiatry, the selling of psychotropics to parents for normal and pathological childhood states and the place of this phenomenon in popular media-driven culture.

In Chapter 8, "False Advertising: Gender Stereotypes, Corporate Manipulation, and Consumer Resistance," C. Richard King and Marcie L. Gilliland address the influence of patriarchy and gender bias in psychiatry and psychotropic drug advertising and their subversion through counterculture advertising.

Notes

1. See T. Szasz, *Ideology and Insanity* (Garden City, N.Y.: Anchor Press, 1970).

2. See M. McLuhan and Q. Fiore, *The Medium Is the Message: An Inventory of Effects* (New York: Bantam, 1967).

3. For a complete discussion of the concept of the asylum, see E. Goffman, *Asylums* (New York: Anchor Books, 1961).

4. For discussions on the concept of hyper-reality, see J. Baudrillard, "Hyperreal America," *Economy and Society* 22, no. 2 (1993), pp. 243–252; and J. Beaudrillard, "The masses: the implosion of the social in the media," *New Literary History* 16, no. 3 (1985), pp. 577–589.

1 The Asylum

Its Construction and Deconstruction
William Wingfield

> From the middle of the seventeenth century, madness was linked
> with this country of confinement, and with the act which des-
> ignated confinement as its natural abode.
> — Michel Foucault, *Madness and Civilization*

Madness and medicine have been associated since the first medicine
man attempted to heal an illness without a detectable physical cause. However, the mad were not segregated and isolated from the community. As
society became more complex, in an attempt to achieve greater social economy, the mad and other deviants were confined. The asylum came into existence as Europe began to modernize and new social institutions began to
emerge.

Origins of the Asylum

When what has been called the Age of Confinement began in the seventeenth century, the mad, along with other deviant classes such as the
poor, the petty criminals, the vagabonds, the sick and the aged were incarcerated in "general hospitals" in France.[1] The hospitals were not places of
treatment, but houses of confinement where those classes that were perceived as a threat to the social order were sequestered.[2] Within the context
of confinement existed changed attitudes and expectations toward the mad
as well as the poor. When such people no longer wandered the European
landscape, madness was confined, with poverty. No longer free to wander,

the insane were expected to work, as were those in other deviant classes. Through labor, the confined groups would reimburse their caretaker, the state. The creation of new houses of confinement reflected

> a new sensibility to poverty and to the duties of assistance, new forms of reaction to the economic problems of unemployment and idleness, a new ethic of work, and also the dream of a city where moral obligation was joined to civil law, within the authoritarian forms of constraint.[3]

The unemployed would be sheltered and fed, but at the cost of their freedom.[4]

The process of confinement spread across France during the latter part of the seventeenth and early part of the eighteenth centuries. By the beginning of the French Revolution, general hospitals had been established in thirty-two provincial cities. Elsewhere, different forms of the confinement process occurred. In German speaking countries, workhouses (*Zuchthausen*) were established during the same period. Houses of confinement in England were called houses of correction, and such institutions were established at about the same time as *Zuchthausen* and general hospitals. By the end of the eighteenth century an entire network of centers of confinement had appeared in England, Holland, Germany, France, Italy, and Spain. An Englishman, John Howard, investigated centers of confinement and in each instance, in every country, found the insane, the profligate, the disturbers of the peace and the unemployed confined within the same walls.[5] On what basis were the mad confined with other deviant groups? Confinement

> marked a decisive event: the moment when madness was perceived on the social horizon of poverty, of incapacity for work, of inability to integrate with the group; the moment when madness began to rank among the problems of the city. The new meanings assigned to poverty, the importance given to the obligation to work, and all the ethical values that are linked to labor, ultimately determined the experience of madness and inflected its course.[6]

As the insane were incarcerated, treatment regimens, modified only by the prevailing medical theories, were promulgated. All of the medical theories of the time pertaining to insanity were based on an organic origin of the disease. Whether insanity was caused by an imbalance of bodily humors or an irritation of the nerves, the affliction was considered somatic in origin.[7] Treatment measures were based on two contradictory views of insanity and treatment: the mad were physically diseased with a bizarre malady, and treatment was consequently heroic — purging, venesection, hot and cold baths, emetics, beatings, and chaining — or the insane were "the afflicted of God," punished with madness for their sins and in need of clerical dispensation.

It follows then, that the curability or incurability of insanity became either a medical issue or a moral issue.[8] The physician either bled, shocked, beat, purged or terrorized[9] the mad into a return to reason or abandoned them to confinement. What constituted treatment in confinement was not treatment, but rather an effort to maintain order. Treatment that debilitated and terrorized the confined was a form of coercion that sought conformity to the norms of the house of confinement.

According to Foucault, the insane were displayed to their fellow townspeople for two purposes: first, by charging an admission fee, the officials of the institution where the mad were confined obtained funds to support the institution; second, to demonstrate that the man of unreason no longer had anything in common with the man of reason. The mad were chained and displayed like captured wild beasts, because they were feared as the realization of the beast in man. The "beast" had crossed the boundaries of "bourgeois order of his own accord and had alienated himself outside the sacred limits of its ethic."[10] Madmen, thus, must suffer the consequences of their behavior—confinement, ridicule, pity—and they must serve as a warning to the reasoning members of the populace.[11]

Reinforced by the increasing pressures of urbanization, industrialization and changing social values and attitudes,[12] the Age of Confinement continued until the end of the eighteenth century in Europe and also in America.[13] The history of the insane in Colonial America followed a pattern similar to that of Europe, although the American experience was, at least initially, not an exact replica of the older culture, as Richard Shryock pointed out:

> It is unlikely that the settlers of the English colonies brought with them many who were recognized as mentally abnormal. Those who were obviously "of unsound mind" were presumably left behind during the Atlantic passage.[14]

As the population of the colonies and the communities within those colonies became more urban, the insane grew in number and in public visibility. As did their European forebears, the colonists grouped together the poor and the mad. In part because of their religious beliefs, the early Americans perceived society as hierarchical:

> At the root of the religious position was the premise that the existing social order had divine approbation, that its form was not accidental or fortuitous, but providential. A higher design made some men rich, eminent and powerful and others low, mean and in subjection.[15]

Furthermore, this perception included a prescription for good works. The rich and powerful had an opportunity to extend Christian charity to the poor. Good works benefited society, for it brought men together and offset self-gratification with brotherly love. Thus the poor performed a necessary function in society and became a permanent part of the social order, not a threat to it. The secular view of colonial society was similarly hierarchical, with the poor accepted as a part of an orderly and cohesive society.[16]

Combined with the religious and secular perceptions of society were the English Poor Law traditions, which inculcated the belief that the community was responsible for poor relief.[17] There were two forms of relief used by the colonists, outdoor and indoor. The term outdoor relief (outside of an institution) refers to that form of charity that maintains the individual or family at home. Indoor (within an institution) relief refers to relief extended the individual housed either in the community's almshouse or workhouse.[18]

The colonists considered the family the most important unit in society so outdoor relief was the dominant form of charity in early American society. With the community directly and intimately involved in the relief of the poor, who were often relatives, friends or neighbors, a provincial insularity developed. Strangers who moved to a particular community were forced to meet extensive and rigid settlement laws that pertained particularly to requirements for legal residency. Residency was realized only after the individual or family had resided in a given locale for a period of one or two years. During the interim, the applicant for residency was required to post a bond to ensure that he and his family would not become dependent on the community or that in the event that dependency became a reality, the community would not have to assume the economic burden.

Individuals or families who could not meet the settlement laws were "warned out," that is, asked to leave the community. The wandering poor, the insane, the disabled, and criminals were thus forced to wander from township to township, occasionally being housed in the town jail overnight before being forced to move on to another community.[19]

As the communities increased in size, both geographically and in terms of population, outdoor relief gave way to indoor relief in the form of almshouses, workhouses and jails. The first almshouses relieved those individuals who were too incapacitated, by reason of insanity, amputation, paralysis, or chronic illness, to be cared for at home or by a neighbor. Other than attending religious services, little was expected of the almshouse inhabitants.

The workhouse was not widespread in Colonial America. Boston built the first workhouse in the colonies, but in reality the workhouse was little different from the almshouse. Built with the expectation that the able bodied indigents would perform some menial tasks for the community and thereby defray the cost of the upkeep, the workhouse domiciled the same type of individuals who inhabited the almshouse: the old, the amputees, the insane, or otherwise disabled persons who could not perform manual labor.[20] Finally, the jails confined the criminals, the criminally insane and the insane whose behavior required confinement away from their homes and who could not be allowed to roam about the community.[21] In sum, Colonial Americans preferred to provide outdoor relief to the poor regardless of the reason for the individual's poverty. Institutional confinement was a result of increasing population, urbanization and behavior or disabilities that could not be tolerated or treated at home.

Urbanization

Urban growth led directly to the establishment of the first hospitals in America, at Philadelphia in 1752 and at New York in 1791. Both hospitals were important in the history of mental illness because they accepted the physically ill as well as insane patients.[22] Treatment of the deranged at these hospitals followed the pattern of European management of the insane. Heroic measures were employed such as venesection, purging with emetics and laxatives, shock treatment in the form of alternating hot and cold baths, and restraints such as iron shackles and the straitjacket. Treatment of the insane in American society occurred within the same perceptual context as European society; insanity was regarded either as an organic illness or as a moral affliction.

As an example of the organic approach, Benjamin Rush, the "Father of American Psychiatry," was associated with the Philadelphia Hospital from 1783 to 1813.[23] According to Norman Dain, a historian of psychiatry in America, Rush served as a transitional figure in the treatment of madness in the United States.[24] He retained the physiological view of insanity that had marked the medical approach to madness. At the Philadelphia Hospital, Rush used bloodletting, purging, physical restraints, shock treatment (alternating hot and cold baths) and, in extreme instances, whippings. These procedures, Rush believed, were cures for mental derangement. Rush's somatic approach to insanity was based on his belief that fever was the source of madness. Fever, for Rush, meant an expansion of the blood vessels in the brain, with resulting delerium or excitation. Consequently, he adopted treatment methods which were intended to reduce blood pressure, which, in turn, would restore equilibrium and then sanity.[25]

Rush invented two mechanical devices, the gyrator and the tranquilizer chair. The gyrator was designed to spin the patient, in a prone position, at a gradually increasing speed, thereby forcing the blood from the patient's brain. The tranquilizer chair completely immobilized the patient in order to lessen his excitement, thus allowing the brain blood to relocate in another area of the body.[26] However, while he remained faithful to the somatic approach, and in spite of what appears to be torture and not treatment, Rush advocated a more humane treatment of the mad. (Although Rush was a contemporary of Philippe Pinel and William Tuke, it is not known to what extent he was aware of their "moral treatment" methods. Pinel's book was not translated into English until 1806 and Tuke's methods were initially transmitted to America by the Quakers in 1813.[27] When Rush published *Medical Inquiries and Observations, Upon the Diseases of the Mind* in 1812, he included an assessment of Pinel's and Tuke's methods.)

When Rush became affiliated with the Pennsylvania Hospital, in 1783,[28] he recommended that the deranged patients be removed from the cellars and that separate quarters be provided for them. Rush also argued for the proper heating and cooling of the living quarters provided to the insane; that the area be kept neat and clean; that the patients be allowed to bathe regularly; that qualified attendants be provided for their supervision; and finally, that the physician should be honest with the patients.[29] So while Rush continued to practice a physiological approach to insanity, he blended with a somatic theory of madness a treatment regimen that in some respects approximated a new therapeutic mode known as "moral treatment."

Deutsch[30] and Riese[31] argued that Rush initiated psychotherapeutic techniques in American psychiatry. Deutsch, in particular, states that Rush anticipated Freud by requesting patients write down their innermost thoughts, no matter how painful. Dain[32] and Shyrock[33] disavow this argument, stating that Rush used what appeared to be psychotherapeutic techniques for humanitarian and empirical reasons, rather than as a rational approach to the cure of mental illness.

In retrospect, the American Rush was a bridge[34] between the two worlds of organic treatment and moral management of the insane. By continuing to use primarily somatic approaches to insanity, he represented the heroic measures of the past, but by introducing to the hospital environment reforms that resembled "moral management," Rush gave medical legitimacy and thus contributed to the acceptance of moral treatment in the United States.

Social Attitudes

Public attitudes toward and treatment of the insane did not begin to change perceptibly until Philippe Pinel unchained the mad at Bicetre and

Salpetriere during the French Revolution. At the same time that Pinel was unchaining the lunatic in Paris, William Tuke was establishing a retreat for the insane at York, England (1792–1796).[35] Both of these men, independent of each other, advocated a more humanitarian approach to treatment of the mad, based on the belief that insanity was a curable disease. Pinel and Tuke theorized that "moral treatment," as their ideas became known, would lead to a recovery of reason if the tenets of moral management were followed.

The philosophy of moral treatment for lunacy wrought a profound change on the landscape of madness, both in Europe and in America. After the intellectual ferment of the Enlightenment and the social, political and economic changes wrought by the American and French Revolutions,[36] moral philosophy was a convergence of different trends in Western thought realized explicitly in the theories of madness promulgated by Pinel and Tuke.[37] Their theories were based on the belief that man was ultimately perfectible and so, therefore, was society. When Pinel unchained the mad at Salpetriere and Tuke established the York Retreat, both advocated a specific treatment regimen that was summarized by Norman Dain in a recent article:

> Although the traditional medical therapies were not wholly discarded, the emphasis was on kindness, compassion, consideration, warmth, good company, freedom of movement, occupation, recreation, the elimination of physical punishment, appeals to the moral sense, persuasion, and training in good habits and self control. Hospitals were to be in a rural setting with considerable acreage not so much to isolate patients as to afford them healthful living, space in which to roam, land on which they could busy themselves gardening or farming, and freedom from disturbing relatives and prying neighbors. Such provision was seen as a vital aspect of treatment, indispensable to the cure as well as the comfort of the patients.[38]

Although Pinel and Tuke advocated similar treatment tenets, there were fundamental differences in their treatment philosophies.

Pinel, a French physician, based his treatment on freeing the mad from their chains (in modern terms, relaxing social control), in order that the external controls of social shackles would be internalized (developing self control). Another aspect of Pinel's treatment philosophy was that of encouraging dialogue between patients so that each madness would be confronted by another madness, and that somewhere in between, "the truth would emerge."[39] Finally, in Pinel's asylum, there was a circumstance "of constant judgement of the patient" by the hospital's staff, so that a patient's inappropriate behavior could be punished.[40] The form of punishment was considerably less heroic than in the past. Punishment consisted primarily of restraints and cold baths; the efficacy of bleeding, purging and whippings was disavowed by Pinel and his European colleagues.[41]

William Tuke, an English Quaker merchant, employed, in addition to the treatments summarized by Dain, religious training and physical labor as a means of ameliorating lunacy. Religious training was intended to soothe the distraught mind, while the order and regularity of physical labor obviated any possibility of the individual "guest" dwelling on those thoughts that perpetuated his madness.[42]

Thus, through Pinel and Tuke, the scientific rationalism of the Enlightenment was combined with the bourgeois moral and work ethics. Rational treatment was deployed to change the man of unreason into the man of reason. Rationalism, religion and labor, in this instance, were perceived as mediators between the society of reason and the subculture of unreason; between the rational, orderly world of civilized man and the chaotic natural world. Tuke, the merchant, and Pinel, the physician, were representative of, respectively, the world of work and the world of science, both of which were opposed to the chaos of nature and committed to the rational order of society.[43]

Both Tuke and Pinel proposed and carried out the segregation of the mad from the rest of society, in asylums erected specifically for the care of the insane. Segregation was essential from their point of view in order to remove the environmental influences that had driven the asylum inhabitants to madness. Another perception of the segregation of the mad was that they represented a threat to the social order. Confinement was intended to protect society and not just the mad[44] (an early precedent of the modern legal committment proceedings determining "danger to one self or others").

Rush, Pinel and Tuke agreed that the insane should be segregated from the general populace and confined in asylums. They also agreed that a more humane approach to treating the mad would result in a higher rate of recovery. Individually, however, they represented the convergence of three components that would alternately submerge and reemerge in modified form throughout the history of psychiatric thought, during the nineteenth and twentieth centuries.

Benjamin Rush's main contribution was in the perpetuation of the belief in a neurological source of insanity.[45] In the twentieth century this belief led to the treatment modes of psychosurgery and psychotropic medication. Tuke incorporated in his treatment scheme the work ethic which became, again in modified form, modern occupational therapy. Pinel inculcated the mediating role of the physician, as diviner between rational society and the irrational mad.[46] These three elements of work ethic, moral treatment and removal from society would be inextricably intertwined in America, from the end of the eighteenth century throughout the nineteenth and into the twentieth century, until the Community Mental Health Center Act in 1964.

While moral treatment in America was the product of the intellectual changes provoked by the Enlightenment and the American and French revolutions, the collapsing and changing of society and modes of conduct reflected itself in the level of acceptance on society's part for a more humane treatment. The continuing change in American demography, the development of an economic elite, and the fusion of religious thought led some to the perception that society was drifting toward anarchy.

Demography was changing as a result of two reciprocally reinforcing factors and the extent of mental illness: urbanization and immigration. Not only were the number of urban areas growing, but the social problems due to the size of the urban areas were also increasing. The change in the pattern of urban development was the result, in part, of the expanding immigration, which also changed the composition of urban areas. As uneducated and unskilled immigrants arrived in America, they tended to congregate in the cities. Unable to find employment that would have allowed them the opportunity of achieving a physically and emotionally healthy life, the new arrivals fell victim to various illnesses, including insanity. Thus the process of urbanization and immigration put added pressure on urban areas to provide adequate care for the physically and emotionally ill who were unable to provide health care for themselves.[47]

But why did society need reforming? Rothman suggests that the social and political changes taking place in America led the leaders of antebellum society to believe that American society was losing its stability and consequently drifting toward anarchy. In order to halt the process, it was necessary to initiate programs of reform, which included the asylum movement.[48]

Finally, all the necessary elements had converged to set the stage for the erection of "insane asylums." Social and intellectual forces held the view that society required reforming, and there ensued a "short lived spurt in the founding of private (and corporate) hospitals"[49] for the mentally ill. The movement was largely confined to New England and other northeastern states. Two American Quaker groups agitated for and succeeded in establishing separate asylums for the insane in New York and Pennsylvania. During this first phase of asylum building in America, William Tuke and the York Retreat had more influence than his contemporary, the Frenchman Philippe Pinel, because of Tuke's contacts with his fellow Quakers in New England. Asylums were also founded in Connecticut and

Massachusetts. The New York Quaker group effected the separation of the insane asylum from its parent, the New York Hospital, through the efforts of Thomas Eddy, and became the Bloomingdale Asylum. The Friends Retreat at Frankford, Pennsylvania, the McLean Asylum at Boston, and the Hartford Retreat at Hartford were opened between 1811 and 1824. The Bloomingdale Asylum began transferring patients from the New York Hospital in 1821.[50]

When the Hartford Retreat began accepting patients in 1824, the private and corporate phase of insane asylums dwindled as the impetus for erecting hospitals for the insane was transferred to the states. With the state (public) asylums, all the inadequacies of moral treatment in the insane asylum would be realized.

The belief that social institutions were failing in their roles reflected an environmental approach to social problems. Social deviancy—crime, poverty, and insanity—could thus be explained in terms of an unsatisfactory environment.[51] In addition to shifts in the population settlement areas, the increase in the population itself heightened awareness by society of the increased deviant groups. The erection of state-supported insane asylums was but one aspect of a broader social reform movement directed at the eradication of various social ills and social deviance, especially poverty, crime and insanity.[52]

The process by which asylum superintendents assisted social critics by placing madness within the context of an industrializing but disordered civilization was complicated. When the Association of Medical Superintendents of American Institutions for the Insane (AMSAII) was formed in 1844, it was not an organization of men with a commonly agreed upon body of knowledge and theories regarding causes and treatment of the insane which sought to mold the approaches society adopted to deal with the insane population. According to Grob, the opposite was true.[53] American society had assigned to the superintendents and the asylums the roles they would play in dealing with a particular deviant group.[54] Ideologies set forth by the asylum superintendents tended to be consistent with the social attitudes toward, and conditions within, the asylums.[55] Because their training and experience were primarily confined to existing structures, the asylum superintendents tended to confirm the social values that had confined the mad. As Foucault pointed out, doctors of the mad were first and foremost agents of society at large, and second, physicians to the insane. So the formation of a professional organization that espoused views in harmony with those of American society at large was consistent with the social roles assigned the superintendents.

The social background of the individual association members themselves reflected social acceptance and perpetuated the use of value systems not embraced or common to the insane, who were regarded as socially deviant. "Before 1860 virtually all of them were from middle class, Protestant backgrounds, college educated and medical school graduates. Minority ethnic and racial groups simply were not represented, nor were women ever employed as superintendents."[56] Furthermore most of the asylum superintendants were from rural communities in the Northeast, where they had been taught an "agrarian and rural" outlook.[57] As a result of their social milieu and educational background, the asylum superintendants and their professional organization perceived madness as conduct which departed from their own ideas of what constituted normal or socially acceptable behavior. As Grob states, "A substantial part of psychiatric theory, therefore, was but a reflection of a particular social ideology, presented as empirical facts."[58] Other factors contributed to the cohesiveness and cliquishness of the association. Membership was limited to the asylum superintendents. Consequently, assistant superintendants and others employed in the asylums were accorded low professional status. The AMSAII refused to affiliate with the American Medical Association when it was organized in 1847.[59]

Among the ideas the AMSAII members exchanged were their theories about the cause of madness. There was general agreement that insanity was the result of physical damage to the brain, whether it was detectable or not. A blow to the head, prolonged illness or general poor health, and irritation of the nerves could lead to insanity. According to contemporary theory, irritated nerves eventually resulted in brain lesions.[60] Brain lesions purportedly were the cause of most insanity. However, medical researchers of the period could not identify pathological brain involvement in a significant number of insane individuals, when autopsies were performed.[61] Thus association members were forced to use either a functional or symptomatic definition of insanity.[62]

Here again a problem emerged. Disorders of the cognitive mind or intellect where hallucinations, delusions or other aberrant behaviors were involved were easy to classify as insanity. But when there was no apparent intellectual disorder, nor a readily discernable organic illness, then the asylum heads were faced with a dilemma. What of those who, for no discernable reason either physical or intellectual, committed senseless, socially unacceptable acts? Were they insane or criminal? The resolution of the dilemma lay in a classification of madness termed "moral insanity." The term became a catchall for ambigious social deviancy during the nineteenth century. But what exactly was moral insanity? James C. Pritchard, an English physician and anthropologist, defined moral insanity in the following manner:

The intellectual faculties appear to have sustained little or no injury, while the disorder is manifested principally or alone, in the state of feelings, temper, or habits. In cases of this description the moral and active principles of the mind are strangely perverted and depraved; the power of self government is lost or greatly impaired; and the individual is found to be incapable, not of talking or reasoning upon any subject proposed to him, for this he will often do with great shrewdness and volubility, but of conducting himself with decency and propriety.... His wishes and inclinations, his attachments, his likings and dislikings have all undergone a morbid change, and this change appears to be the originating cause, or be at the foundation of any disturbance which understanding itself may seem to have sustained, and even in some instances to form throughout the sole role manifestation of the disease.[63]

The "morbid change," because it was without physical or intellectual cause, must be the result of the apparent decline of civilization, therefore in the social environment of the morally insane individual. With this theory in mind, the asylum superintendents were confronted with the additonal need to provide facilities for morally insane indigent individuals. Moral treatment, in the meantime, was enjoying exceptional success in the "cure" of madness. Since the inception of asylums for the insane in America, statistics had been kept regarding the rate of recovery from the affliction. Between 1830 and 1850, these statistics reflected a gradually increasing rate of recovery. Deutsch calls this "the cult of curability" and gives little credence to the asylum superintendents' purported recovery rates. Norman Dain, in disagreement with Deutsch, cites a more recent study by Bromberg that substantiated to a large degree the figures for recovery claimed by the asylum superintendents.[64] Deutsch does make a very telling comment about the ambiguity and disagreement among the superintendents concerning what the term "recovery" meant. Grob, Dain and Rothman point out that the methods of keeping statistics during the period were crude, at best.

By the early 1840's, the recovery rate was said to have reached the 90 percent level and in 1843, the cure rate was reported to have reached 100 percent.[65] These inflated claims regarding the efficacy of moral treatment certainly lent impetus to the establishment of state-supported asylums. Asylum superintendents whose backgrounds were similar to those of other social reformers, and who reflected that group's attitudes and values, felt that the failure of other social institutions must be arrested or new institutions must be found to replace the older institutions. A new successful institution, the insane asylum, would inculcate, in a controlled environment, order, regularity and discipline in the insane. Thus the insane asylum would serve two functions: first, it would restore the great majority of the mad to reason; second, the success of moral management would serve as an example that the whole of society could follow. The emphasis, however, was on the segregation of the insane from the environment that was perceived as the cause of the illness.

While there was no indication that as an organization the AMSAII cooperated closely with social reformers in other movements, there was evidence that individual association members did so, particularly in New England. At least three of the New England social reformers, Horace Mann, Samuel Gridley Howe and Dorothea Dix, played significant roles in establishing and perpetuating the belief in the necessity of insane asylums. But of all the New England reformers, Dorothea Dix was the most important for the history of insanity in America. A member of the same social class as other reformers and the asylum superintendents, she shared their views toward society and insanity.[66] Dix believed that insanity and its arrival were the direct result of changing civilization. Along with Mann and Howe, Dix believed that the insane were the victims of social institutions and social attitudes, and were therefore the responsibility of society, specifically state and local governments.[67]

She began her crusade for adequate facilities for the insane with a casual inspection of the East Cambridge jail. In the jail, she found the insane inmates housed in deplorable conditions, filthy, poorly clothed, and without heat in the dead of winter.[68] Shocked by what she had seen, Dix began a two-year tour of jails and almshouses, throughout Massachusetts.[69] Dix presented testimony to the state legislature in which she outlined the conditions she had observed. She proposed either the enlargement of the present state asylum or the establishment of a new state asylum for the insane.[70] When the furor aroused by Dix's testimony subsided, the legislature agreed to an enlargement of the Worchester State Hospital.[71] After her success in Massachusetts, Dorothea Dix spent the next thirty-eight years (1843–1881) lobbying and campaigning for the establishment of state asylums throughout the United States.

With support and encouragement from Mann, Howe, and the asylum superintendents, Dix was eminently successful. She was credited with being "directly responsible for the founding or enlarging of thirty two mental hospitals in the United States and abroad."[72] Why was Dix so successful? According to Gerald Grob, "Dix's insistence upon institutional care for the mentally ill ... struck a responsive chord among those who were committed to the creation of a better society by diminishing the role of the family and other traditional institutions and increasing sharply the role of government."[73]

The additional impetus and direction given the social reform movement produced profound results for the insane in America. Fifty-three insane asylums, most of which were state supported, were erected between 1825 and 1865, bringing the total number of asylums in America to sixty-two.[74] During the same period, the total number of asylum admissions in America grew from 353 to 7,253 per year. The total American inmate population increased from 594 in 1825 to 15,806 in 1865.[75]

This remarkable increase in asylums and patient population had a significant effect on the role of the asylum superintendents. Moral management, with the goal of creating a moral environment for the insane, was vulnerable to the unrealistic expectations of the reformers and the implementation of the asylum superintendents. With the increase in patient population came a tendency for the superintendents to emphasize institutionalization itself as a cure for insanity. As Rothman states, the belief persisted that:

> The institution would arrange and administer a disciplined routine that would curb uncontrolled impulses without cruelty or unnecessary punishment. It would recreate fixity and stability to compensate for the irregularities of the society. Thus, it would rehabilitate the casualties of the system. The hospital walls would enclose a new world for the insane, designed in the reverse image of the one they had left.[76]

The patient's daily schedule was carefully arranged so that the times for rising, partaking of meals, work, entertainment, doctor's visits, and sleeping were rigidly precise. In addition to the daily schedule, emphasis was placed on orderliness and neatness. The facilities must be kept neat and activities carried out in an orderly fashion.[77] The reason for such internal organization was simple. "A precise schedule and regular work were the two chief characteristics of the best private and public institutions, and in the view of their managers, the key to curing insanity."[78]

The emphasis on asylum administration and facility planning or architecture demonstrates that the institutions did not accomodate themselves to the inmates. Quite the contrary, the inmates were forced to accomodate themselves to the institution. The inmates were indeed managed or, in more modern jargon, "their days were structured." There can be no question that the institution was the mediator between the insane and society. Segregated, organized, regulated and regimented, the insane were to be forced by a new approach of medicine — socio-psychological medicine — to return to reason, and resume a productive role in society. The superintendents were society's representatives in the institutions that wanted the mad confined. The superintendents approached all forms of insanity from their particular background and imposed upon the insane those external constraints that recreated at least the appearance of reason within the asylum.

The asylums had been "discovered" (David Rothman called the years of the Jacksonian period in America, the period of the Discovery of the Asylum in America), and erected against the background of a changing society and the belief by American social reformers that this changing society needed reform. The goal of the reform movement was the removal of social obstacles to growth and productivity of the society itself, an idea articulated by Ralph Waldo Emerson. He wrote: "The power which is at once spring and regulator in all effort of reform is the conviction that there is an infinite worthiness in man, which appears at the call of worth, and that all practical reforms are the removing of some impediment."[79] The reformers emerged to remove social impediments to their idea of what constituted an ideal society, one of which was the problem of insanity. In America, as in Europe, the asylum symbolized the estrangement of the deranged from what had been their society. Society's reformers felt that if the problem of insanity was not resolved it was, at least, confined. Located at some distance from communities, the asylums housed those whom society felt were impediments to attaining the goal of an ideal society, and also confined the world of madness, which threatened and challenged social order, within the asylum walls. It was believed that estranged and isolated, the mad would have no alternative but to cease being a hinderance to society's quest for the ideal American society; that is, to cease being mad.

The Decline of the Asylum

American social reformers' and the asylum superintendents' apparent victory over the illusory social monster of insanity appeared certain after the introduction of the state asylum as a new therapeutic tool. However, the so-called victory was short lived. By the end of the 1850's, the asylums as social institutions were a fixture in American society, but the reputation of the asylums rested on a shifting foundation. Between the beginning of the Civil War and the end of the century, the asylums where moral management was practiced drifted into a period of disrepute and decline as viable solutions to the problem of insanity.

The insane continued to be confined in asylums, but public optimism concerning the efficacy of asylums as examples of social reform and, more particularly, as a solution to the problem of insanity, became gradually pessimistic and finally fatalistic. As American social attitudes changed toward the asylums, so did the characteristics of the asylums themselves and the attitudes of the superintendents toward insanity.

Many factors were directly and indirectly responsible for the decline in popularity of the asylums. There was continuing social pressure to increase the number of inmates at each asylum, without a commensurate increase in the size of the facility or the asylum's staff. There was a constant increase in the number of chronic patients admitted and, in the local community, a lack of an overall rationally and adequately planned welfare program, of which asylums were a part. In addition, there was increasing demand from the asylum superintendents for public economic support. These factors, in concert, mitigated against the continued public acceptance and unquestioned success of the asylums. The conditions of overcrowding, lack of monies, and suspect success statistics, appeared within the context of a society that was rapidly industrializing and adopting a new social philosophy that was laissez-faire. As a result, support for the asylums eroded as society directed its energies to other needs and appeared reluctant to assume responsibility for the long term institutionalization of the deranged. The combined effect of the Civil War and a new social philosophy, Social Darwinism, exacerbated instrinsic problems in the administration of asylums and the care of inmates.

Social Darwinism (a term coined by Herbert Spencer was directly opposed to the philosophy of governmental intervention in social problems that had led to the rapid expansion of the asylum system. Two men in the 1850's promulgated the basic theses that were the foundation of Social Darwinism. The English social philosopher Herbert Spencer published two papers in 1852 that were concerned with the evolutionary character of society[80] and seven years later, in 1859, Charles Darwin published *On the Origin of Species*, which lent scientific credibility to the concept of the "survival of the fittest" and, therefore, impetus to Spencer's social theories.[81] Spencer and particularly Darwin had a profound effect on American religious thought. Richard Hofstadter points out that Spencer and his philosophy were far more acceptable and consequently more important in America than in his native country of England.[82] Darwin's theory of evolution, as set forth in *On the Origin of Species*, refuted a literal interpretation of the Bible and forced American religious leaders to deal with a more naturalistic view of man, nature, and man's relationship to nature.

Herbert Spencer began publication of his *Synthetic Philosophy* in 1860. Intended as a comprehensive philosophical system, Spencer's first volume raised great intellectual controversy in America. His perception of society, that change in society was continual but gradual, buttressed the emerging conservativism in the aftermath of the Civil War.[83] Man, in Spencer's philosophical system, was placed in a position of constantly adapting himself to social change. Those who failed to adapt did not survive; such individuals had the least "power of self-preservation." Men who successfully adapted and survived had the greatest "power of self-preservation" and were, therefore, the "select of their generation."[84] Spencer's philosophy of "survival of the fittest" supported the view that the "best" men competed most successfully, and that change was slow and natural.[85] This view, of course, coincided with the conservative viewpoint of the need for unconstrained competition in American society and commerce.

One of Spencer's American apostles, William Graham Sumner, extended Spencer's philosophy of society even further. Sumner stated that by tampering with the natural social process, man can only ensure the downfall of civilization and bring on chaos.[86] Predicated on a thesis of natural social evolution, both Spencer and Sumner were opposed to charity or the support of those who were unable to adapt to society. Spencer wrote that supporting social failures was done at the expense of social successes and would be paid for by future generations. Organized charity, according to Spencer, interfered with the natural process of selection by supporting "good-for-nothings" in great numbers.[87] Sumner concurred, "A law may be passed which shall force somebody to support the hopelessly degenerate members of a society, but such a law can only perpetuate the evil and entail it on future generations with new accumulation of distress."[88]

"Degenerate" was a key word in Sumner's context, for concurrent and compatible with Social Darwinism was a theory of insanity labeled "degeneration" or "degeneracy." Introduced by Philippe Morel in 1857,[89] the theory of degeneration argued that insanity was indicative of a "pathological deviation," which was hereditary. The theory stated that degeneration was caused by abuse of spirits (alcohol), the social environment, a disturbed personality, heredity and "acquired or congenital insults of various kinds."[90] Once tainted by such deviations, future generations went "inexorably to their doom." Mental illness was as good an example of a degenerative conditions as could be found in society at that time.[91]

This fatalistic and pessimistic view of insanity had a powerful influence in post–Civil War America because it served as a useful theory for the asylum superintendents. The theory of degeneration shifted the burden from the environment to the individual or the forebears of the individual who was insane (heredity). The individual must adapt himself to the natural social environment. Violating natural law meant suffering the consequences himself, or accepting the inevitable consequences for his progeny.[92] By shifting the burden from social environment to personal responsibility of the individual, the philosophy of degeneracy aided the asylum superintendents in their approach toward custodial care. No longer impelled toward social reform, the asylum superintendents were able to justify, to themselves at least, the failure of moral management. Moral management could modify the insane person's environment in an efficacious manner but the new American social perspective now perceived moral management, with its emphasis on order, regularity and discipline, as a means of managing the population that society had labeled insane. That the insane were excluded from society was justifiable, for the insane had violated natural law, by engaging in unacceptable social and personal behavior not common to the group. Within the context of Social Darwinism, by failing to adapt, the insane deserved confinement.

The asylum superintendents accepted this basic tenet of insanity, but now carried it one step further. While the superintendents did not rule out the possibility of recovery, the emphasis shifted to custodial care after 1865, to reflect society's view of the insane as hopelessly degenerate, and deserving of exclusion, or confinement. That degeneracy and custodial care were related can be most clearly explicated in the issue of chronic inmates. The chronic insane had been an increasing problem since the state asylums began opening their doors to the deranged. Formerly housed in almshouses, jails or private homes, there was a rapid influx of these individuals into asylums when the institutions initially opened. With the passage of time, these inmates occupied proportionately more of the available beds in state asylums.[93]

The difficulty of managing and treating the chronic insane lay in the tenets of moral management and the manner in which American asylum superintendents in America believed the goals of moral management could be realized through order, regularity and predictability.[94] Achievement of these goals required close interpersonal relationships between the asylum staff and inmates.[95] Most asylum superintendents believed that recovery from insanity was most likely if treatment began in "the early stages of the illness."[96] Treatment in the first six months of the affliction had not been possible with the large number of insane who previously had been confined in jails or almshouses throughout each state. As a consequence, as each state erected insane asylums, there was an extant chronic population to be admitted.

Second, in addition to the almshouse and jail refugees, there was an increasing national population accompanied by a broadening definition of insanity by society. This increased the demand for the insane to be admitted to the asylums as well as the number of insane to be admitted. From this increased asylum population, there would be a number of the insane who did not recover, for one reason or another; consequently, new inmates would be added to the existing chronic asylum population.

By 1866 the AMSAII increased the maximum number of inmates recommended per asylum from 250 to 600, even though many institutions already had as many as 1000–1200 inmates.[97] The increasing number of inmates was not accompanied by a commensurate increase in the size of the asylum facilities or the asylum staff. Consequently there was a decline in the interpersonal relationships between the staff and the inmates. Emphasis shifted from treatment to custodial care, which further emphasized the administrative functions of the superintendent's role. Thus, chronicity resulted in a vicious cycle: chronic inmates directly contributed to the increasing population of the asylums, which in turn interdicted moral management, which in turn caused a disillusionment with moral treatment. As there was not a viable treatment alternative to moral management, at least in America, disillusionment meant an increased reliance on the institutionalization of the insane and an emphasis on maintaining the status quo.

Another of the factors that led to the decline in popularity of the asylums was Pliny Earle's examination of the asylum superintendents' statistics for recovery. Earle, the superintendent of Northhampton State Lunatic Hospital,[98] criticized the superintendents' statistics on three bases: first, the "proportion of cures represented the ratio of recoveries to cases discharged, rather than to cases admitted"[99]; second, the figures did not include readmissions, and therefore the total number of cases was much larger than the number of individuals admitted; third, many individuals were discharged as recovered, more than once.[100] Earle explained the inaccurate statistics on the basis that the superintendents were inexperienced at keeping records. In addition, Earle showed that the superintendents deliberately skewed the statistics to show a high rate of recovery in order to encourage public and monetary support for the continued erection of asylums. According to David Rothman, Earle's expose of the "soft" recovery statistics resulted in loss of public support.[101] According to Barbra Sicherman, a historian who has written about the mental health system in late nineteenth century America,

> Earle probably overstated his case, he accurately reflected, and probably reinforced, the disillusionment of the period. The disenchantment was all the greater because earlier expectations had been so high.[102]

Developments in Neurology

Concurrent with developments in psychiatry and the asylums, neurology, which had begun to emerge as a medical specialty during the Civil War,[103] reinforced the growing perception that derangement was an organic disease. Discoveries in neurology such as the cause of some forms of paralysis, epilepsy and locomotor ataxia[104] lent credibility and legitimacy to the neurologists' claim that insanity was organic. American neurologists Edward Spitzka, E.C. Seguin, Silas Weir Mitchell and George M. Beard insisted that "some as yet undiscovered organic causality"[105] of insanity existed. George M. Beard was fairly representative of his profession in how neurologists in the latter part of the nineteenth century perceived mental illness. Beard was one of the physicians who developed the concept of neurasthenia (weak nerves), a term he used to describe those individuals who lacked sufficient nervous energy to successfully adapt to the demands of nineteenth century society. From Beard's perspective[106] each individual possessed a unique and finite quantity of nervous energy; and those endowed with insufficient nervous energy to adapt to the demands of every-day life would sucumb to neurasthenia. For Beard, individual differences in nervous energy were the consequence of heredity. During the late nine-teenth century, as Rosenberg declared, "Hereditary explanations of mental illness were in the air."[107] Neurasthenia conformed to the prevalent Social Darwinist philosophy and the idea of degeneracy, because from Beard's perspective (and others'), a complex and moral civilization was a reflection of an increasingly complex nervous system.

> Unfortunately however, this highly evolved nervous system was, by virtue of its very "fineness of organization," vulnerable to the tensions characteristic of the civilization its evolution made possible.[108]

In sum, Beard and his contemporaries were somaticists and heredi-tarians. They regarded civilization as a causal factor of mental illness, in order to explain psychological issues through organic concepts. Late nine-teenth century physicians agreed that insanity was a disease of the brain; that is, physical, tangible occurrences in the brain caused mental illness. They were as equally certain that

> environmental and emotional causes, tension, anxiety, grief—"moral" causes in the vocabulary of the time—might exacerbate or even cause mental illness (especially in those with some hereditary weakness or predisposition).[109]

Although acquiescing on the cause(s) of insanity to psychiatrists, neu-rologists were critical of the asylum superintendents. To the neurologists, asylum superintendents were no more than asylum administrators, not physician-scientists concerned with clinical practice and medical research regarding the origins and treatment of mental illness. The conflict between the two medical specialties was further exacerbated when the asylum super-intendents refused to admit neurologists, as well as any other physicians, to the AMSAII. Membership was limited to only those physicians who were superintendents of asylums. To make matters worse, the conflict was con-ducted in the two specialties through their respective professional journals, in testimony before a variety of state and local governmental bodies and in the popular press, particularly during criminal proceedings where a plea of "not guilty by reason of insanity" was entered. The debate grew increasingly ascerbic until its culmination with the speech of Silas Weir Mitchell to the asylum superintendents in 1894.[110] Dr. Mitchell's speech, though highly critical of the superintendents, met with few objections. It was delivered at the annual meeting of the American Medico-Psychological Association — the title the AMSAII adopted in 1892. The superintendents' lack of objection to the speech and the change in their organization's title was indicative of reforms implemented in the asylums during the preceding decade. According to Barbra Sicherman, asylum care was expensive and as a consequence the state boards of charities gradually became more involved in supervising the asylums.[111] Grob indicated that placing the publicly funded asylums under the aegis of the state boards of charities was part of the process of centralization and rationalization of the public welfare system: the administrative control of the asylums was shifted to the boards of charities as states discovered they were spending the largest percentage[112] of their budgets for staffing and maintaining insane asylums. During the latter part of the century, twelve states established boards of charities; this had the effect of regrouping the mentally ill with other dependent and deviant groups,[113] vis-à-vis the seventeenth century general hospitals. As a further consequence of this process, "slowly but surely the shift in the sources of funding led municipalities and counties to transfer their mentally ill from almshouses to state hospitals and to redefine senility in psychiatric terms."[114]

This altered relationship with government, the change in the asylums' social function and the increased politicization of the superintendents' positions occurred in the context of psychiatry's declining reputation.[115] Understandably the superintendents resented what they considered outside interference in the internal affairs of the asylum[116] by lay people. Resisting criticism from neurologists, resentful of changes forced on them by the state boards of charities, psychiatrists were ultimately confronted with an alliance between neurologists and charity workers in the form of the short-lived National Association for the Protection of the Insane and Prevention of Insanity in 1880. The stated purpose of the NAPIPI was to reform psychiatric practice and inform the public about mental illness.[117] With the death or resignation of a number of its leaders, the association lost impetus. Moreover, the asylum superintendents initiated reforms such as improved medical standards in the asylums, the development of outpatient clinics and psychopathic hospitals for acute cases, the inclusion of research in the asylums and psychiatry in general, expansion of the asylum staff to include new disciplines and the admission to full membership in the American Medico-Psychological Association (AMPA) of other asylum physicians and a variety of medical disciplines.[118]

As for the neurologists, they had acknowledged the legitimacy of superintendants' claims concerning under-funding and staffing and their objections to outside interference. Consequently on the eve of Mitchell's address to the AMPA, psychiatry and neurology had reached an accomodation that was to be maintained in the twentieth century. But even with an amicable relationship with neurologists, and asylum reform, psychiatry — both institutional and office — had reached an impasse. From the close of the eighteenth to the end of the nineteenth centuries the profession had converted the asylum into its primary therapeutic tool, and one had been erected in almost every state.[119] However, from optimism regarding the efficacy of moral management — a psychological approach — psychiatry had retreated to a renewed pessimism predicated on a pervasive organic theory of insanity. Psychiatry had established a professional organization and a journal, and rectified, to some extent, the decline in professional status since the Civil War through asylum reform and the adoption of Emil Kraepelin's nosology and classification system.[120] Ultimately though, the asylums and implicitly the superintendents had become a vital component of the expanding public welfare system.

What official psychiatry lacked was an organized psychology, which in Europe had begun to emerge in the form of psychoanalysis. By the first decade of the twentieth century, psychoanalysis had made its debut in America and had begun to revolutionize psychiatric practice. But psychoanalysis was not an abrupt discovery; rather, to Henri Ellenberger and Gregory Zilboorg, it embodied a number of elements extant throughout the nineteenth century. Fundamentally those elements revolved around what could be loosely called the psyche, or unconscious mental life. Both authors trace the development of psychoanalysis through the Enlightenment, Romanticism and Positivism, the Scientific and Industrial revolutions and more esoteric subjects such as phrenology, mesmerism, hypnosis, sexual pathology, faith healing and spiritualism. Zilboorg and Ellenberger contend that the old Cartesian Dualism enacted in psychiatry during the first half of the nineteenth century with "soma" eventually became predominate in the latter half. Psychoanalysis represented to both authors the culmination — literally the systemization — of centuries of speculation in a variety of arenas. Zilboorg felt psychoanalysis represented a revolution in thought and labeled it "the Second Psychiatric Revolution"[121]; Ellenberger took a more gradualist approach. To Ellenberger a number of factors converged at the end of the nineteenth century that assisted Sigmund Freud personally and intellectually in synthesizing and systematizing psychoanalytic theories and techniques:

> The general faith in science was maintained, not only by the positivists' worship but also through the innumerable discoveries and inventions that ceaselessly came to increase that belief, following one another so rapidly that one could, so to speak, see the face of the earth modified under their impact. The progress of medicine and hygiene was changing the conditions of human life, the average length of which had never ceased to increase from the beginning of the nineteen century. This progress had deep social and biological implications. Finally, the discovery of surgical anesthesia between 1840 and 1850 not only made the progress of surgery possible but eliminated the experience of physical pain, which was furthered by the subsequent discovery of analgesics and sedatives. Man was no longer conditioned to pain as he had been previously and he became more sensitive and also more fearful of pain. Thus, man at the end of the century was not quite the same biological being as he had been at its beginning, and it is therefore not surprising that he did not have quite the same psychopathology.[122]

From Ellenberger's perspective the development of psychoanalysis—to him the rationalization of the unconscious—was more a slowly evolving cultural development than a revolution. However, Zilboorg and Ellenberger agreed that the evolution of psychoanalysis represented a watershed in Western cultural development. More to the point, psychoanalytic concepts would be assimilated by American society during the Progressive Era and emerge in a uniquely American style.[123] By 1909 when Freud lectured at Clark University in the United States, the Progressive Era was well under way. Psychiatry and psychoanalysis were entangled in a number of issues—criminal insanity, mental hygiene, sexual pathology—in the American Progressive social agenda. Throughout the nineteenth century the evolving American civilization had been suspect as a cause of mental illness—in the Progressive Era "civilization" was accorded a new label, "the environment." Psychiatry, and its new ally, psychoanalysis, would play a role in shaping the "environment" during, and after, the Progressive Era. But the changing society would generate a redefinition of mental illness.

Twentieth Century

In the decades that followed to the close of the twentieth century, there were three important developments: continuing developments in medicine that directly affected the treatment of mental illness; expanding government participation in funding and oversight of patient care; and a proliferation of psychotherapeutic schools, most a response to the growing popularity of psychoanalysis.

Medical discoveries continued to redefine diagnostic categories and influence treatment for mental disorders. Therapeutic procedures appeared to revert to the former "heroic" measures of the past with the application of metrazol, insulin and electric shock therapies between 1937 and 1940. All three induced severe convulsions in the subject, who were typically chronically psychotic, with questionable results and at some risk to the patient. More effective and benign treatment appeared in the early 1950's in the form of chemical compounds known today as tranquilizers or, more accurately, psychotropic medication. The continuing evolution and effectiveness of these drugs has had a profound effect on treatment for the mentally ill, enabling many hospitalized patients to return to home and work or precluding hospitalization in the first place. As more effective treatment regimens appeared and in response to public demand, government took a more active role in allocating funds for research and the establishment of model programs for the mentally ill. In 1946, the National Mental Health Centers Act provided for the establishment of the National Institute of Mental Health; in 1963, the federal government ratified the National Communities Mental Health Act, which effectively deinstitutionalized most chronically ill patients and brought to an end reliance on custodial care facilities for the most severely disturbed individuals. The legislation anticipated that most former chronic patients would be managed by medications provided through local community mental health centers, but this expectation was not realized. The unfortunate consequence of this legislation has been to create an indigent homeless population in larger municipalities that absorbs law enforcement, medical and other community resources. None the less, state and federal governments have assumed a seemingly limitless role regarding mental disorders and the mentally ill.

Perhaps even more startling than any other development regarding mental illness in the United States has been an explosion of mental health professionals during the past one hundred years. From an extraordinarily small group of psychiatrists, two hundred and twenty-two in 1900, the number and variety of mental health professionals has grown enormously. No longer is psychiatry the only discipline concerned with treatment of the mentally ill. Today there are more than thirty-two thousand psychiatrists, seventy thousand psychologists and many hundreds of thousands practicing in related professions—psychiatric social work, pastoral counseling, sex therapy, marriage counseling, and a myriad of other quasi-professional and lay practitioners. Moreover the number of psychotherapeutic approaches has grown to nearly three hundred competing therapies, various forms of psychoanalysis, individual and group psychotherapy, marriage and family counseling, primal scream therapy, EST, transactional analysis, Gestalt therapy and so on. Public and private hospital expenditures have surpassed sixty-nine billion dollars and continue to increase, while private outpatient expenditures are undetermined. There is a vast array of psychoactive medications available, either over the counter or by prescription. What were once private, personal problems are now the subject of radio, television talk shows and newspaper advice columns.

Mental illness in America has been transformed during the past century. The single therapeutic tool of the nineteenth century, the brick-and-mortar asylum, has virtually disappeared. Once the stepchild of medicine, psychiatry has become a recognized medical specialty, a requirement in most medical schools. Underlying causes for mental illnesses are now recognized as a combination of environment and biology. One constant remains. As the medical and natural sciences continue to make new discoveries, what constitutes mental illness will continue to be redefined.

The asylum emerged as the institution to cure madness. At its inception, it was perceived as a facility to segregate the mad from the community and enable them to confront their madness as directed by the medical staff and return to their community, rehabilitated. Ultimately, the asylum failed to eliminate madness from American society. Underfunding, understaffing, overcrowding and limited community follow-up or support reduced the insane asylums to "snake pits," institutions of last resort. The perception that asylums were snake pits and the advent of an ever increasing variety and effectiveness of psychotropic medications led to deinstitutionalization forty years ago. But, at the same time, the incidence of mental illness has steadily increased to the point that experts suggest a large percentage of the American population experiences a psychiatric disorder.

The demise of the old asylum has led to a new asylum, located in Americans' medicine bottles and perceptions of what are normal, tolerable feelings and behavior. Life, it seems, should be pain free — no anxiety or depression associated with everyday life is to be tolerated. Medical science and pharmaceutical companies have provided a vast (and growing) pharmocopeia to eliminate psychic pain. And both have used mass media to inform and persuade Americans that it is normal to be emotionally numb, thus creating a society where the majority are "mad" and medicated.

Through TV's Looking Glass

Psychiatry and the American Public

The American public's perception of mental illness has undergone a sea-change since World War Two and the advent of psychotropic medications. What was once an embarrassing, unmentionable condition to the individual, family and community, has become a relatively normal condition, experienced by an ever-growing number of Americans. The growing influence of American television over the past half century has reinforced the "medicalization of deviance" (transformation of moral and legal issues into medical matters) that began in the eighteenth century with the emergence of the insane asylum. American television as a social and socializing agent has assisted in shifting the cultural boundaries of mental illness to include an ever-expanding segment of the population. The dawn and subsequent media proliferation of "direct to consumer advertising" (DTCA) of psychotropic medications in the late 1990's has been instrumental in removing the final bricks of the asylum. The proliferation of television drug advertisements and incorporation of psychotropic references into television dialogue for treatment of disorders such as depression, attention deficit disorder, anxiety, erectile dysfunction and sleep problems has changed the social landscape of mental illness and the reduced the necessity for psychiatric hospitalizations.

The Growing Influence of Television

The formal rituals associated with labeling an individual deviant, whether at criminal proceedings or psychiatric examinations, inform the individual and society of the characteristics of his deviance and the sanctions for it. One of most recognizable labels for deviance in American society has been the label of mental illness, which traditionally required medical intervention in the form of psychiatric hospitalization. However, the influence of the mass media, specifically television, has blurred the cultural boundaries around mental illness. Entertainment programs and advertisements commodify and help to portray mental illness as a normal human experience. Their message, both explicit in the form of news programs and implicit in the context of show dialogue, is that relief is readily available. By doing so, the stigma historically attached to madness and insanity is incorporated into mainstream thinking. As a social agent, the mass media has shifted American society's cultural boundaries so that being designated mentally ill no longer carries the shame it did fifty years ago. More and more Americans suffer from depression, anxiety, adjustment, (post-traumatic) stress disorders, and attention deficit, for which there appears to be a readily available magic pill. According to news reports, Americans are the most heavily medicated society in the world. "About 130 million Americans swallow, inject, inhale, infuse, spray, and pat on prescribed medication every month.... The number of prescriptions has swelled by two-thirds over the past decade to 3.5 billion yearly and Americans devour even more nonprescription drugs."[124] Simply stated, American society is awash in a vast pharmocopeia of over the counter and prescription drugs— most advertised in the mass media.

Mass media in the United States comprises print, motion pictures, the Internet and television. Based on numbers alone, television is the most influential of all the mass media. Consider the following statistics, which are based on a 2005 special report on television use and viewing habits by the U.S. Census Bureau.[125] In 2000, the American population was 281 million with 248 million television sets. The percentage of households with at least one television set had risen from 87.3 percent in 1960 to 98.2 percent in 2001. American homes had an average of almost 2½ televisions per household, which were watched 1,669 hours or 70 days a year. Ninety-four percent of Americans eighteen or older watched television; 97 percent of those Americans 65 and older were "glued to the tube," watching one of the 1,937 television broadcasting networks and stations in the United States. In addition to the purchase price of each television set, the typical American spent $255 on cable and satellite connections. In other words, a normal American watched television, courtesy of his local cable or satellite provider, as much time as he worked or slept, on one of the two or three television sets in his home.

With such incredible penetration into the American household and consciousness, television is a marketing force to be reckoned with. The images seen on television have the power to influence the audience's perception of reality. It has been argued that "a wide variety of media messages can act as teachers of values, ideologies, and beliefs and can provide images for interpreting the world whether or not the designers are conscious of this intent."[126] The mythical images presented on television screens appeal to the unconscious as symbolic narrative, and the underlying themes are repeated in various forms, similar to dreams. According to Adler and Cater, "Both TV and dreams are visual; both are symbolic; both TV and dreams contain a high degree of wish fulfillment; both include much that is trivial and meaningless; dreams and TV have significant and powerful content, most of which is easily forgotten; both make use of concrete and symbolic images from recent experiences."[127] The degree of television's influence is controversial; however, it is possible that individual imaginations are persuaded to organize portions of daily life, that is, "the way they live in the world and imagine it."[128] Michael Kammen, in *American Culture, American Tastes,* argued that American television has become the most significant form of mass media, in part because of "the growing power of advertising in the world of entertainment."[129] Television and television advertising have assisted in producing a mass culture that is "a form of entertainment, a glorified tranquillizer or anti-depressant, something to while away the empty leisure hours when one is not at work or on holidays."[130]

In general traditional network audiences have declined, despite the growth in total audience size and increase in average hours watching television. Cable networks now claim to have 60 percent of the total television audience. Even though cable television audiences are fragmented, divided among hundreds of networks and super-stations, individual channel or network content is similar to the traditional networks: entertainment and advertising. Only subscription services such as HBO, Showtime and Starz provide commercial-free viewing to their subscribers. (Subscription services fill the gap between scheduled shows with advertisements for the next, or "coming soon," presentation.)

Television entertainment has taken good advantage of the growing use of psychotropic medication in American society. Between 1993 and 1999, shows as diverse as *Frazier* and *The Sopranos* commented on one of the character's use of Prozac, the most recognizable label for antidepressants. Niles, Frazier's eloquent but indelibly neurotic brother, comments that the only way he could persuade his wife from under a bed during a storm was to use Prozac on a string.[131] The following year Phoebe, one of the female stars on the wildly popular *Friends* series accused another character of being like Santa Claus on Prozac ... in Disney Land getting laid.[132] Even Tony, the charismatic and sociopathic mob boss on HBO's critically acclaimed crime drama *The Sopranos,* asks when taking lithium and Prozac will finally end.[133] Even shows targeted at young audiences are potential sales boosters for psychotropic drugs. On one episode of the coming-of-age drama *Dawson's Creek,* the main character, Jen Lindley, warns her friend that she is heading to a lifelong showdown with Prozac.[134] After a particularly successful day tormenting his teacher, Bart, the demonic child on the animated series *The Simpsons,* is forced to write "I will not hide my teacher's Prozac" one hundred times on the blackboard.[135]

Not all psychotropic TV drug references are entertaining. As noted in the above U.S. Census Report on television use and viewing habits between June 2000 and June 2005, CBS News had 136 stories regarding antidepressants and another 457 entries for mental illness. The news bulletins are typically brief and the reports usually highlight either the effectiveness of antidepressants or the risks associated with some medications. News bulletins warned of the increased risk of suicide among some consumers, particularly children and adolescents. Other reports have focused on use of antidepressants among older Americans and the effectiveness of antidepressants for menopause in some women, headaches, chronic fatigue and terrorists attacks.[136] In other words, if television news is to be taken as a credible source of information, antidepressants have become a virtual panacea for what could be argued to be normal life experiences. (ABC, Fox, NBC and CNN have reported similar news stories during the same period.) Perhaps the most dramatic news story regarding antidepressants appeared on CNN. The network convened a panel of experts to identify and rank the twenty-five medical miracles over the past quarter century. Prozac, introduced in 1987, was rated number seven with an accompanying story that 54 million people around the globe have taken Prozac. Network news all reported the Nobel Prize for medicine was awarded to researchers Arvid Carlsson, Paul Greengard and Eric Kandel for the neurological discoveries that led to the development of Prozac and similar medications.[137]

Television advertising is effective. According to Harris Interactive, 92 percent who discuss medication with their physician say they saw an advertisement on television.[138,139] Zoloft's little egg commercial and the current Welbutrin advertisement list common symptoms of depression — weight, appetite and mood disturbance — and they imply that medication might alleviate the symptoms and suggest the viewer contact their physician and quickly mention adverse effects and contraindications. Such advertisements encourage self-diagnosis and requests for medical care. When reinforced by local advertisements for mental health services and television dialogue that conveys the message that psychotropics are like aspirin or candy, the message to the viewing audience must be "better living through chemistry." No longer is mental illness a shameful, embarrassing condition — to the contrary, it is just like the common cold because everybody is infected sooner or later. What better example of the medicalization of deviance!

The deconstruction of the insane asylum in American society will continue. Mass media has, and will, continue to shift the boundaries of mental illness until the entire society could be considered mentally ill. The power of television to persuade and educate has been enhanced by the development of increasingly sophisticated computer technology that significantly increases the attractiveness and interest in television entertainment and advertising. As high definition television (HDTV) is acquired by consumers, television broadcasting will become even more dominant. No doubt the controversy regarding the degree to which television affects individual and collective behavior will persist. Consumer response to pharmaceutical advertising demonstrates that television influences behavior, at least in regards Americans' desire to live a psychic life free of discomfort. It is reminiscent of Huxley's "soma" in *Brave New World*, a chemical that makes everyone happy and content no matter how grim their existence.

Notes

1. Michel Foucault, *Madness and Civilization: A History of Insanity in the Age of Reason*, trans. Richard Howard (New York: Random House, 1965), p. 39.

2. Ibid.

3. Ibid.

4. Ibid.

5. Ibid.

6. Ibid.

7. Ibid.

8. Ibid.

9. Ibid.

10. Ibid.

11. Ibid.

12. George Rosen, *Madness in Society* (New York: Harper Row Publishers, 1968), pp. 268–271; Gerald N. Grob, *Mental Institutions in America: Social Policy to 1875* (New York: MacMillan Publishing Co., 1973), p. 65; Richard Harrison Shyrock, *Medicine and Society in America: 1660–1860* (New York: Cornell University Press, 1960), pp. 8, 13.

13. Ibid.

14. Shyrock, op. cit., p. 2.

15. David J. Rothman, *The Discovery of the Asylum: Social Order and Disorder in the New Republic* (Boston: Little, Brown and Co., 1971), p. 7.

16. Ibid.

17. Ibid.; Grob, op. cit. pp. 5–7; Shyrock, op. cit., p. 7.

18. Rothman, op. cit. pp. 30–56, passim; Grob, op. cit., p. 13.

19. Rothman, op. cit., pp. 20–25.

20. Rothman, op. cit., pp. 28–29, 41.

21. Rothman, op. cit., pp. 52–56.

22. Grob, op. cit., pp. 19–31.

23. Albert Deutsch, *The Mentally Ill in America* (New York: Doubleday Press, 1937), pp. 77–89, passim.

24. Norman Dain, *Concepts of Insanity in the United States, 1789–1865* (New Brunswick, New Jersey: Rutgers University Press, 1964), p. 15.

25. Ibid.; Deutsch, op. cit., pp. 72–87; Shyrock, op. cit., pp. 12–15.

26. Dain, op. cit., p. 19; Deutsch, op. cit., p. 79.

27. Grob, op. cit., p. 28; Dain, op. cit., p. 15.

28. Deutsch, op. cit., p. 77.

29. Dain, op. cit., pp. 15–21; Deutsch, op. cit., p. 84.

30. Deutsch, op. cit., p. 85.

31. Walter Riese, in *Historic Derivations of Modern Psychiatry* by Iago Goldston (New York: McGraw Hill Book Co., 1967), pp. 110–112.

32. Dain, op. cit., p. 20.

33. Shyrock, op. cit., p. 13.

34. Dain, op. cit., p. 15.

35. Grob, op. cit., p. 28.

36. Grob, op. cit., p. 42; Rothman, op. cit., p. 109.

37. Dain, op. cit., pp. 11–12.

38. Norman Dain, "American Psychiatry in the 18th Century," in *American Psychiatry Past, Present and Future*, eds. George Kriegman, Robert D. Gardner, and Wilfred Abse (Charlottesville: University Press of Virginia, 1975), p. 24.

39. Goldston, op. cit., p. 115; George Mora and Jeanne L. Brand, eds., *Psychiatry and Its History* (Springfield, Illinois: Charles C. Thomas Publishers, 1970), pp. 162–163.

40. Mora and Brand, op. cit., pp. 162–163.

41. Dain, op. cit., p. 13.

42. Grob, op. cit., p. 45.

43. Foucault, op. cit., pp. 241–278, passim.

44. Foucault, op. cit., pp. 40 and 51; Rothman, op. cit., pp. 109–129, passim.

45. Dain, op. cit., p. 64.

46. Foucault, op. cit., pp. 269–273.

47. Grob, op. cit., pp. 36–38.

48. Rothman, op. cit., pp. 125–126.

49. Grob, op. cit., p. 51.

50. Grob, op. cit., pp. 51–83, passim.

51. Rothman, op. cit., p. 78.

52. Grob, op. cit., pp. 84–85.

53. Grob, op. cit., p. 132.

54. Ibid.

55. Ibid.

56. Dain, op. cit., p. 57 and Grob, op. cit., p. 136.

57. Grob, op. cit., p. 159.

58. Grob, op. cit., p. 157.

59. Grob, op. cit., p. 148.

60. Rothman, op. cit., pp. 110–111.

61. Rothman, op. cit., p. 110.

62. Dain, op. cit., p. 70.

63. Dain, op. cit., p. 73.

64. Dain, op. cit., p. 71.

65. Deutsch, op. cit., pp. 132–157, passim.

66. Dain, op. cit., p. 168.

67. Dain, op. cit., p. 170.

68. Deutsch, op. cit., p. 158.

69. Deutsch, op. cit., p. 165.

70. Deutsch, op. cit., p. 169.

71. Ibid.

72. Deutsch, op. cit., p. 184.

73. Grob, op. cit., p. 108.

74. Dain, op. cit., p. 55.

75. Grob, op. cit., pp. 374–395, passim.

76. Rothman, op. cit., p. 133.

77. Rothman, op. cit., p. 144.

78. Rothman, op. cit., p. 144.

79. Allan Nevins and Henry Steele Commager, *A Pocket History of the United States*, 5th ed. (New York: Washington Square Press, 1967), p. 173.

80. Richard Hofstadter, *Social Darwinism in American Thought* (Boston: Beacon Press Books, 1955), pp. 3–5.

81. Ibid.

82. Ibid.

83. Ibid.

84. J.D.Y. Peel, *Herbert Spencer* (Chicago: University of Chicago Press), pp. 3, 36, passim.

85. Hofstadter, op. cit., pp. 6–7.

86. William E. Leuchtenberg and Bernard Wishy, *Social Darwinism: Selected Essays of William Graham Sumner*, Classics in History Series (Englewood Cliffs, New Jersey: Prentice Hall, Inc., 1963), pp. 18–19.

87. Cynthia Eagle Russett, *Darwin in America: The Intellectual Response, 1865–1912* (San Francisco: W.H. Freeman and Company, 1976), p. 89.

88. Ibid.

89. George Rosen, *Madness in Society* (New York: Harper Torchbooks, 1969), p. 254.

90. Ibid.

91. Ibid.

92. For a thorough discussion of "degeneracy," see Benedict-Augustin Morel, *Traité des Degenerescences Physiques, Intellectuelles et Morales de l'espece Humaine* (Paris: Masson, 1852) and Max Nordau, *Degeneration* (1892). There is extensive discussion of "degeneracy" in histories of psychiatry; see Gerald Grob, Norman Dain and Edward Shorter.

93. Grob, op. cit., pp. 177–178.

94. Grob, op. cit., p. 176.

95. Grob, op. cit., p. 181.

96. Grob, op. cit., p. 182.

97. Barbra Sicherman, *The Quest for Mental Health in America, 1880–1917* (Unpublished Ph.D. dissertation, Columbia University, 1967), p. 18.

98. Grob, op. cit., pp. 182–184.

99. Ibid.

100. Ibid.

101. Rothman, op. cit., p. 169.

102. Sicherman, op. cit., p. 19.

103. Deutsch, op. cit., pp. 276–277.

104. Erwin H. Ackerknecht, *A Short History of Medicine*, revised printing (New York: The Ronald Press Company, 1968), pp. 203–205.

105. Deutsch, op. cit., p. 329.

106. Charles E. Rosenberg, "The Place of George M. Beard in Nineteenth Century Psychiatry," *Bulletin of the History of Medicine* 36 (May–June 1962), pp. 245–259.

107. Ibid.

108. Ibid.

109. Barbra Sicherman, pp. 84, 94 95; Charles E. Rosenberg, *The Trial of the Assassin Guiteau: Psychiatry and Law in the Gilded Age* (Chicago: University of Chicago Press, 1968), p. 64.

110. Grob, op. cit., pp. 61–62.

111. Sicherman, op. cit., pp. 28–35.

112. Grob, op. cit., pp. 50, 72.

113. Grob, op. cit., p. 79.

114. Grob, op. cit., p. 107.

115. Grob, op. cit., pp. 79–91, passim.

116. Sicherman, op. cit., pp. 22–23.

117. Grob, op. cit., p. 55; Sicherman, op. cit., p. 46.

118. Sicherman, op. cit., pp. 60–72, passim.

119. Grob, op. cit., p. 4.

120. Ackerknecht, pp. 77–81, Henri F. Ellenberger, *The Discovery of the Unconscious: The History and Evolution of Dynamic Psychiatry* (New York: Basic Books, Inc., 1970), p. 285.

121. Gregory Zilboorg, *A History of Medical Psychology* (New York: The Norton Library, W.W. Norton and Co., Inc., 1969), p. 479.

122. Ellenberger, op. cit., p. 228.

123. Bruno Bettelheim, *Freud and Man's Soul* (New York: Alfred A. Knopf, 1983), p. 33.

124. Jeff Donn, "Experts Warn on Expense of US Drugs," Associated Press, April 16, 2005, <http://abcnews.go.com/Health/wireStory?id=676656> (viewed June 1, 2005). (archived)

125. U.S. Census Bureau, Newsroom, Special Edition, "50th Anniversary of 'Wonderful World of Color' TV," March 11, 2004, <http://www.census.gov/Press-Release/www/releases/archives/facts_for_features/001702.html> (viewed May 27, 2005). (archived)

126. William A. Gamson, David Croteau, William Hoynes, and Theodore Sasson, "Media Images and the Social Construction of Reality," *Annual Review of Sociology* 18 (1992), p. 374, JSTOR, stable URL: <http://links.jstor.org/sici?sici=0360–0572%281992%2918%3C373%3AMIATSC%3E2.0.CO%3B2-Z> (viewed May 30, 2005).

127. Richard Adler and Douglass Cater, *Television as a Cultural Force* (New York: Praeger, 1976), pp. 21–23.

128. Claire O'Farrell, "Theory, Practice and Imagination in the Creative Industries," Foucault Resources, 2000, pp. 2–3, <http://www.foucault.qut.edu.au/ci.html> (viewed June 3, 2005). (archived)

129. Michael Kammen, *American Culture, American Tastes: Social Change and the 20th Century* (New York: Alfred A. Knopf), 1999, p. 152.

130. Claire O'Farrell, op. cit.

131. *Frazier,* producers Marta Kauffman, David Krane and Kevin Brite, NBC, 1994.

132. *Friends,* producers David Crane and Marta Kauffman, Warner Bros., 1994.

133. *The Sopranos,* producer David Chase, HBO, 1999.

134. *Dawson's Creek,* producer Kevin Williamson, Columbia Tri Star, 1998.

135. *The Simpsons,* producers James Brooks, Sam Simon and Matt Groening, NBC, 1994.

136. CBS News, key word "antidepressants," <http://www.cbsnews.com/htdocs/search/search.php?source=cbsnews&searchString=antidepressants&sort=1&type=all&num=10&offset=0> (viewed June 20, 2005).

137. CNN, "Top 25: Medical Stories," June 19, 2005, <http://www.cnn.com/2005/HEALTH/01/31/cnn25.top.medical/index.html>.

138. Arnold, Matthew, "Changing Channels," *DTC Outlook,* pp. 38, 39, <http://offlinehbpl.hbpl.co.uk/Misc/MMM/Features/APR05%2034–42%20DTC%20OUTLOOK.pdf> (viewed June 15, 2005).

139. Dr. Anne Axelrod and Darren Moore, "Direct-to-Consumer (DTC) Advertising: A Classic Case of Cognitive Dissonance," p. 29, <http://www.harrisinteractive.com/productsandservices/pubs/DTC_Perspectives_Dec04.pdf> (viewed June 15, 2005).

2 Hollywood Rx

MEREDITH KNEAVEL *and* ANN KNEAVEL

"Take a holiday from reality whenever you like."
— Advertising slogan for Soma,
the euphoria drug in Aldous Huxley's *Brave New World*

Michael Radford's film version of George Orwell's *Nineteen Eighty-four* opens with a shot of the population of Oceania massed in front of giant screens where they are shown films designed to indoctrinate them with the norms of their totalitarian dystopia. "These are our people," a voice intones over scenes of rippling wheat fields; "This is our land."[1] In the actual year 2004, 1,506.9 million people[2] thronged into movie theaters to watch Hollywood's version of "our people" and "our land" on the big screens. And this figure does not take into account the home video sales and rentals of more than $25 billion[3] or any statistics about movies channeled into American homes through cable and satellite. Obviously, therefore, the movie industry has enormous penetration and potential for widespread influence and possible control over American society, dictating what is acceptable, what is desirable, what is *normal*. For the last forty years, Hollywood has filled the silver screens with the features of an American brave new world of "better living through chemistry," to quote a former advertising slogan,[4] a world in which there is a pharmaceutical prescription for every possible mental state.

The power of movies to shape opinion and behavior is rooted in the origins of the film industry. As Garth Jewett points out in his seminal work, *Film: The Democratic Art*, much of the movies' influence on our world derives from the chronological coincidence of their development with the vast influx of immigrants in America, eager for instruction on the manners and mores of their new world.[5]

Hortense Powdermaker studied the way modern cinema influences contemporary Americans in her anthropological study *Hollywood, the Dream Factory.* According to this observer of the film media phenomenon, "a unique trait of modern life is the manipulation of people through mass communications.... In a time of change and conflict such as we experience today, movies and other mass communications emphasize and reinforce one set of values rather than another, present models for human relations through their portrayal by glamorous stars, and show life, truly or falsely, beyond the average individual's everyday experiences."[6]

Given this fascination with glamour, some of the most compelling stories on the silver screen are movies about the people who make movies. In 1967, Marc Robson presented *Valley of the Dolls,* the shocking exposé of Hollywood lives regulated by "dolls—the instant turn on for instant love, instant excitement, ultimate hell."[7] The film shows the drug culture on two levels—the level of the story of glamorous stars and the level of the famous actresses themselves, whom the audience identifies as sharing the drug problems of the characters they portray. The trailer introduces us to

Anne (Barbara Perkins) who took green pills
Neely (Patty Duke), an alcoholic who took red pills
Jennifer (Sharon Tate), who became a porn star and was addicted to blue
pills and
Helen Lawson (Susan Hayward), an aging star who used yellow pills.[8]

In the 40 years since the release of *Valley of the Dolls,* the pharmacopeia of "uppers, downer, and every-mood-in-betweeners" has expanded vastly from that handful of primary colored pills. No longer shocking behavior reserved for the scandal-page celebrities, instant mood fixes are very much a part of every facet of American life. In fact, Shankar Vedantam reported in the *Washington Post* (December 3, 2004) that use of antidepressant drugs has almost tripled in the last ten years. Vedantam cites a government report that "1 in 10 American women takes an antidepressant drug such as Prozac, Paxil or Zoloft," and adds information from Amy Bernstein, director of the project which produced a report on drug use for the Center for Health Statistics of the Center for Disease Control and Prevention, that more than one in three doctor's office visits by women in 2002 included getting or renewing a prescription for an antidepressant.[9] Antidepressants account for only one segment (albeit a large one) of the increase in drug use by the American public. The use of other psychotropic prescription drugs is also sharply up.

As these statistics show, many Americans live in a world seen through the lenses of these psychotropic drugs. This analysis examines specifically the role of contemporary films in portraying and, in fact, shaping this world.

A study of the multitude of varied references to psychotropic drugs in films reveals the American public's broad cultural awareness and uncritical acceptance. Drugs that were once specialized treatments used by psychiatrists in clinical settings are now recognized by the general movie-going public by their brand names, much like Starbucks or Krispy Kreme. Closer analysis of Hollywood's prescriptions uncovers several sub themes in the way these psychiatric drugs are viewed in the world of the silver screen and, by extension, in American society as a whole. While intricately intertwined, the attitudes expressed by the references in movies to psychiatric drugs fall into three distinct categories: First, psychotropic drugs are qualitatively similar to or worse than street drugs. Second, everyone is using these drugs or, at least, the use is quite widespread. Third, one or more of these medications can serve as a panacea for any and all problems.

Psychotropic Drugs Are Similar to Other Substances

An aspect of today's wide spread acceptance of psychotropic drugs is the way they are often compared to other drugs or substances. It is not uncommon to view films that reference the highly addictive and widespread street drug heroin alongside prescription drugs used to treat psychiatric symptoms. For instance, *Trainspotting*, the 1996 film that captured the ethos of a certain segment of Generation X, presents Valium specifically as helpful for someone trying to overcome his heroin addiction. Mark "Rent Boy" Renton lists the supplies gathered in stage one of "relinquishing junk." He includes such items as tomato soup, ice cream, mouthwash, vitamins, milk of magnesia, buckets for excrement, a television and one bottle of Valium. He indicates that he has obtained Valium from his mother and comments that this is an indication of her own drug addiction, an addiction which is admittedly more socially acceptable and is often relegated to housewives.[10] This reference points to the mixed social message regarding these prescription drugs. On one hand, they are acknowledged as less threatening than street drugs such as heroin; on the other hand, they are recognized as just as likely to be abused and perhaps as even more dangerous because of their wide-spread social acceptance and the veneer of legitimacy conferred by their prescription status. Of course, when the prescription is used incorrectly as in a Valium addiction or in counteracting side effects of withdrawal from other drugs, any aspect of legitimacy is voided. Ironically, immediately after reflecting on his mother's drug abuse, Rent Boy concludes his preparations by saying that he is now ready and just needs one final hit of heroin while the Valium kicks in to ease the pain of the heroin withdrawal.[11] Thus Rent Boy is assuring failure on several counts. First, despite his extensive preparation, the assumption that one can take a final hit of heroin shows complete naiveté regarding the insidious nature of heroin addiction. Second, the idea that Valium will be enough to counteract the suffering of heroin withdrawal vastly underestimates the intensity of that experience (or wildly overestimates the curative power of Valium). Finally, even if the Valium-assisted sobriety had succeeded, one expects from his mother's experience that Rent Boy would simply have replaced one addiction with another. This last point highlights society's incorrect assumption that it is better to be addicted to a prescription drug than to a variety of other street or illegal drugs. This assumption misses the point that incorrect use of these psychiatric drugs is illegal and often reflects underlying addictions or lack of coping resources.

A similar pairing of addictions is presented in *Requiem for a Dream* (2000).[12] This movie depicts parallel drug stories across various aspects of American society. Initially the movie depicts Sara Goldfarb as she portrays a middle-aged woman who begins taking pills from a "diet doctor," just to look better in her favorite red dress. Dieting soon becomes an obsession, and very shortly she is taking barbiturates to counteract the diet pills and other stimulants to wake up from her sedative-induced slumbers. Her acceptance of barbiturate and sedative use may have stemmed from her initial acceptance of the "quick fix" diet pill. Now she finds herself needing medicinal magic for every mood, situation, and time of day. So she begins mixing and matching prescription pills. Meanwhile, as she becomes more and more addicted to these drugs, the film traces the parallel downward spiral of her son and his girlfriend, both of whom become addicted to illicit narcotics. In a particularly gruesome sequence, the camera shifts between two emergency room scenes— in one, the mother's persistent drug cocktail has led to a psychotic breakdown, and in the other, her son is being treated for a near lethal hit of heroin. The outcome is no better for the girlfriend, who slips into a cycle of prostitution and drug abuse. The film accurately reflects the dangers of both illicit narcotics and prescription drugs as well as their similar prevalence in our society. The message is clear that the younger generation may have rejected the use of barbiturates and sedatives as not being strong enough, not producing a good enough high, or simply being too old-fashioned; yet, the devastating effects of any kind of drug abuse remain the same. As is often the case, the generational divide is evident in the type of drug that is abused.

Besides the parallels with illicit drugs, these psychotropic medications are often paired with another legal, widely accepted substance — alcohol. Sometimes, the pills are simply a substitute for alcohol. Where in a previous generation, someone would take a drink in a moment of crisis or heightened emotion, today's characters are just as likely to reach for a pill.

In *The Life of David Gale*,[13] Prozac abuse is compared favorably to alcoholism. David Gale, the philosophy professor and anti–death penalty activist, was dismissed from his college because of a false charge of rape. After an unsuccessful interview for a faculty position at another university, he asks why he was not considered for the job. The dean assures Gale that his alcohol problem is not an impediment. In fact, the college administrator says that it would nice to have someone who did not use Prozac as a crutch, as the rest of the faculty do, thus highlighting the prevalence of the overuse of this antidepressant, in this case among the intellectual elite.

The movie *Antitrust* (2001)[14] is the story two young computer geniuses, fresh out of college, who are on the brink of introducing software that will revolutionize the industry. One of the pair, Milo, goes to work for a large corporation. The first indication of wrongdoing is a TV news story heard in the background while Milo works. The TV screen shows a wrecked vehicle while a voiceover tells that alcohol and Prozac were found in the car. The implication is that the man has emotional problems for which he was being treated by a professional with an antidepressant and simultaneously self-medicating with the alcohol. This serves to allay suspicion of foul play by suggesting not only that he was already suffering from emotional problems, but that he was also adding to those problems by using alcohol. By pairing these two substances, the corporate villains are playing on the audience's immediate recognition of these drugs and the ramifications of their combined use.

Other movies show characters casually washing down their pills with alcohol. In *Basketball Diaries* (1995),[15] the high school basketball stars turned drug addicts are often shown swallowing uppers and downers with cheap liquor when they can afford it. As the movie progresses, they begin to use heroin exclusively and forgo the other drugs that supposedly initially helped them counteract heroin's effects. In *Valley of the Dolls*, alcohol is used to enhance the effects of stimulants because, as Neely explains, the drinks make the pills work better and faster.[16] While this hyperaddive effect may exist, alcohol can be a very dangerous combination with most of these psychiatric drugs, particularly when the person decides for himself what the "most effective" use is. For example, research suggests the synergistic effect of mixing sedative drugs with alcohol can be lethal.[17]

The dual use of alcohol and psychoactive drugs was part of a 1977 research survey of the 1 million members of Alcoholics Anonymous. Eighteen percent of all survey respondents said they were addicted to other drugs as well as alcohol. Significantly, young women were the largest group of dual addicts. These results are not surprising, considering that women are far more likely to be given prescription tranquilizers or antidepressants than men.[18] Captain Joseph Pursch, director of the Long Beach Rehabilitation Center where Betty Ford was treated, refers to this condition as "sedativism." And the addiction to psychoactive drugs can be far more devastating than alcoholism. Hughes and Brewn, authors of *Tranquilizing of America*, report that many people who work with recovering addicts say they would rather take someone off heroin than Valium.[19]

Rarely does the character recognize the inefficacy of using combinations of different substances to deal with emotional problems. In *Heat* (1995), Justine Hanna snaps at her husband that his emotional withdrawal is in many ways worse than her own withdrawal through the combined use of Prozac and marijuana.[20] Ironically, while she is obviously self-medicating with marijuana and antidepressants for the frustration she feels at the void in her marriage, she at least recognizes that she must also deal with the situation emotionally. As she points out, her husband has failed to face the reality that their relationship is not working and that he has thus fallen into a pattern of wandering through life on autopilot. He uses his job as an excuse to avoid the relationship—a practice that Justine even on her drug mixture clearly recognizes as ineffective. Not only does this movie highlight the combined use of street drugs such as marijuana with psychiatric drugs such as Prozac, it also reveals insights about the emotional danger of avoiding problems. While Justine recognizes, to some extent, the ineffectiveness of her drug use in avoiding problems, she is more critical of her husband's throwing himself into his work to escape confronting their situations. The implication in her line is that if he would just avoid his problems like everyone else by taking drugs, she would have more respect for him or would be able to deal with their problems on an equal playing field—one in which both partners are high on some drug.

Everyone Is Doing It

A second prevalent theme in recent movies is the attitude that psychotropic drugs are widespread and commonly accepted as forms of avoidance or self-medication. Today, psychiatric drugs are so prevalent that offhanded, lighthearted references abound in Hollywood's comedies. Contrary to the shocking nature of the Hollywood exposé in *Valley of the Dolls*, the more recent *America's Sweethearts* (2001) makes drug use in Hollywood the subject of offhanded humor. This romantic comedy about a celebrated Hollywood couple, whose marital squabbles are interfering with the publicity for their new release, references a myriad of different prescription drugs that Americans are using to medicate themselves for every possible condition. In an early scene Eddie, the romantic male lead, pours a handful of drugs into his palm while seated in the backseat of his limousine. As the driver looks askance at him, Eddie assures him that these are herbal medications and not the Zoloft that the tabloid magazines allege he is using.[21] The driver's only response is to note that Eddie certainly has a large amount, although one gets the impression that the driver is judging Eddie's need for all these so-called herbal medications as well as his honesty about the actual nature of the pills. Moments later, Eddie reveals just how plentiful his supply is when he chucks big white pills at his obviously agitated agent who is in the process of trying to negotiate the appearance of the stars' entourages. The audience immediately gets the non-verbal message, "When dealing with a stressful situation, take some happy pills."

At the press conference that follows, Lee, the agent, explains away Eddie's belligerence toward the security guards by confiding, "diet pills."[22] This offhanded dispersal of drugs for any situation and the casual explanation of drugs as an acceptable cause of negative behavior are meant to reflect Hollywood's acceptance of and even reliance on these drugs. Eddie himself tells the assembled press that he has just taken a large quantity of Vicodin and therefore should be feeling the effects for months.[23] He has no qualms about sharing his drug use with the public or using this as an explanation for behavior. His reference to Vicodin here indicates his belief that it is perfectly acceptable and perhaps even desirable behavior. While the film is replete with references to a myriad of drugs for every known purpose, perhaps the most telling and comedic reference is the incident in the movie star's home. As Lee is seated on the sofa, he witnesses a dog dragging a man along the ground. He tells his estranged wife that her dog has "just swallowed" the window washer. On hearing this, Kiki, the assistant, jumps up and runs out of the room explaining that she must go get Prozac. At this bizarre reaction, Lee is curious and asks whether the star is taking Prozac. The response he gets is that no, Kiki is not giving the Prozac to the overwrought diva; rather, it is the dog which is being medicated.[24] This interaction reflects a Hollywood where even the moods of animals are regulated by drugs and this practice is perfectly acceptable.

Oddly enough, comedic references to psychotropic medication of animals are not uncommon. These references seem on the surface to be evidence of just how over-prescribed our society has become as we now offhandedly recommend psychiatric drugs for pets as well as people. As far back as the 1989 film Turner and Hooch, an irate neighbor shouts for Turner to manage the dog's behavior with Valium and suggests that it might not be a bad idea for Turner to take some himself.[25] In point of fact, this junk-yard dog has witnessed the violent death of his owner, so the advice may not be far off the mark. The neighbor is actually fairly accurate in his "pre-scription" that a relaxant may help the dog to overcome or to deal with the trauma that it has witnessed. This somewhat accurate prescription is reflective of common understanding of appropriate uses for psychotropic drugs. Similarly, the little pet in *Picking up the Pieces* has also suffered a psy-chological trauma. Tex (played by Woody Allen) has chopped his partner into little pieces during a magic trick gone wildly wrong. The dog is incon-solable at the loss of his mistress. In response to the dog's mopey behavior, Tex wonders aloud what is wrong with the dog and speculates that he may have to begin giving his wife's pet Prozac in its Alpo.[26] Here it is noted that while the dog has possibly suffered a significant trauma, the layman's pre-scription for Prozac is a reference to use of this antidepressant to cure any-thing that may be making one feel bad. Quick dispersal of Prozac that supplants the natural grief process is often not beneficial to the grieving individual. However, the point in the movie is that it is too much bother to deal with the dog's emotional problems and thus Prozac, a quick fix, is recommended. Also, it is interesting to note in this quote the linking of two brands (dog food and antidepressant) that are so widely advertised that their names are synonymous with their product types. In both these movies, these prescription psychiatric drugs are so well known and universally dis-tributed that even dogs are not immune to their use.

In point of fact, it is not uncommon for dogs to be on Prozac for rea-sons as varied as those of their human owners. An article in *Veterinary Forum* lists nineteen clinical indications for prescribing Prozac, including any obsessive-compulsive, stereotypic-repetitive behavior, attention seek-ing, eating disorders, inappropriate urination, and separation anxiety. This latter obviously was the reason Prozac was suggested for the silver screen canines in two of the movies mentioned above. Nor are dogs the only ani-mals in America on Prozac. Dr. Melmen also recommends its use for enhancing training of horses, cats with behavioral problems, feather pluck-ing disorder in birds, and pigs with bulimia.[27]

While psychotropic drugs are treated as commonplace, reference to them is often a kind of shorthand symbol for sophistication, signaling that the user is trying to assuage some generalized anxiety resulting from a hypersensitive nature or to modify a mood of world-weary ennui. Exam-ples are the showbiz glitterati mentioned at the beginning of this chapter, the well-to-do suburbanites of *Ordinary People*, Woody Allen's neurotic urban sophisticates—in other words, the upper echelon of every facet of American society.

This phenomenon of drug use as status symbol is sometimes linked to another symbol of privilege — being under the care of a therapist. After all, these are prescription drugs, so the initial source has to be a medical doctor. Most often, however, in the newer films, the characters themselves are using the drugs inappropriately or are passing the medications along to friends as in the following exchange from *Six Days, Seven Nights*.

As their small plane is buffeted off course and damaged in a sudden violent storm, Robin Monroe, the sophisticated magazine editor played by Anne Heche, shakes pills out of a prescription medicine bottle. As she is doing this, the pilot questions what she has in the bottle. She responds that her doctor has given her Xanax for tense situations, and that being in a damaged airplane flying out of control certainly meets the definition of "tense." The pilot then asks for several himself, but Robin refuses and orders him to focus on piloting the plane. Several minutes (and several pills) later, Robin grabs the microphone as the pilot is trying to place a mayday call and starts announcing "blue light specials" just before passing out.[28]

A variation of this idea of drug use as a sign of sophistication, particularly in the more recent films, occurs when young people are given drugs by adults. In the horror movie *28 Days Later*, for example, 12-year-old Hannah asks for some of the Valium the adults are sharing. Her father initially forbids it, but at the urging of the pharmacist relents and allows her half a pill. His lay assessment of the proper dosage just to take the edge off her anxiety and allow her to sleep adds extra dimension to a later scene in which Selena gives her several Valium when the soldiers are planning to rape her.[29] Mark Renton uses his mother's Valium in *Trainspotting* in an abortive attempt to kick his heroin habit, and the priest in *Desecration* gives valium to Bobby Rullo.[30]

The widespread use of prescription medications for children and adolescents was highlighted non-cinematically yet dramatically in 2005 by the murder trial of Christopher Pittman. Defense counsel argued that Zoloft was responsible for the violent murder of Pittman's grandparents by the youth, who was twelve at the time of the crime. This contention was based on a 2004 FDA Public Health Advisory that identified a greater risk of suicide among children and adolescents who were taking antidepressant drugs, including SSRIs, for major depressive disorders, obsessive compulsive disorders, and other psychiatric problems.[31] Prosecutors countered with the fact that no connections had been established between such drugs and violent behavior toward others. Apparently the jury did not agree that Zoloft, so widely prescribed for the disorders listed above, could have such a catastrophic effect on a child's personality, since they found him guilty. The case, however, brought to public attention the dramatic increase of use of these SSRIs in children. An article for CNN.com which discusses the case reports that currently, children under 18 make up 7 percent of all the people in the U.S. taking antidepressants.[32]

Hollywood characters themselves use drug references as a proof of their sophistication. In *Mean Guns* (1997), for example, Lou pronounces Valium, Prozac, and Ritalin "Breakfast of champions."[33] This clear corollary between the popular culture reference to the breakfast cereal Wheaties resonates on several levels. First, it makes the breakfast cereal associated with the best athletes equivalent to a psychiatric drug cocktail. (And, in recent years, we have seen that many famous athletes do, indeed, use performance-enhancing drugs on a daily basis.) Second, it demonstrates the familiarity with all these brands, the psychotropic drugs and the General Mills cereal. Finally, it indicates another reality in American life — that drugs like Prozac and Ritalin are marketed in exactly the same way today as breakfast cereal.

In fact, references to brand name drugs have become so common that the game of one-upmanship has risen to another level. It is now not enough to casually refer to prescription medications; one must have the latest and best; as for example in the 1997 film *Grosse Point Blank*. In one scene, the rival hit men are having a conversation. Mr. Grocer is trying to convince Martin Blank to join his syndicate. When he observes Martin taking pills ("nutrients," Martin calls them), Grocer offers pills of his own which he refers to as the newest thing — Durazac 15, which makes Prozac seem like a "decaf latte."[34] The implication is clear — Grocer has the latest and the best, and joining him will greatly improve Martin's status.

Similarly, in *Wisegirls* (2002), Rachel is the experienced waitress who initiates the naïve Meg into the lucrative drug business being run through the restaurant. When Meg appears to be breaking down after witnessing a mob hit in the restaurant, Rachel tries to pull her together and asks what Meg is taking. Meg acknowledges two glasses of wine and a few Valium and asks Rachel if she wants any. To which the streetwise Rachel crudely scoffs that no one takes Valium anymore. When Meg responds resentfully, Rachel counters that perhaps she should be Meg's "pharmacist" because she can offer much better than Valium and cheap wine (referring to the illicit hard narcotics).

The fact that the three movies discussed above deal with organized crime brings up an interesting sideline. Similar to the parallels made between illicit and legal drugs, the connection of these prescription medications and underworld activities somehow casts a shadow over the pharmaceuticals as well.

Psychiatric Drugs as Panacea

The theme that everyone is doing these drugs serves as a logical precursor to the third common theme with reference to these drugs—that one or more of these medications serves as a panacea for all of one's problems. Drugs are everywhere in movies as a viable treatment for whatever ails the movie characters. *Ordinary People* (1980), for example, reveals the general view of these drugs as necessary and acceptable. Conrad, who has previously been institutionalized briefly for a suicide attempt following his brother's drowning, confronts his psychiatrist about his need for a tranquilizer. In reply to the doctor's response that tranquilizers are not indicated in this case, Conrad snaps back that he is paying him well and the doctor should be able to make him feel better with a pill. The doctor answers that people are not necessarily always supposed to feel better.[35] This interaction indicates the clear trend that "ordinary people" are diagnosing themselves and have become convinced by society, media, and the prevalence of these drugs that they are supposed to feel good all the time. In addition, Conrad's attitude reflects the conviction that the pharmaceutical industry can and should provide a vast array of feel-good pills and that doctors should concede this quick fix solution rather than worrying about actually fixing the underlying problem.

So ingrained is this conviction that mental health professionals are being considered unnecessary. In response to a stressful and confusing situation, one of Woody Allen's angst-ridden characters in *Manhattan Murder Mystery* (1993) is discussing consulting a psychiatrist to reevaluate her life. Her husband advises her that she does not need a psychiatrist and says she has no problems "a little Prozac and a polo mallet can't cure."[36] While one gets the impression that the only real problem is that the woman is just over-involved in the life of her neighbor, her perspective is that she can not deal with anything. Her rush to consult with a psychiatrist indicates people reliance on therapy or something outside of themselves to deal with problems. Her husband's response indicates society's acceptance of circumventing the therapist and going directly for the quick-fix drug.

The movies are replete with such advice. As early as 1985, in *Desperately Seeking Susan*, Leslie, whose sister is missing, reproaches her husband and her brother-in-law (the missing woman's husband). She is outraged that the two are eating in the midst of the crisis of trying to find Susan. Her husband responds that this is a natural reaction to their nervousness. Leslie instructs them that the normal response is to take a Valium and implies that they should take some immediately rather than assuaging their anxiety with food.[37] What is most significant here is the reference to the idea that taking Valium is the widely accepted norm and that it will somehow allow these characters to deal with the traumatic anxiety of not knowing where their loved one is. Disturbingly, in *Unhook the Stars*, taking Valium is presented as sound parenting advice. The woman is nervous as a young boy rides off to begin a paper route on his own for the first time. "Take a Valium" is the advice that she is given by an experienced mother.[38] In another reference in *Manhattan Murder Mystery*, Larry is upset by officers investigating a possible crime scene in which he was involved. As he is pacing and clearly tense, he rambles through a list of his needs, which include a drink and a large quantity of Xanax or anything that will calm him down.[39] Here, rational approaches to the situation or other methods of calming oneself are replaced by the immediate reaching for large quantities of anti-anxiety drugs. This is not uncommon for characters in Woody Allen movies, as illustrated by "Broadway" Danny Rose, who opines, "I need a Valium the size of a hockey puck."[40] Not only are the characters in seemingly desperate need of these drugs despite the fact that the situations they face are not very traumatic, but they also need quantities larger than would be recommended by any doctor.

In *Mambo Italiano*, the tranquilizer is a way to cope with family stress. Angelo is a young gay man who has come home to reveal his sexual preference to his family. When he asks his sister how she is doing in response to his news, she confides that she will be all right once the Valium takes effect.[41] Once again, we see a reflection of the dangerous trend of substituting pills for the sometimes difficult, but ultimately necessary, effort of facing up to a situation and dealing with the inevitable emotions surrounding something difficult. This family, like the Jarrett family in *Ordinary People*, does not need to be emotionally anesthetized; they need to deal with their conflicting emotions, not bury them with pharmaceuticals.

Not only does Hollywood show movie characters represented as regular people using these mood-altering drugs to combat the stresses of their everyday lives in twentieth century America, they are also used by the victims in the most extreme situations of the horror genre.

In *Child's Play 2*, Andy, the intended victim of Chucky, the homicidal doll in the first movie, is living with foster parents, Joanne and Phil. Joanne is worried about Andy's adjustment and indicates to her husband that they should do something to make the transition to their home easier for the young boy. Phil's suggested antidote is to give Andy some Valium.[42] While most experts on parenting would probably not advocate sedatives to make a child "feel more at home," this use perhaps seems more appropriate than the avoidance usages discussed above, since the child has previously been attacked by a monster doll. However, the appropriateness of giving a child such a strong drug should be examined closely and not offered as a quick fix before other avenues have been explored.

Teenagers, perhaps because they figure so prominently in horror movies, are often found using these prescription drugs. In *Final Destination 2* (2003), a group of kids "cheat death" from a terrible car crash and spend the rest of the movie anxiously awaiting the grim fates they have narrowly avoided. At one particularly tense moment, one of them polls the group in a search for Valium (which is referred to by name). Of course, since these are typical movie teenagers, one of the girls produces a bottle of the prescription pills. When a third character reaches for the bottle, the audience understands that everyone in this scene needs the medicinal solace because the burden and stress of waiting for death is overwhelming.[43]

The 1994 horror film *Desecration* tells the tale of a young Catholic boy, Bobby Rullo, who loses control of a remote control airplane, causing the death of a nun on the playground at his school. This accident begins a chain of horrific events, which the movie audience sees as related to his mother's death when Bobby was an infant. Brother Nicholas, one of the priests at Bobby's school, offers the child a pill. When Bobby asks the priest where he got the pills, the priest responds that the Valium is his. At the boy's surprise, Brother Nicholas assures him that indeed priests can and do take Valium (just like everyone else).[44]

Further evidence of the use of these drugs to combat severe situations encountered in horror films is found in the film *28 Days Later,* in which England has been overrun by enraged beings infected by a terrible virus. On the grounds of a ruined farmhouse, a small band of survivors settles down for the night when Selena, the female lead character, pulls out numerous packets of Valium. Her male companion remarks with awe at the large quantity she has.[45] She tells him that she didn't need a prescription because she was qualified as a chemist. Thus in this situation, the drugs are being dispensed by someone who, while not a mental health professional, is at least a pharmacist and therefore familiar with proper use and dosage. Jim, of course, is also familiar with the drug, not as a professional, but as every layman is. He indicates that even if they do get attacked in the middle of the night, the assault will not bother them because of the effects of the drug.[46] Here the Valium which may have been intended to take the edge off an admittedly stressful situation is recognized for its ability to combat the most horrible scenario that these characters can imagine.

Later, Valium is used for precisely this purpose of voiding any negative thoughts, feelings or emotions associated with extreme trauma. Selena and Hannah, a young girl who is traveling with them after her father was infected by the dreaded virus, are being held prisoner by a rogue army troop. Selena knows that the soldiers are planning to sexually violate them. To dull the impending horror for the young girl, Selena gives her a handful of the Valium. As they sit on a sofa under guard waiting for the soldiers to return, Hannah remarks that she can feel the effect of the drug but that she is not feeling sleepy.[47] They successfully elude the soldiers and escape from the stronghold, but despite the girl's assessment of the drug's effects, the film depicts her soporific state and implies that if she had been raped, the effects of the drug would have prevented any recognition or experience of that horror.

In Wes Craven's 2002 horror flick, *They*, three young adults are talking at their friend's funeral. One asks if the deceased had given any indication as to his mental state before he died. The friend replies that he didn't have any indication that there was a psychological problem, but that the deceased was rambling and incoherent and possibly on drugs again. To this, the deceased's college roommate interjects that the deceased was taking Prozac and remarks that obviously the drug was not effective in this case.[48] The background story is that Billy was part of a group of children who had been abducted by alien creatures. Eighteen years later, they return to claim him. In despair and panic, Billy shoots himself in a coffee shop in front of his childhood friend. The conversation at the funeral reveals that the young man had probably been appropriately given a prescription to combat legitimate depression or anxiety related to his impending re-abduction. Given the bizarre circumstances, it is not surprising that the antidepressant was not effective.

Even in spoofs of horror films, the characters attempt to relieve the terror of the situation through the use of psychiatric drugs. In *Scream 2* (1997), the news photographer, Joel, announces that he is going out to get donuts, Prozac, and hopefully more powerful drugs such as crack in response to the group's discussion of horrible urban legends.[49] Here, Prozac is recommended as a way to deal with the frightening conversation and resultant fears that emerge.

While references to drugs for anxiety and depression span the range of movie genres from horror flicks to comedies, references to drugs used to treat psychotic symptoms tend to be dealt with by more serious characters and are not as common. Still, these drugs are referenced panaceas even for serious psychotic breaks with reality.

One of the most accurate portrayals of schizophrenia is found in *A Beautiful Mind*, the biographical depiction of John Nash, a Nobel Prize winner in physics who suffers from schizophrenia. Interestingly, the movie portrays John's struggle with schizophrenia at a time when psychotropic treatment was in its infancy. His first introduction to medication occurs as he is having a severe psychotic break and a doctor injects him with Thorazine and later advises him that he has been given Thorazine and that he should ease back into reality.[50] Following this, the audience finds John's wife watching as he is put into an insulin coma. It is a fairly gruesome and perhaps even barbaric-appearing treatment that essentially puts John's body into severe shock. Once home, John has been given pills to take daily, which are assumed to be used to treat his symptoms of seeing things and hearing voices which do not really exist. While the drug is never mentioned by name in this scene, based on the time period, it is most likely Thorazine or some close relative of that drug. It is in this biographically based movie, that we see an accurate depiction of the treatments used at the time and a movement toward more independence for the patient (being able to be home and even work some) with the introduction of pharmaceutical treatments.

However, most mentions of Thorazine occur in movies in which the audience has difficulty determining where reality lies. In the film *Twelve Monkeys* (1995), a convict named Cole is sent back in time from the year 2035 to 1996 to discover the origins of a deadly virus that is threatening to eradicate the human population. Unfortunately, he ends up in 1990 and is locked up in a mental institution for his ramblings about the end of society and life as we know it. His proselytizing about the doom of the virus leads others to believe that he is insane and lands him in a mental institution where he meets Dr. Railly and her son, Jeffrey. At one point, he is having a conversation with Jeffrey, who is portrayed as mentally imbalanced himself. On speculation about what happened to Cole in the mental hospital, Jeffrey lists Thorazine and Haldol as possible drugs Cole was given and asks how much of each he was given.[51] Even though the time period is 1990, the character is still referring to some of the earliest drugs known for the treatment of schizophrenia, reflecting a limitation in the public's knowledge of current treatments for psychotic symptoms but continued clear identification of early drugs with these symptoms.

Similarly, in the film *K-PAX* (2001), the character Prot is found in Grand Central Station in New York in a dazed state and is taken in by the police, where he is questioned about where he came from. To this he answers that he is an alien from the planet K-PAX. This leads to hospitalization in a psychiatric ward. After unsuccessful treatment of Prot's symptoms, Dr. Powell is brought in as an expert in psychosis to consult on the odd responses of this patient. The referring physician indicates how different this patient is when explaining to Dr. Powell that he has been delusional for an entire month, as indicated by his unshakable belief that he is an alien from another planet. Dr. Powell, looking at the patient's chart, reads the dosage and duration of Prot's Thorazine treatment and expresses his disbelief that at this dosage for this duration the patient's behavior and beliefs have remained unchanged.[52] Thus the audience's understanding of the power and effectiveness of this antipsychotic is implied; however, it is not assumed that the general audience has familiarity with dosage and thus this is explicitly stated. This is the first indication that Prot may not be a typical psychotic, and the seed is planted that perhaps he really is an alien. Throughout the course of treatment, he claims to have intimate and exceptional knowledge of space, space travel, and astrophysics. To verify that he has this knowledge, Prot is brought before a group of elite astrophysicists, where he explains planetary alignment and orbiting related to his home planet, K-PAX. The astrophysicists are stunned at his having this knowledge when they themselves had just discovered some of the information and were having difficulty understanding the relationships between the planets in this particular system. This leaves the audience and the psychiatrist questioning whether the patient really might be from a distant planet. The movie continues to trace the growing skepticism of Dr. Powell in a conference with other psychiatrists at the hospital where he discusses the specifics of Prot's case and begins to reveal his doubts about Prot's psychotic diagnosis to his fellow physicians. He questions how it is possible that Prot failed to respond to the Haldol that he was given. It is here that we find out that in addition to the initial treatment, another antipsychotic, Haldol, has also been tried. Interestingly, the two drugs mentioned in this movie are part of the early class of typical antipsychotics, again reflecting the public's limited knowledge of newer treatments.

The general public is probably not as familiar with the second generation drugs which include Clozaril (chemical name: clozapine) and Risperdal (chemical name: risperidone) or the recent third generation drug Abilify (chemical name: aripirazole). In the psychiatrists' meeting, none of these alternative, second- or third-generation drugs are mentioned as a possible course of treatment for one of several reasons. It is common for several first-generation drugs to be used initially as they can have some of the strongest effects, but more importantly because they are the least costly. In the case of someone who does not have insurance or a family, as in Prot's case, the most cost effective solution would be advised. However, it is more likely that the other possible treatments are not referred to in the movie because of the audience's lack of knowledge of these drugs. In a final twist at the end of the movie, Dr. Powell challenges Prot's claims of hailing from the planet K-PAX and being able to travel faster than light, even though it is still clear to the audience that he may believe the alien story. To this challenge, Prot replies with the knowledge of a psychiatrist and he himself recommends a Thorazine drip to treat the doctor's implied delusion.[53] Again, the reference signifies the widespread acceptance and knowledge of the antipsychotic drug Thorazine, such that even the patients are well aware of its use. This last reference is, however, somewhat incorrect as Dr. Powell has simply made an error in judgment or thinking and is not actually experiencing psychotic symptoms.

On a much lighter note, a reference to Thorazine as a treatment for unbelievable or fantastic thoughts is also found in the comic movie *Freaky Friday*. The premise for the movie is that a mother and her teenage daughter are at odds with each other and frustrated by the other's inability to empathize with the difficulties each faces. In a science fictional twist, the two switch bodies. Upon waking up and discovering that they are in different bodies, they discuss what they should do and how to handle this bizarre switch. At one point, the daughter, who is in the mother's body, suggests that they go to the emergency room. The mother, a psychiatrist, recognizes that the results of telling other people, particularly authorities, will result in psychiatric hospitalization and medication with Thorazine.[54] Similar to the reference in *K-PAX*, this reference indicates that Thorazine will be administered for any claim that might be unusual, unreal, or unbelievable. Although simply having one bizarre belief does not usually constitute a psychotic break or a need for pharmaceutical treatment, and Tess Coleman, as a trained professional, should recognize that fact, this is Hollywood, and therefore she expresses the common social attitude that antipsychotics are a cure-all.

The Future of Psychotropia?

While these three themes have reflected popular culture's attitudes toward psychotropic drugs, there are indications that American society may be reevaluating the Psychotropia it has created. For the past forty years, films have shown us a world in which psychotropic drugs are similar to other mind-altering substances, one in which use of these drugs is widespread and accepted, and finally a world that offers pills as panaceas for any and all problems. In 2004, one movie questioned the Utopist implications of this world.

The movie, *Garden State*, depicts the all-too-common use of psychotropic medications for covering up a range of problems that one does not want to deal with. The movie opens with scenes in which we find out that Andrew's mother has just passed away and he has come home to New Jersey from California for the funeral. While home, he visits a neurologist for treatment of headaches which he describes as intense, short-lived, and like lightening. The neurologist in reviewing Andrew's history recognizes that he has been given Lithium and asks Andrew about the duration of that treatment. Andrew replies that he has been on this or similar drugs since he was ten years old. The doctor then looks further into the chart and questions the duration of treatment and effectiveness of the myriad of other psychotropic drugs including Paxil, Zoloft, Celexa, and Depacot that Andrew has been on.[55] This exchange between doctor and patient highlights the myriad of psychotropic drugs that Andrew has been on and leaves the audience curious as to why he has been on them. From what the movie has depicted to this point, Andrew's affect and environment have been very flat and seem to lack any emotion or variety. His apartment is stark, his relationship with his father is clinical, and his reaction to his mother's death is blasé. The neurologist clearly questions the appropriateness of this many psychotropic medications, and it is soon revealed that Andrew himself has been questioning whether to stay on the medications. The doctor then advises Andrew to discuss any change in psychiatric medication use with his psychiatrist, It is here that the audience and the neurologist learn that Andrew's father, a psychiatrist, has been treating him and prescribing the medications. Assuming that the Lithium is being prescribed for an inability to cope with everyday demands, the doctor suggests that stress and anxiety can have adverse reactions on health and well-being. When Andrew reflects that he does not think that he is under stress and anxiety and does not feel much of anything, the neurologist advises that the dosage of Lithium may be quite high and may result in a numbing of any feeling. He comments on the high dosage of Lithium and Andrew's proclamation that he feels little. The doctor's response and advice indicate his surprise and concern that the Lithium has been given at too high a dosage, for too long, and has been prescribed inappropriately by the father, as he should not be treating to his own son. The doctor also offers his opinion that these drugs are not particularly useful in the long run to treat psychological disorders outside of the context of therapy designed to address the core issues.[56]

This interaction between patient and doctor reveals many different ethical and moral issues surrounding the use of psychiatric drugs. First, it is unethical for Andrew's father to serve as his psychiatrist. Secondly, as is revealed later in the movie, the reason that his father has been maintaining him on these drugs is because of an incident that happened when Andrew was nine years old in which he pushed his mother in a moment of anger; she fell over an open dishwasher and was permanently paralyzed. The father's response to prescribe and then maintain his son on these multiple drugs reflects exactly the reason that it is unethical for a parent to treat a child — that there can often be lack of objectivity. In this case, this lack of objectivity seems to indicate that Andrew's father projected his own feelings of sadness and sense of loss onto Andrew and then was actually trying to treat himself. In Andrew's conversation with the neurologist and as a theme throughout the movie, one gets the sense that it has been easier for the father to maintain his son on medication than to actually face any dysfunctional family dynamic. In fact, Andrew specifically indicates at one point that he thinks his father wants him to stay on the Lithium because he believes it makes Andrew, and by extension the entire family, happy.[57] That has been the theme throughout the films studied: Do not deal with the realities of a world that might make you feel bad. Take a pill and create a world in which there are no problems.

Gradually, Andrew (and the audience) comes to an awareness that this carefully cultivated "garden state" that he is in, this world where thoughts, emotions, and feelings are controlled by medication, may not be the ideal world we have been led to believe. Andrew lashes out about how much he despises his home town because of the widespread use of every type of drug. He then compares his town to the drug-maintained utopia in *Brave New World*.[58] Andrew's observation reflects insight into the condition of America today. Like the inhabitants of Huxley's dystopia, who had their pleasure pill, "Soma," everyone in America has access to happiness in a pill. Determinedly, Andrew turns his back on the psychotropic solution and resolves to try to confront his life without the fog of medication. Like the heroes of *Brave New World* and *Nineteen Eighty-four*, Andrew becomes the one voice that questions blind acceptance of society's prescription for happiness.

Although it is too soon and there is not enough evidence to positively identify a shift in public attitude, and it must be noted that *Garden State* is an Indie film and thus possibly not representative of Hollywood's view, still the movie may signal the beginning of a realization on the part of the American public that Psychotropia is actually a dystopia. The Psychotropia shown on the Hollywood screens as "our land" and "our people" is like Huxley's Brave New World and Orwell's Oceania, a world of false promise and beliefs that are ultimately destructive. And, perhaps, in 2004, the American public began to recognize this.

Notes

1. *Nineteen Eighty-four* (1984), Michael Radford, director, 113 minutes, International Video Entertainment, videocassette.

2. Based on a chart in Box Office Mojo, <www.boxofficemojo.com/yearly/> (viewed March 9, 2005).

3. 2004 home video wrap, Hollywood Reporter.com, January 19, 2005, <http://www.hollywoodreporter.com>. (archived)

4. Advertising slogan of E.I. Nemours DuPont Company.

5. Garth Jewett, *Film: The Democratic Art* (New York: William Morrow, 1976), p. 35.

6. Hortense Powdermaker, *Hollywood, the Dream Factory* (New York: Little, Brown and Company, 1950), 11.

7. *Valley of the Dolls,* 1967, Mark Robson, director, 123 minutes, 20th Century Fox Home Entertainment, videocassette.

8. Ibid.

9. Shankar Vedantam, "Antidepressant Use by U.S. Adults Soars," *Washington Post,* December 3, 2004, Friday, A15, <http://www.washingtonpost.com/ac2/wp-dyn/A297 151–2004Dec2?language=printer> (viewed January 14, 2004). (archived)

10. *Trainspotting,* 1995, Danny Boyle, director, 94 minutes, Buena Vista Home Entertainment, 2004, DVD.

11. Ibid.

12. *Requiem for a Dream,* 2000, Darren Aronofsky, director, 102 minutes, Artisan Entertainment, 2001, DVD.

13. *The Life of David Gale,* 2003, Alan Parker, director, 131 minutes, Universal Pictures, 2003, videocassette.

14. *Antitrust,* 2001, Peter Hewitt, director, 108 minutes, MGM Home Entertainment, 2001, DVD.

15. *Basketball Diaries,* Scott Kalvert, director, 102 minutes, Polygram Music Video, 1995, videocassette.

16. *Valley of the Dolls.*

17. Richard Hughes and Robert Brewin, *The Tranquilizing of America* (New York: Harcourt, Brace, Jovanovich, 1979), p. 42.

18. Ibid., pp. 26–27.

19. Ibid., p. 42.

20. *Heat,* Michael Mann, director, 171 minutes, Warner Home Video, 1996, videocassette.

21. *America's Sweethearts,* Joe Roth, director, 103 minutes, Columbia Pictures, 2001, videocassette.

22. Ibid.

23. Ibid.

24. Ibid.

25. *Turner and Hooch,* Roger Spottiswoode, director, 99 minutes, Buena Vista Home Entertainment, 2002, videocassette.

26. *Picking up the Pieces,* Alfonso Arau, director, 95 minutes, Artisan Entertainment, 2001, videocassette.

27. Steven A. Melman, VMD, "Use of Prozac in Animals for Selected Dermatological and Behavioral Conditions," *Veterinary Forum,* August 1995, available <http://www.dermapet.com/articles/art-06.html> (viewed January 28, 2005).

28. *Six Days, Seven Nights,* Ivan Reitman, director, 102 minutes, 1998, Buena Vista Home Entertainment, videocassette.

29. *28 Days Later,* Danny Boyle, director, 113 minutes, 2004, 20th Century Fox Home Entertainment, videocassette.

30. *Desecration,* Dante Tomaselli, director, 88 minutes, 2000, Image Entertainment, Inc., videocassette.

31. U.S. Food and Drug Administration, FDA Public Health Advisory, "Suicidality

in Children and Adolescebnts Being Treated with Antidepressant Medications," October 15, 2004, available <http://www.fda.gov/cder/drug/antidepressants/SSRIPHA200410.htm> (viewed January 21, 2005).

32. Elaine Cassel, "Did Zoloft Make Him Do It?" CNN.com, Monday, February 7, 2005, available <http://www.cnn.com/2005/law/oz/07/cassel.pittman/> (viewed February 16, 2005). (archived)

33. *Mean Guns*, Albert Pyum, director, 110 minutes, 1999, Trimark Home Video, videocassette.

34. *Grosse Point Blank*, George Armitage, director, 106 minutes, 1998, Buena Vista Home Entertainment, DVD.

35. *Ordinary People*, Robert Redford, director, 124 minutes, 1996, Paramount Home Entertainment, videocassette.

36. *Manhattan Murder Mystery*, Woody Allen, director, 107 minutes, 1994, Sony Pictures Home Entertainment, videocassette.

37. *Desperately Seeking Susan*, Susan Seidelman, director, 104 minutes, 1994, Orion Home Video, videocassette.

38. *Unhook the Stars*, Nick Cassavetes, director, 105 minutes, 1997, Buena Vista Home Entertainment, videocassette.

39. *Manhattan Murder Mystery*.

40. *Broadway Danny Rose*, Woody Allen, director, 85 minutes, 1995, Orion Home Video, videocassette.

41. *Mambo Italiano*, Emile Gaudreault, 89 minutes, 2003, Sony Pictures Home Entertainment, videocassette.

42. *Child's Play 2*, Tom Holland, director, 87 minutes, 1999, MGM Home Entertainment, videocassette.

43. *Final Destination 2*, David R. Ellis, 100 minutes, 2003, Warner Home Video, videocassette.

44. *Desecration*.

45. *28 Days Later*.

46. Ibid.

47. Ibid.

48. *They*, Robert Harmon and Rick Bota, directors, 89 minutes, 2002, Dimension Home Video, videocassette.

49. *Scream 2*, Wes Craven, director, 120 minutes, 1998, Buena Vista Home Video, videocassette.

50. *A Beautiful Mind*, Ron Howard, director, 136 minutes, 2002, Universal Studios Home Video, DVD.

51. *Twelve Monkeys*, Terry Gilliam, director, 130 minutes, 1996, Universal Studios Home Video, videocassette.

52. *K-Pax*, Iain Softley, director, 121 minutes, 2002, Universal Studios Home Video, videocassette.

53. Ibid.

54. *Freaky Friday*, Mark Waters, director, 97 minutes, Buena Vista Home Entertainment, videocassette.

55. *Garden State*, Zach Braff, director, 103 minutes, 2004, 20th Century Fox Home Entertainment, videocassette.

56. Ibid.

57. Ibid.

58. Ibid.

3 Cheerful Robots in Cyberspace

Prozac, Postmodernism, and Politics

SIMON GOTTSCHALK

Among contemporary men, will there come to prevail and even flourish, what may be called The Cheerful Robot?
— CW Mills, 1959, p. 171

"Better than well," "personality enhancer," "euthanasia of the soul," "designer drugs," "normalizing drug," "cosmetic psychopharmacology." These are some of the terms that have been used to discuss the effects of a new category of drugs (Selective Serotonin Reuptake Inhibitors, henceforth SSRIs) that are increasingly manufactured, prescribed, advertised in a variety of media, and consumed.[1] Chief among these new drugs is Prozac, which has been the subject of countless magazine articles, televised debates, and jokes. In some sense, Prozac does not only refer to a particular drug manufactured by the E. Lilly corporation, but has also come to signify other SSRIs, a trend in the social construction of the self, a cultural phenomenon, perhaps even a *Weltanschauung*.[2] That a therapeutic technology prescribed to relieve psychological problems gains so much popularity is a bit puzzling and requires reflection.

The purpose of this chapter is neither to reject outright the use of these drugs, nor to resolve the philosophical debates about human nature they have prompted, nor to deny that biology might very well be *among* the causes of the disorders that Prozac and other SSRIs promise to alleviate. Rather, it is to accomplish two interrelated tasks: first, to critically examine the articulations between these drugs and the postmodern condition or "structure of feeling" which, as many theorists suggest, characterize the present moment[3]; second, critically explore some social implications of these drugs for symbolic interaction theory. This chapter will also examine the effects of these drugs at a more macro-social level. Since every chapter in this book examines the representation of psychotropic drugs in a variety of media, this discussion will be grounded in an analysis of the major official Web sites that advertise them.[4] After all, few other technologies symbolize the postmodern moment as the computer and the virtual world it enables us to experience.

The reading presented here of these Web sites is neither the "true" nor the only one possible. Depending on her or his paradigmatic orientations, any reader could easily suggest another analysis and provide different interpretations. No reading is ever innocent and neither is this one. On the contrary, it is purposefully informed by, and seeks to contribute to, both symbolic interactionist and critical-postmodern sociological theories.

The reader looking for tight logic, unarguable facts, and cold analysis should be patient, as this essay is not disciplined in that way. As commentators suggest, the unpredictable social changes introduced by the SSRI "revolution" might be as profound and disturbing as those introduced by the atomic bomb, the computer, and genetic engineering, among others. Accordingly, the changes resulting from this revolution defy quick answers, absolutes, and traditional models. Like the effects of SSRIs themselves, these changes prompt us to think differently. Accordingly, grounded in (inter-textual) analysis of these Web sites and inspired by the theoretical traditions mentioned above, this essay can only propose interpretations, critical reflections, and theoretical interrogations. Hopefully, this essay will be sufficiently interesting to keep the reader's attention, to inspire her or his own interpretations, and to pursue the critical examination of this worrisome phenomenon in this most bizarre and (self-destructive) postmodern moment.

* * *

The chemical asylum is increasingly replacing the physical one. In other words, SSRIs accomplish chemically what the concrete bricks-and-mortar buildings achieved physically: the control and "rehabilitation" of people whose behaviors are considered abnormal and undesirable. However, this chemical asylum is different from its physical predecessor in a number of ways that require critical attention.

First, in contrast to the physical asylum, commitment to the chemical one is often a voluntary decision — albeit a decision that is encouraged and normalized daily by countless commercial ads. Second, whereas admission to and length of stay in the physical asylum were typically influenced by all sorts of variables (staff, number of beds, budget, family decisions, community factors, etc.), these variables are no longer relevant in the chemical one. Virtually anybody can "check in," for as long as necessary. Third, whereas the physical asylum was typically reserved for particularly troublesome behaviors, the chemical one has significantly expanded the list of conditions it proposes to regulate. Fourth, by ingesting SSRIs, the virtual patient no longer *metaphorically* internalizes the medical discourse but chemically re-calibrates his and her brain in accordance with this discourse, which radically re-defines the meaning of the self, of one's emotions, and of what is normal. Fifth and finally, the physical asylum was regulated by public officials and was open to public scrutiny and potential reform. It still enabled patients to develop micro-communities, and to play a part in their own and others' progress towards mental health. Located in one's head, the chemical asylum eliminates this potential. Since, like its physical predecessor, the chemical asylum also serves powerful professional, organizational, economic, ideological, and political interests, it urgently requires sociological attention.

This essay is divided into three sections. The first analyzes the official Web sites of the companies producing the three main SSRIs, explores the main themes they articulate, and draws parallels between these and various aspects of the postmodern condition. The second section uses a number of key insights from symbolic interaction theory to discuss, at the micro level, some implications of the effects of SSRIs for the self and the social relations that construct it. The third section uses critical theory to consider more macro-social and political implications of the increasing normalization of SSRIs and the effects they produce. It goes without saying that these sections are interwoven; they have been separated for the purpose of (hopefully better) organization and communication.

SSRI Web Sites and the Postmodern Condition

> Welcome to MyTherapy.com — Computerized Psychiatric Diagnosis
> — http://mytherapy.com, Phillip W. Long, M.D., 1995–2005

Choosing to examine SSRI Web sites as strategic cultural texts that articulate the postmodern moment seems obvious. The recent emergence and rapid proliferation of the computer and its increasing colonization of both public and private spheres are changing every aspect of daily life in ways we cannot fully understand, and will continue to do so in ways we cannot presently imagine.[5] Importantly, it is not solely the growing number of computers *per se* which is truly baffling, but the exponentially multiplying number of Web sites, discussion lists, e-mails, links, and the resulting volume of information, which swells faster than we can think. Everywhere we turn, we can both see this increasing colonization, and experience it in the growing number of tasks that we now perform with or on computer screens rather than with a real and physically co-present human being. From virtual sociology classrooms to guitar lessons, from romance to sex, from the airport to the versateller, an increasing number of face-to-face interactions are rapidly being replaced by person-to-terminal ones.

Virtual Consultation on the Terminal Screen

A particularly telling example of this replacement of human beings by computer screens is concretized on the Paxil,[6] Prozac,[7] and Zoloft[8] Web sites, which all feature psychological quizzes that readers concerned about their states of mind are urged to answer. Although the questions which appear on these quizzes are standard and can also be found on TV and in printed commercial ads, what is unique about the on-line quiz is the instantaneity of this virtual "consultation" which provides an immediate "diagnosis": "Your answers suggest that you may have experienced panic disorders"— the Paxil Web site concludes from my own answers to the electronic McQuiz.[9] Although these Web sites repeatedly remind us that the electronic quiz cannot replace a consultation with a real doctor, in the solitude of the interface, it is still a first point of contact between the (we hope) anonymous reader and the equally anonymous and abstract psychopharmacological-medical complex. The faceless terminal does not substitute for the doctor, but it might have already replaced a friend's sympathetic ear or sustained self-reflection.

These Web sites do not only encourage readers to take these quizzes but also recommend that you "bring your doctor a printout of your responses."[10] This simple suggestion already implies the complicit links between the Web sites, drug companies, and the medical institution. "Only your doctor can make a diagnosis" and only your doctor can prescribe SSRIs.[11] By recommending that we bring the printout to our doctor, the SSRI Web sites also legitimize the information they present, the drugs they promote, the companies that manufacture them, the usefulness of the quiz, and a decidedly strange approach to psychological and emotional problems. Through such links, the Web sites also position the isolated reader as inescapably dependent for her and his emotional well-being on a virtual network of large, faceless pharmaceutical companies and medical organizations.

Neurotransmitters R Us: Medical Absolution, Chemical Self-Esteem, and Therapeutic Narcissism

> If knowing yourself is the road map, liking yourself is the vehicle.... Try not to overanalyze or be too critical of yourself. Recognize the good things about yourself. You are a worthwhile person
>
> — Prozac Web page, p. 2, 2004

On the SSRI Web sites, the different sections that explain the various disorders the drugs can alleviate repeat the statement that some people find comfort just by learning that depression (or social anxiety disorder or panic attacks, or post-traumatic stress disorder) is a medical condition.[12] Repeating this like a mantra, the Web sites reconstruct a wide variety of emotional pains which have probably always characterized the human condition as "a medically recognized psychological condition with a suspected biological component,"[13] "a common medical illness,"[14] "a real medical condition," "a serious illness"[15] "as real as diabetes or arthritis,"[16] "heart disease,"[17] or "high blood pressure."[18]

This medical framing of unruly emotions both reassures and absolves the reader for experiencing the "wrong" feelings. Depression is "An Illness, Not a Weakness," it is "not something you've brought on yourself, and it doesn't reveal a personal weakness or an inability to cope," "it's not a character flaw," "it's neither a 'mood' nor a personal weakness that you can change at will or by 'pulling yourself together,'" claims the Prozac Web site.[19] The Zoloft Web site offers similar reassurances and suggests that "depression doesn't mean you have a flawed character or aren't strong enough emotionally."[20] Like many other physiological dysfunctions, the Web sites tell us, those seemingly emotional problems can also be chemically altered and recalibrated to ensure better functioning.

Challenging our everyday logic and dismissing centuries of theorizing and philosophical reflection on the symbiotic and symbolic relationship between self and others, the Web sites reconstruct the self through stories of cells, serotonin, and synapses.[21] As Crossley puts it,

> We are increasingly attuned to hear references to "brains," "neurotransmitters," etc. as more real, truer and deeper accounts of what and who we are.

We are less trustful of our own everyday language of self-hood and personal life, more enamoured by the "facts" of the "hard sciences" of the brain. "Misery" is not enough, we believe only in "low serotonin."[22]

The swallowing of this rather bizarre approach to such a complex issue as the emotional self is facilitated by an equally strange but tasty two-layered coating. The first promises that this chemical recalibration will enable the emergence of an enhanced self. As SSRI proponents tell us, the self that the drug liberates will be more uninhibited, smiling, charming, anxiety-free, extroverted, outgoing, confident, flexible, and accepting than the self sans SSRI. We will be better than well, claims Kramer, the author of *Listening to Prozac*.[23]

The second layer suggests that this enhanced self is really our true self. The Prozac Web site, for example, promises that "with treatment, you can feel like *yourself* again."[24] Following the same logic, the Paxil Web site's main page shows the picture of a young healthy and attractive white woman, who looks straight at the reader, smiling with self-confidence. Conspicuous on her sport jacket is a label showing a bold "Hello" in print and, underneath (in supposedly her own handwriting), the word "Me."[25] Paxil is thus presented as having rescued the young woman's real, peppy, relaxed and confident self from the throes of social anxiety disorder, panic disorder or depression. As the Web site implies, those emotional experiences did not express her "real" self but resulted from serotonin deficiency or other neurochemical dysfunctions for which neither she nor anybody else can reasonably be held responsible.

Equating the "enhanced" self with the "true" self articulates both a medical promise and endorsement of our cultural obsession with narcissism[26] that is repeated daily by countless commercial ads hailing us in a variety of mass media. "Feel good about yourself," "be kind to yourself," "enjoy yourself," "treating yourself like the wonderful person you are is a good way to affirm your self-worth," and "write down everything you like about yourself," the virtual therapist recommends on the Prozac Web site.[27]

These recommendations, claims and promises suggest an interesting parallel between Baudrillard's characterization of the postmodern moment as "hyper-real"[28] and SSRI proponents who declare that the drug will enable us to become "*better* than well."[29] Gone is the necessary confrontation with those emotional limitations we all suffer from and which, if successfully resolved, might make us "just" well. More is promised. With very little effort, we can become better than well, better than we have ever been, and better than we ever hoped to be. Flattered by such promises and ideas, we might be increasingly encouraged to believe that the self we have always experienced as limited, limiting, and subject to a variety of painful experiences is in fact false, and that it can easily be replaced by its chemically enhanced, ideal, yet curiously "true" version. Although quite delusional, this approach to the self should hardly be surprising and is perfectly attuned to the logic of our throwaway society. Constantly encouraged to replace defective appliances by sexier, sturdier, and lower-maintenance models, and reminded daily that we can surgically correct our less-than-perfect body parts, the medically approved recommendation that we chemically alter our very sense of self appears increasingly reasonable.

Additionally, the promise that we can effortlessly and chemically achieve emotional bliss and a better self is not that different from the truly hallucinatory assault by countless other ads which repeat *ad nauseam* and 24/7 the delusional guarantee that the frenetic consumption of disposable objects and services will also instantly gratify complex social, psychological and emotional needs as well as increase the likelihood of uncomplicated sexual encounters. In a hyper-consumerist society which promises virtually everybody "instant pre-approval" and "immediate delivery" with "0 dollars down" or "no credit," it is hard not see the relationship between the peddling of SSRIs in the media and the promotion of a multitude of other objects which all serve to gratify narcissistic needs, keep depressive tendencies at bay, and calm realistic anxieties. In fact, the Prozac Web site explicitly endorses this link between "feeling good about yourself" and consumption by suggesting that the therapeutic project of self-discovery *cum* self-esteem should include "buying something," and "watching a funny movie or TV show." Echoing most other commercials, the Web site thus also proclaims that, in addition to SSRIs, self-esteem requires a trip to the mall and passive entertainment by moronic spectacles.[30]

Resonating with our postmodern fixation on the private lives of stars and celebrities, the Prozac Web site also encourages self-esteem by reminding us that many famous political figures (Lincoln, Roosevelt, Churchill, Princess Diana, Calvin Coolidge, Richard Nixon, Menachem Begin, General Patton) and artists (Van Gogh, Hemingway, Mark Twain, Marilyn Monroe, Nijinsky) have all suffered from depression.[31] Interestingly, this Web site conveniently omits the simple fact that most of those illustrious people managed to accomplish great political feats or works of art without the benefit of SSRIs. The Zoloft Web site develops this idea and tells the abridged story of country singer Naomi Judd's "triumphal" victory over panic disorder, thanks to a combination of Zoloft and cognitive-behavioral therapy.[32] Juxtaposed to other stories of everyday unknown people who also successfully struggled against different disorders ("Alan Chambers," the CEO who defeated depression, and "Drusilla," who overcame panic disorder), the Zoloft Web site invites the reader to experience affinities with celebrities, or at least the reasonably successful.

The reduction of emotional, cognitive, or interactional problems that have probably always challenged individuals living in vastly different societies and historical periods to simple deficiencies in neurotransmitters legitimizes the medical discourse by stimulating narcissistic needs, by absolving the troubled individual of all responsibility, and by suggesting that the "enhanced" self equals the "true" self. Whereas the attainment of genuine and enduring self-esteem typically requires sustained personal investment, some worthy accomplishment, the realization of one's goals, or, at the very least, the repeated experience of positive interactions with people who matter to us, the friendly virtual therapist insists that none of these inconvenient efforts are necessary in the mellow and cheerful Land of Prozac.

Neurochemical Reductionism and Social Isolation: Alone in Psy/cyberspace

In tandem with self-esteem and narcissism, these Web sites also promote a particularly strange approach to self-other relationships. Asides from the commonsensical observation that Web-surfing is typically a solitary activity, these sites also promote a sense of social and psychological isolation in the reader by suggesting that, except for the drugs-prescribing doctor, the therapeutic endeavor is essentially a solitary one. In fact, while almost every "disorder" section on these Web sites repeats that we must talk to our doctor, the multitude of other people who fill our lives and influence our sense of self, those others who are always and complexly implicated in our emotional conditions, are completely absent. None of the very scientific explanations or quiz questions ever mentions these others' possible influence, importance, and inevitable presence in the very fibers of our being. We are never encouraged to ask these others how they see and "feel" us, to discuss the quiz questions with them, or to engage them in a heart-to-heart conversation. Establishing an exclusionary monologue with the reader, the terminal *virtually* eliminates all these others from consciousness or, at best, relegates them to the status of residual and negligible variables in the neurochemical equation.

Two exceptions deserve attention. The first is the Zoloft Web site, which, in the various "disorders" sections, mentions that friends and relatives can help. Interestingly, however, the role of these significant others is often reduced to their ensuring that disturbed family members or friends seek medical assistance and continue to take their medication:

> One important thing family members and friends can do for those who are depressed is to help them get appropriate diagnosis and treatment. This may mean getting them to see a doctor in the first place, or encouraging them to stay with treatment until they feel better.[33]

While the other two sections which discuss panic and obsessive-compulsive disorders also provide advice to relatives and friends, these are always the same, regardless of the disorder:

> Learning as much as possible about the ... disorder.
> Adapting to changes that take place during treatment.
> Understanding that stressful periods may be difficult for everyone.
> Encouraging the patient to stay on his or her prescribed medication and/or therapy.[34]

The providing of exactly the same advice to those "caring others" who want to help friends or relatives who are suffering from different disorders implicitly suggests that, except for these four rather commonsensical injunctions, their contribution to the therapeutic enterprise is limited and perfunctory at best.

The second exception is the Prozac Web site, which also indicates that relatives and friends can help. However, the extent of this help is limited to "accepting that depression is a real illness—not a weakness or a character defect," and that loved ones "can't 'snap out of it' and it won't go away with time." Implicitly recruited as agents of the medical discourse, friends and relatives are told to

> help the depressed person understand that ... depression is a medical condition, and that it can be successfully treated. Also, your friend or loved one may need your help to find treatment. Until the chemical imbalance in the brain is corrected, it is difficult for the people with depression to find the strength and energy necessary to get their lives back on track.[35]

This implicit assumption of social and psychological isolation is even reproduced in the pictures of "successful patients" which appear on all these Web sites. Interestingly, and with one exception on the Paxil and Zoloft Web sites, these people are always displayed alone. Although seemingly benign, these depictions of single individuals reinforce the individualistic assumption guiding our approach to psychological and emotional problems—an assumption which remains essentially ideological. Here again, the pictures represent enhanced individuals as people who have suffered from, confronted, and overcome their various emotional problems alone, under the intermittent professional guidance of an invisible but benevolent physician.

The Web sites' curious assumption of socially and psychologically isolated individuals is not only implied in the quizzes, the explanations of the disorders, and the therapeutic options, but also in the prognostic promises. More specifically, the Web sites' complete lack of attention to the social dimensions of the self is matched by their utter neglect of the social consequences of the chemically regulated self. Here too, the absence of significant others in the post-illness phase betrays the same inadequate understanding of the importance of social relations in individuals' lives. There is, for example, no mention of the simple facts that those others who always also suffer with us will have to somehow re-adjust their ways of interacting with the new enhanced self, that they may question its authenticity, or simply feel weird around it. On the contrary, evoking an optimistic and self-sufficient mindset reminiscent of the effects of SSRIs themselves (and the logic of most commercials), these invisible significant others will, it is implied, naturally and joyfully greet the Prozac-regulated family member, colleague or friend, embrace without questioning the new qualities which she now displays, and show her the same approval they would express upon seeing her new car, plasma TV, furniture, nose job, stomach tuck, or breast implants. And whereas the Web sites provide cautionary statements that different people react differently to SSRIs, they never discuss the rather commonsensical fact that different people may react very differently not to SSRIs but to their colleague, relative or friend who has been chemically altered. For all intents and purposes, those others who are—for good and ill—so implicated in our emotional lives have completely disappeared from the electronic and emotional picture. As we will see below, this tacit and asocial elimination of significant others from the pre-illness, illness, and post-illness phases resonates quite well with the effects of SSRIs on social relations.

Interestingly, the Web sites' sections that discuss different disorders remind the reader that the therapeutic interventions for most of those disorders may also entail talk therapy, group therapy, cognitive-behavioral therapy, or a combination of those with SSRIs. But since, as we are repeatedly told, these disorders are *medical* illnesses which, like high blood pressure, arthritis, or diabetes, are caused by biological dysfunctions, it is difficult to precisely understand how talking could possibly help restore healthy neurotransmitter traffic between cells. Further, since, as we will see below, SSRIs reduce emotional reactivity to both oneself and others, it is not clear whether the purpose of such talk is to assess how a patient really feels or how SSRIs work. Accordingly, the title *Listening to Prozac* (rather than to the patient) must be read literally.

Overall, the Web sites represent us as quite isolated individuals who can only have meaningful conversations about our inner souls with doctors and psychotherapists. Web surfing, taking the quiz, the informal and personal mode of address on those Web sites, and the very explanations they provide about what ails us effectively repeat the same message: Mental disorders are purely private (and neurochemical) troubles. Talk to your doctor because s/he is the only one who can understand you, properly diagnose you, and, in the absence of any compelling alternative, heal you with drugs which alter the circulation of those unruly neurotransmitters. Your significant others are relatively irrelevant to what you are experiencing and, in any case, cannot really help you overcome your condition, except by showing encouragement and optimism, listening to you, refraining from judging you, and ensuring that you see a doctor and take your medication.

Chilled: The SSRI Feel and the SSRI Web Sites

Considering the psychochemical effects of SSRIs, it is difficult to resist exploring the various ways these Web sites conjure — in both content and form — the effects of the very drugs they promote. The Web sites are obviously pitched to a troubled yet rational and educated reader who seeks a quick solution to problems that reduce happiness, focusing, self-control, productivity, and a general *joie de vivre.* The tone of the "voice" speaking to us in those Web sites is relatively unemotional, relaxed, even, and friendly. It uses a sensible, informal language to explain a variety of disorders to "you," the reader. Depression is "not something *you*'ve brought on *yourself,*" "with treatment, *you* can feel like *yourself* again,"[36] claims the Prozac Web site (my italics). Reassuring the reader on every page that depression or other disorders are probably caused by neurotransmitter malfunctions, the voice sounds indeed like that of a friendly virtual doctor who does not judge, condemn or insist on difficult self-reflection, genuine conversation, or a radical reassessment of one's lifestyle and relations. Rather, it gently produces textually what the drug induces chemically. It soothes, calms, removes responsibility, and encourages us not to feel the guilt, shame or anxiety that we might normally experience upon realizing that we cannot control our emotions. But in so doing, it invites a kind of alienation between one's self and the emotions one experiences, and hence within the self.[37]

The Web sites also communicate this SSRI "state of mind" through pictures of (typically solitary) individuals whose general characteristics and clothing style typify members of an ethnically diverse, economically comfortable, conforming, but guilt-prone and threatened middle class. Neither too fat nor too thin, neither too young nor too old (although the few older faces look amazingly healthy and wrinkle-free), neither poor nor outrageously wealthy, they look like our friends, acquaintances and relatives who roughly belong to the same social class we identify with or aspire to. They are the executives, administrators, high-ranking bureaucrats, and professionals with whom we are likely to interact and collaborate in our everyday lives. Their facial characteristics are also revealing. They are convulsed by neither ecstatic laughter nor cathartic tears. They show no sign of surprise, fear, anger, disgust, anxiety, curiosity or conflict. They are smiling and relaxed, reasonably cheerful and satisfied, pleasant and accepting. In effect, they graphically project the kinds of disposition people experience once they have been properly regulated by Prozac or other SSRIs.[38] By themselves, therefore, these pictures not only already evoke the emotional temperament of the chemically enhanced self, but also invite identification by the middle class reader who is implicitly reminded that those "medical" conditions are indeed not unusual in people "just like us" or, considering the bleak alternatives in contemporary society, like we would like to be.

Since the occupations that characterize the comfortable middle class often entail emotional skills, an outgoing nature, the ability to work in small and large groups, adaptability, a conciliatory disposition, a general smoothness of character, and extensive and often difficult "emotion work,"[39] one cannot help but wonder whether we should not also chemically regulate our own emotions in order to remain competitive. Together, these faces, success stories, and promises of restored productivity implicitly communicate the professional and economic advantages these personality enhancing drugs obviously bestow. As Zita remarks,

> Prozac is more than a medical remedy for a mental dysfunction. It appears on the contemporary scene with a promise to reconstitute out of the chaos of unlimited postmodern disintegration the individual-based, white middle-class norms for gender, sex, and work.[40]

Having medicalized emotions insisted on our social isolation, and encouraged alienation from self and others, the Web sites conjure the seductive mindset we will enjoy on SSRIs, provide visual "proof" that those who have been properly medicated enjoy success, peace of mind, attractiveness, and productivity, and promote a fake sense of identification with a virtual community of people who appear very similar to us. They just seem more mellow and successful.

Symbolic Interaction Theory on Prozac

> Prozac disrupts two of the neurotransmitters most involved in frontal-lobe function — serotonin and dopamine — and in that process can rob us of our sensitivity, self-awareness, and capacity to care or to love. Put simply, the SSRIs are anti-empathic agents. That means they are anti-life — anti human life in the fullest sense.
>
> — Breggin and Breggin, 1994, p. 210

Exploring all the ramifications of the SSRIs trend for Symbolic Interaction theory is well beyond the scope of this paper.[41] Still, as a modest step in that direction, several questions can be addressed that this trend raises with regard to Cooley's metaphor of the "looking-glass" self, and more recent theorists' approaches to the self as "narratively constructed."

The Looking-Glass Self and Prozac: Blurred Reflections and Distortions

In Cooley's metaphor of the "looking-glass self," we derive a sense of self by interpreting how those with whom we interact react to us.[42] Depending on the reflections these human mirrors send back to us, we derive positive feelings such as pride or negative ones such as mortification and shame. According to this assumption and the theories derived from it, the sense of self thus necessitates the ability to correctly self-reflect from another's point of view. Following Breggin and Breggin's discussion of the chemical effects of SSRIs,[43] we should reevaluate the emphasis we place on this "reflected self." More precisely, since SSRIs produce a disassociation and diminished emotional sensitivity to both self and others, it seems reasonable to suggest that those who consume SSRIs will suffer from a weakened ability to "read" others, and hence, logically, to correctly self-reflect from their points of view. More importantly, people chemically altered by SSRIs will also be less concerned about this weakened ability, the misreadings it unavoidably causes, the emotional reactions such misreadings frequently trigger, and the rituals of readjustment they typically require among "normal" people. In other words, the SSRI-regulated individual will not only likely be less able to "read" others' reflections but will also care less about these reflections in terms of his emotional well-being, self-esteem, and self-concept. Accordingly, as others are less immediately relevant for his positive feelings, and as SSRIs chemically reduce his experiencing of negative ones, he will quite naturally be inclined to radically re-assess the very essence of the interactions and relationships that used to be primordial for his sense of self.

Symbolic Interaction theorists have typically assumed that self-reflection was a rather rational process and that a correspondence existed between how others reflect us and how we interpret these reflections. In contrast, Freudian theory suggests that our readings of other people's responses to us are most often distorted by unconscious ego-defense mechanisms which protect the fragile ego and its narcissistic needs. Still, the Freudian discourse claimed that such distortions could be brought out of the unconscious into conscious awareness, analyzed, and ideally corrected.

With SSRIs, the systematic distortion of others' reflections is chemically engineered, and medically defined as "normal."

Regulated by SSRIs, we are less able to correctly self-reflect with others, but it no longer matters since we can experience a positive sense of self by ingesting chemicals that make us feel good, regardless of what other people think. Moreover, the reduction of emotional reactions to serotonin imbalances so frequently repeated on the Web sites not only encourages a new approach to the self but also, logically, to others. Since, according to the SSRI discourse, my own emotional experiences result from neurochemical imbalances, and since my mind functions in ways that I cannot control, predict, or regulate, it is only logical to perceive other people in the same light. Since we are little more than the effects of neurochemical processes, emotional alienation from self easily translates into emotional alienation from others. Their emotional needs become similarly re-framed and re-constructed as mysterious chemical imbalances that can rapidly be calibrated to better fit the requirements of their social and psychological environments. Will such a reframing lead to a decreased amount of emotional work we are willing to invest in order to heal the emotional pains and needs of those who matter to us? Since it is chemical anyway, will we echo the old doctor's suggestion to "take an aspirin and call me in the morning" by telling our emotionally upset loved ones to "take some Prozac and chill out"?

The flip side of the story is that when emotional detachment and reduced sensitivity to others and self are increasingly normalized, individuals *not* regulated by SSRIs will, with increasing frequency, encounter everyday situations and interactions where they will logically self-reflect with individuals very emotionally different from themselves. In such a situation, it is not too far-fetched to suggest that these "normal" individuals will increasingly question their own (now) unreasonable emotional reactions, and will be more likely to re-define them as exaggerated, or as signs of childish over-sensitivity.[44] They will increasingly feel the growing social pressure to get "in synch" with the new and improved emotional "program."

The Narrated Self: (Prozac) Web Site Stories

Many contemporary Symbolic Interactionists and others have increasingly developed the idea that the self is "narratively constructed," that the self can be understood as stories we tell different audiences in various situations.[45] Accordingly, following Breggin and Breggin's discussion of the SSRIs' blunting of empathy, "sensitivity, self awareness, and capacity to care or to love," these drugs and the discourse which promotes them will also guide the stories we tell about ourselves and others in worrisome directions. In both form and content, these new stories will now construct the self in terms of cells, synapses, and serotonin.[46] But what are consequences of tracing our own and others' biographies in neurochemical terms? What happens when such stories are increasingly circulated, validated as "normal," and reciprocated? The Web sites' constant reminders to "caring others" that "depression is a medical illness" whose causes are essentially neurochemical certainly seem to encourage such an approach. By reducing the most complex concept of selfhood to neurochemical deficiencies, accidents, or fitness, these stories necessarily narrate selfhood and humanness in a terribly heartless and soulless prose. In such stories, ethical dilemma, moral responsibility, love, empathy, compassion, patience, modesty, passion, and all these experiences which make us uniquely human, become pure chemical reactions. More worrisome yet, the "genetic" dimension frequently appearing in these SSRI Web site stories also suggests that a transition (or return) to a new genetic discourse about personality is not far away.[47] In light of the disastrous consequences such a discourse has typically brought about, we should pay a great deal of attention to these new stories which hail us on our TV screens, computer terminals, magazines, other media, and the people we will increasingly interact with.

From the Asylums to the Chemical Gated Communities

> Swallowing, half an hour before closing time, that second dose of *soma* had raised a quite impenetrable wall between the actual universe and their minds.
> — Huxley, 1969, p. 52

As Breggin and Breggin suggest, Prozac and other SSRIs alleviate painful emotional experiences and conditions by chemically weakening our emotional responsiveness to self and others, by producing a disconnection from self and between self and others.[48] Whereas the medical success of these drugs is typically explained by their ability to selectively act on certain neurotransmitters rather than many (thereby reducing unpleasant side-effects), at a social emotional level, their advantage is that they alleviate our symptoms by blunting our affect. Yet, this blunting also seems to increase happiness, a relaxed attitude, outgoingness, sociability, approachability, acceptance of both others and self, and — in the worst cases— desensitized violence.[49] By increasing the circulation of serotonin between cells,

SSRIs increase the feelings of well-being, a relaxed attitude, and self-confidence. In other words, they produce chemical mental-emotional "comfort zones" which screen out whatever might cause too much emotional upset, anxiety, or justifiable depressive bouts.

In social psychological — and even political — terms, these drugs provide the ability *not* to pay too much attention to the self's and others' emotional difficulties, or to pay a different kind of attention — a more detached one. If frequent watching of TV violence has been shown to cause a certain desensitization to real life violence, then perhaps SSRIs accomplish very rapidly and chemically the same result. The claim that such a chemically-engineered self is "better than well" is, to say the least, rather worrisome as it both implicitly and explicitly repositions "normal" (or "just well") emotions as inferior and lacking. In other words, by suggesting that reduced emotional reactivity and empathy are signs of an enhanced self or that they express one's "true" self, these Web sites implicitly promote a particularly troubling vision of what the healthy self should be and feel like. And behind the young, pseudo-hip, accepting and attractive faces smiling at us on the Web site, there is something quite chilling about these drugs which seem to produce people whose shyness, insecurities, anxieties, and depressive tendencies have been effectively dulled; people who are basically well-disposed, cheerful and accepting because they might have simply ceased to care enough to react with appropriate emotional vigor.

The replacement of the self one experiences as painful but real by its chemically enhanced version which seems much less vulnerable to emotional interference reproduces, at the neurochemical level, the same kind of distortion Baudrillard and other postmodern theorists detected in the mass media and postmodern culture generally.[50] As they saw it, television mediated our perceptions of real social conditions and hence also disabled our very ability to appropriately understand and confront them. SSRIs function in a similar fashion. They not only mediate our perceptions of our own and others' emotional conditions, but also disable our very ability to appropriately understand and confront them. Both, in effect, facilitate our acceptance or tolerance of conditions (macro and micro) which used to trigger pain, outrage, anxiety, revulsion, or justified anger. As an especially astute bumper-sticker claims, "if you are not completely appalled, then you haven't been paying attention."

Such effects are particularly well attuned to the postmodern moment that seems to precisely require a constant "adiaphorization,"[51] a "narcosis of the senses."[52] Like those TV commercials showing a happy couple dancing around a bucket of greasy fried chicken which so frequently interrupt important and unpleasant news, SSRIs may very well chemically interrupt and displace the important, unpleasant and emotionally trying experiences which inevitably punctuate our daily existence. In both cases, dulling spectacles, commodities, or pills discharge a sense of mild euphoria that conveniently eliminates the real and difficult work that we must often undertake in order to implement necessary changes in both macro and micro social spheres. Thus, if the Prozac Web site recommends, as part of our "feel good" self-discovery therapy, that you "avoid people who make you feel bad,"[53] it is only a short while before these recommendation will be extended to other difficult aspects of our environment that also make us feel a little too guilty, sad, anxious, or panicked, those that seem too demanding, those that spoil our mood, or those that threaten our newly FDA-approved right to self-love and emotional escape. Judging by the vertiginous increase in the number of children who are unwillingly medicated with Ritalin,[54] it is difficult not to imagine a future when we might also be increasingly advised to take Prozac, Paxil or Zoloft "for our own good," to enhance our emotional performance and fitness at the office, at home, on vacation, or on business trips. As Lyon observes,

> According to some commentators, Prozac is commonly prescribed for persons who do not at all fit the criteria for depression, but who are labeled as "dysthymic," or even "sub or borderline dysthymic." Dysthymia, meaning emotion inappropriate to the circumstances, surely a social judgment is, in the words of one review, jargon for those who are "perpetually crabby, under the weather, insecure, malcontent" or simply "people who realise they're more unhappy than the situation calls for."[55]

Although it is hard not to fall into clichés after Huxley's *Brave New World,* we should also consider the political implications of the increasing chemical pacification of the middle and professional classes which have, overall, remained rather complacent in the face of daily news of a growing body count in Iraq, of the torturing of civilians, of deportations, of the erosion of civil rights in the name of freedom and security, of increasing ecological devastation, and of a long list of other crises. It is similarly difficult to resist the conclusion that the new drugs so celebrated on these Web sites constitute an individualistic psychochemical solution to the seemingly unsolvable and always violent crises that terrorize us on the high-definition screens of the mediascape. Bombarded daily with news of anthrax and high-school shootings, of plane crashes and random murder, of sudden poverty and mutant viruses, of terrorism and lethal dangers lurking in everything we eat, breathe, drink and drive, the Web sites' descriptions of generalized anxiety disorders as "worry when there is no sign of trouble"[56] or of panic attacks as "intense fear in the absence of any external threat"[57] sound almost comical.

Whereas these Web sites use complex diagrams, high-tech animations, chemical formulas and fancy-sounding words to explain why so many of us may be suffering from depression, social anxiety disorders, or panic attacks, they cannot allow themselves to ask different questions. They cannot (and choose not to) discuss all the threats which we must confront without any sense of community, authentic solidarity, a viable future, guidance and inspiration from any form of leadership, or even a modest belief in its competence. Rather, they propose to treat the emotional reactions these threats would reasonably trigger in any normal person by advocating self-satisfaction, consumerist narcissism, mellowness, and emotional detachment in the face of growing disaster.

At some level, this emotional bluntness, this decreasing ability to feel with the appropriate human intensity is the price we pay for enjoying an easier social and emotional life under conditions of "fun" capitalism. More spectacles and better visuals; more bargains at the mall and sexier cars; bigger burgers and more free toppings on your pizza; more movie channels and faster downloads; the rewarding of mediocrity, the celebration of one-dimensional thought, and a self-righteous arrogance on the international scene that is reproduced as infantile and self-indulgent patriotism in the neighborhood. In this respect, the seemingly delusional claims on the SSRIs Web sites and other media texts that the chemically regulated, enhanced self is indeed one's true self is not only narcissistic but also ideological. In other words, this self is not only preferable at the individual "feel good" level but also at a more macro-social one. In such a light, this mellow, attractive and satisfied "me" they promise us might perhaps become the ideal role model, the preferred disposition we should all emulate in order to fit more smoothly and cheerfully in the brave new postmodern world.

Whereas critical theorists such as Marcuse and Fromm proclaimed that citizens of "civilized" societies would be "brainwashed" into conformity and submission by mindless media spectacles, a more tolerant approach to sexuality, and the promises of increasing consumption for all, this concept of "brainwashed" has now taken an eerily literal meaning.[58] For Marcuse, the purpose of this brainwashing was to manipulate our sense of reality in order to ensure our willing resignation to, and satisfaction with, everyday life under capitalism. In Marcuse's time, however, such a metaphorical brainwashing necessitated the coordinated efforts of the mass media and the economic and political institutions. Today, this project is much more easily achieved through the individual's voluntary swallowing of pills which—chemically—promote the same credo of adaptation to the existing system, absorption in asinine spectacles, ever-escalating consumption of all the toys the economy turns out (at reduced prices), and above all, the self-satisfied resignation that there is simply no alternative. And while Marcuse still pinned some hope on the discontent permeating "civilized" societies, SSRIs eliminate this critical potential. Chemically.

This situation has, of course, profound consequences for the kinds of people we will become, how we will socialize our children, the kind of emotional guidance and tolerance we will have at our and their disposal, and the social-emotional landscape we prepare for them. Environmentalists have long remarked that our ravenously hedonistic lifestyle which requires the increasing release of toxic substances in nature and the exponential depletion of its precious resources, *de facto* rips off the next generations. The parallel with how we treat our emotional environment is obvious. The medically recommended decision to maximize one's level of serotonin in order to enjoy the promises of an individualistic and instant emotional utopia follows the same destructive logic.[59] It means that we are also depleting, at both individual and social levels, rich "natural" emotional resources without thinking too much about the effects of such fast food solutions on the near and distant future. Accordingly, Mick Jagger's famous song might have become obsolete. Thanks to Prozac, I *can* get *now* satisfaction.

The medically sanctioned turn towards SSRIs might very well constitute a sort of abdication of social and emotional responsibility in the face of worsening social crises. It is the chemical version of the increasing retreat behind the exclusionary fences of gated communities. Pleasant, subdued, orderly, daily landscaped by an invisible cheap minority workforce, they offer relaxing spaces, security, and the welcome architectural/neurochemical exclusion of unpleasant realities in the public space outside and the private space within.

Conclusion: The Prozac Paradox

> Two thousand pharmacologists and bio-chemists were subsidized in A.F. 178.... Six years later it was being produced commercially. The perfect drug... Euphoric, narcotic, pleasantly hallucinant... All the advantages of Christianity and alcohol; none of their defects.... Stability was practically assured.
> — Huxley, 1969, pp. 36–37

Because SSRIs weaken our emotional sensitivity, we must seriously contemplate the conclusion that, as chemically regulated citizens, we will increasingly lose the ability to correctly assess our actions and their consequences—from the personal to the international level. Since interactions at all these levels always include an emotional dimension, an inability to properly attend to it means that our decisions will be permanently misguided by very incomplete and distorted information. To use the Prozac metaphor of oneself as "the vehicle" on the road to self-knowledge, while we would reasonably refuse to be driven around by a person inebriated by alcohol or other substances that distort his perception, we should consider that the SSRI-regulated self is no less impaired.[60] Since it is emotionally desensitized and suffers from a weakened capacity for empathy and care, it should perhaps not be trusted for important decisions. But while an alcoholic can decide to sober up and stop drinking, the chemical recalibration of our brains seems more permanent.

Additionally, whereas the social and psychological effects of SSRIs are problematic enough in terms of "proper" emotional intensity and ability to care, Stephen Braun points at another danger of the neurochemical solution:

> What sets antidepressant drugs apart and makes an inquiry into drug company assertions about their value and effectiveness so vital is that these drugs act directly on the very organ we use to decide whether to take drugs. Unlike antihypertensive, anti-ulcer drugs, and all other types of drugs, antidepressants have the unique power to change our *attitude* toward things. They can change the degree to which we *care* about issues—issues such as the appropriate use of new drug technologies.[61]

If SSRIs not only blunt our emotional sensitivity but also impair our ability to make intelligent decisions about their very use, we are indeed confronting a most unusual crisis and danger, about which the SSRIs Web sites remain conveniently silent.

It is too early to really comprehend and anticipate the revolutionary changes that SSRIs have introduced, and in any case, such changes cannot be fully examined without also taking into consideration a plethora of other permanent revolutions we currently experience as a matter of routine in the postmodern moment. Still, as scientists of the self and society, it is imperative and urgent that we do so. To quote C.W. Mills one last time,

> I do not know the answer to the question of political irresponsibility in our time or to the cultural and political question of the Cheerful Robot. But is it not clear that no answers will be found unless these problems are at least confronted? Is it not obvious, that the ones to confront them, above all others, are the social scientists of the rich societies?[62]

Notes

1. Peter Breggin and Ginger Breggin, *Talking Back to Prozac* (New York: Prentice Hall, 1994); Peter Kramer, *Listening to Prozac* (New York: Viking, 1993); M.L. Lyon,

"C. Wright Mills meets Prozac: The relevance of 'social emotion' to the sociology of health and illness," in Veronica James and Jonathan Gabe, eds., *Health and the Sociology of Emotions* (Oxford: Blackwell Publishers, Ltd., 1996), pp. 60–61.

2. Breggin and Breggin, *Talking Back to Prozac*, op. cit.; N. Crossley, "Prozac nation and the biochemical self: a critique," in Simon Williams, Lynda Birke and Gillian Bendelow eds., *Debating Biology: Sociological Reflections on Health, Medicine and Society* (London: Routledge, 2003), p. 249; M.L. Lyon, "C. Wright Mills meets Prozac," op. cit., p. 58; Peter Kramer, *Listening to Prozac* (Viking: New York, 1993).

3. Norman Denzin, "The Postmodern Sensibility," *Studies in Symbolic Interaction* 15 (1993), pp. 179–188; David Dickens and Andrea Fontana, eds., *Postmodernism and Social Inquiry* (New York: Guilford Press, 1994); Mike Featherstone, *Consumer Culture and Postmodernism* (London: Sage, 1991); Mark Gottdiener, "Alienation, everyday life, and postmodernism as critical theory," in F. Geyer, ed., *Alienation, Ethnicity, and Postmodernism* (Westport, Connecticutt: Greenwood Press, 1996), pp. 139–148; Simon Gottschalk, "Uncomfortably numb: countercultural impulses in the postmodern era," *Studies in Symbolic Interaction* 21 (1997a), pp. 115–146; Simon Gottschalk, "The pains of everyday life: Between the D.S.M. and the postmodern," *Studies in Symbolic Interaction* 21 (1997b), pp. 115–146; Simon Gottschalk, "Videology: Video-games as postmodern sites/sights of ideological reproduction," *Symbolic Interaction* 18, no. 1 (1995a), pp. 1–18; Simon Gottschalk, "Ethnographic fragments in postmodern spaces," *Journal of Contemporary Ethnography* 24, no. 2 (1995b), pp. 195–238; David Harvey, *The Condition of Postmodernity* (London: Basil Blackwell, 1989); Robert Hollinger, *Postmodernism and the Social Sciences: A Thematic Approach* (Thousand Oaks: Sage, 1990); Frederic Jameson, "Postmodernism and consumer society," in H. Foster, ed., *The Anti-aesthetic* (Port Townsend: Bay Press, 1983), pp. 111–125; Frederic Jameson, "Postmodernism, or the cultural logic of late capitalism," *New Left Review* 146 (1984), pp. 53–92; E. Kaplan, ed., *Postmodernism and Its Discontents* (London: Verso, 1988); Douglas Kellner, *Media Culture* (New York: Routledge, 1995); M.D. Levin, "Clinical stories: a modern self in the fury of being," in M.D. Levin, ed., *Pathologies of the Modern Self: Postmodern Studies on Narcissism, Schizophrenia and Depression* (New York: New York University Press, 1987), pp. 479–530; David Morris, *Illness and Culture in the Postmodern Age* (Berkeley: University of California Press, 1998); Steven Seidman, ed., *The Postmodern Turn: New Perspectives on Social Theory* (New York: Cambridge University Press, 1994); R. Williams, *Marxism and Literature* (New York: New York University Press, 1977).

4. I am referring here to the information appearing on the Web pages of the three main SSRIs— Prozac, Paxil and Zoloft.

5. Mary Chayko, "What is real in the age of virtual reality?: Reframing frame analysis for a technological world," *Symbolic Interaction* 6, no. 2 (1993), pp. 171–181; Mark Poster, *The Second Media Age* (Polity Press: Cambridge: n.p., 1995); Mark Poster, *The Mode of Information* (Chicago: Chicago University Press, 1990); Howard Rheingold, *Virtual Reality* (New York: Touchstone Books, 1991); Sherry Turkle, *The Second Self: Computers and the Human Spirit* (New York: Simon and Schuster, 1984).

6. GlaxoSmithKline, 1997–2004, <http://www.Paxil.com> (viewed November 29, 2004).

7. E. Lilly and Company, Florida, 2005, <http://www.Prozac.com> (viewed March 1, 2005).

8. Pfizer, Inc., <http://www.Zoloft.com> (viewed November 29, 2004).

9. Paxil Web site, p. 1.

10. Ibid.

11. Zoloft Web site; ibid., p. 4.

12. Prozac Web site, p. 2; Paxil Web site, p. 1.

13. Paxil Web site, "Panic Disorders" section, p. 1.

14. Prozac Web site, "Depression" section, p. 1.

15. Zoloft Web site, "Social Anxiety Disorder" section, p. 1.

16. Ibid., p. 2.

17. Paxil Web site, "Post-Traumatic Stress Disorder" section, p. 1.

18. Prozac Web site, "Depression" section, p. 2.

19. Prozac Web site, "Disease Information" section, p. 3.

20. Zoloft Web site, "Depression" section, "Myths and Facts," p. 1.

21. Prozac Web site, "Disease Information" section, p. 3.

22. N. Crossley, "Prozac nation and the biochemical self: A critique," in S.J. Williams, L. Birke and G.A. Bendelow, eds., *Debating Biology: Sociological Reflections on Health, Medicine and Society* (London: Routledge, 2003), p. 248.

23. Peter Kramer, *Listening to Prozac* (New York: Viking, 1993).

24. Prozac Web site, "Disease Information" section, p. 3.

25. Paxil Web site, p. 1.

26. Christopher Lasch, *The Culture of Narcissism* (London: Abacus, 1978). See also Jonathan Friedman, "Narcissism, roots and postmodernity: The constitution of selfhood in the global crisis," in S. Lash and J. Friedman, eds., *Modernity and Identity* (Oxford: Blackwell, 1992), pp. 331–336; M.D. Levin, ed., *Pathologies of the Modern Self: Postmodern Studies on Narcissism, Schizophrenia and Depression* (New York: New York University Press, 1987).

27. Prozac Web site, "Practicing Self Discovery" section, p. 1.

28. Jean Baudrillard, *Simulations* (New York: Semiotext[e], 1983). Hyper-reality refers to a condition where simulations (such as TV representations) seem more real than what they are representing.

29. Prozac Web site, "Practicing Self Discovery" section, p. 1.

30. Prozac Web site, "Disease Information" section, p. 1. That Marilyn Monroe might have died from an overdose of antidepressants is conveniently glossed over.

31. Zoloft Web site, "Panic Disorder" section, pp. 1–2.

32. Zoloft Web site, "Depression" section, p. 3. In addition, the Zoloft page mentions that it is also important to offer emotional support in the following ways: Acknowledge that the person is suffering. Express affection, offer kind words, give compliments. Show that you respect and value the person. Help the person keep active and busy. **Don't** expect the person to just "snap out of it." **Don't** criticize, pick on, or blame the person for his/her behavior. **Don't** say or do anything that might worsen the person's poor self-image. **Don't** ignore any talk of suicide: notify a member of the person's family or his or her doctor immediately.

33. Zoloft Web site, "Panic Disorder" section, pp. 2 and 3; "Obsessive-Compulsive" section, p. 3.

34. Prozac Web site, "Depression" section, "Caring for Others," pp. 1 and 2. Family members and friends of the depressed person are also told to "encourage the person to stick with the treatment," "give emotional support by listening carefully, being optimistic, and offering hope," "invite the person to join you in activities he or she used to enjoy," "keep in mind that expecting too much too soon can lead to feelings of failure," "do not accuse the person of faking illness or expect him or her to 'snap out of it,'" and "take comments about suicide seriously: seek professional advice."

35. Prozac Web site, "Disease Information" section, p. 3.

36. N. Crossley, "Prozac nation and the biochemical self: a critique," in S.J. Williams, L. Birke and G.A. Bendelow, eds., *Debating Biology: Sociological Reflections on Health, Medicine and Society* (London: Routledge, 2003), p. 253.

37. While still mostly alone, the faces appearing in the different "disorders" sections on the Paxil Web site seem to display the disorders being discussed. The cute, egg-shaped, cartoonish Zoloft figure is also drawn as showing emotions which evoke various disorders, and it smiles on those sections of the Web site which describe Zoloft's effects on various disorders.

38. Arlie Hochschild, *The Managed Heart: The Commodification of Human Feelings* (Berkeley: University of California Press, 1983).

39. Jacquelyn Zita, *Body Talk: Philosophical Reflections on Sex and Gender* (New York: Columbia University Press, 1998), p. 63.

40. I cannot, in the space of this chapter, offer a crash course in Symbolic Interaction theory. Interested readers should consult the founding texts such as Herbert Blumer, *Symbolic Interactionism* (Berkeley: University of California Press, 1986); Charles Cooley, *Human Nature and the Social Order* (New York: Scribners, 1922); Erving Goffman, *The Presentation of Self in Everyday Life* (Harmondsworth: Penguin, 1959); Erving Goffman, *Behaviour in Public Places* (New York: Free Press, 1963); Erving Goffman, *Interaction Ritual* (New York: Pantheon, 1967); Erving Goffman, *Relations in Public: Microstudies of the Public Order* (Harmondsworth: Penguin, 1971); George Mead, *Mind, Self, and Society* (Chicago: University of Chicago Press, 1936). Other useful texts include Joel Charon, *Symbolic Interaction: An Introduction, an Interpretation, an Integration* (New Jersey: Prentice Hall, 1985); E. Goffman, *Relations in Public: Microstudies of the Public Order* (New York: Basic Books, 1971, for example, as well as the journal *Symbolic Interaction.*

41. Charles Cooley, *Human Nature and the Social Order* (New York: Scribers, 1922). Note that we also self-reflect with imaginary "others" whose reactions can also be imagined and rehearsed.

42. Peter Breggin and Ginger Breggin, *Talking Back to Prozac* (New York: Viking, 1994), p. 208.

43. Ibid.

44. D. Grodin and R. Lindlof, eds., *Constructing the Self in a Mediated World* (London: Sage, 1996); Jaber Gubrium and James Holstein, "Grounding the Postmodern Self," *The Sociological Quarterly* 35, no. 4 (1994), pp. 685–703; Stuart Hall, "Introduction: Who needs identity?" in S. Hall and P. Du Gay, eds., *Questions of Cultural Identity* (London: Sage, 1996), pp. 1–17; Sheila McNamee, "Therapy and identity construction in a postmodern World," in Grodin and Lindlof, op. cit., pp. 141–153; Laurel Richardson, "Narrative and sociology," in J. Van Maanen, ed., *Representation in Ethnography* (Thousand Oaks, California: Sage, 1995), pp. 198–221.

45. Breggin and Breggin, *Talking Back to Prozac*, op. cit., p. 210.

46. GlaxoSmithKline, 1997–2004, <http://www.Paxil.com> (viewed November 29, 2004); E. Lilly and Company, Florida, 2005, <http://www.Prozac.com> (viewed March 1, 2005); Pfizer, Inc., <http://www.Zoloft.com> (viewed November 29, 2004).

47. Breggin and Breggin, *Talking Back to Prozac*, op. cit., pp. 210–218.

48. Ibid., p. 211.

49. Jean Baudrillard, *Simulations* (New York: Semiotext[e], 1983).

50. Zygmunt Bauman, *Life in Fragments* (Oxford: Blackwell, 1995), p. 149.

51. Ken Robbins, "Forces of consumption: From the symbolic to the psychotic," *Media Culture and Society* 16 (1994), pp. 449–468. See also Simon Gottschalk, "The pains of everyday life: Between the D.S.M. and the postmodern," *Studies in Symbolic Interaction,* 1997, pp. 115–146.

52. Prozac Web site, "Depression" section, "Practicing Self-Discovery," p. 1.

53. Richard De Grandpre, *Ritalin Nation: Rapid-Fire Culture and the Transformation of Human Consciousness* (New York: W.W. Norton and Co., 1999).

54. M.L. Lyon, "C. Wright Mills meets Prozac: The relevance of 'social emotion' to the sociology of health and illness," in V. James and J. Gabe, eds., *Health and the Sociology of Emotions* (Oxford: Routledge, 1998), pp. 60–61.

55. Paxil Web site, "Disorders" section, p. 2.

56. Ibid.

57. Erich Fromm, *The Sane Society* (New York: Doubleday, 1956); H. Marcuse, *Eros and Civilization* (Boston: Beacon, 1955); Herbert Marcuse, *One-Dimensional Man* (Boston: Beacon, 1968).

58. David Morris, *Illness and Culture in the Postmodern Age* (Berkeley: University of California Press, 1998), p. 237.

59. Prozac Web site, "Disease Information" section, p. 3.

60. Stephen Braun, *The Science of Happiness: Unlocking the Mysteries of Mood* (New York: John Wiley and Sons, 2000).

61. Charles W. Mills, *The Sociological Imagination*, Oxford University Press, Oxford, 1959, p. 171.

4 Advertising Madness

LAWRENCE C. RUBIN

It has been said that truth in advertising is an oxymoron!
— Anonymous

Introduction

A little more than a half century ago, the drug Thorazine was discovered by Henri Laborit, and soon after widely used to ease the suffering of the severely mentally ill and those who cared for them. This was, as history would reveal, the beginning of the modern era of psychopharmacology.[1] Since that epochal discovery, an incalculable number of children, adults, and the elderly have been diagnosed with an ever-expanding cadre of psychiatric illnesses. This growth has been chronicled through the evolving *Diagnostic and Statistical Manual of Mental Disorders* (DSM), first published by the American Psychiatric Association in 1952. Since that maiden edition, in which a scant 66 psychiatric illnesses were identified, there have been several iterations of the volume, culminating in the current *DSM-IV-TR*, which identifies nearly four hundred forms of psychiatric illness. Inextricably coincident with this seeming psychiatric pandemic has been a boom, or more accurately, a nuclear proliferation, of medicines developed to combat or control the symptoms of anxiety, depression, psychosis, and more recently eating disorders, substance abuse, weight loss, smoking cessation and sexual dysfunction. Given these trends, it becomes logical to ask, "Has the American public become that much more psychiatrically ill, necessitating in turn, the development of literally hundreds of psychotropic drugs over the last several decades?"

The statistics are awe-inspiring. Over the last six years, the retail value

85

of drugs to treat depression, psychosis, mania, neuropsychiatric conditions and anxiety has been estimated at $123 billion.[2] Antidepressants, most prominently SSRIs and SNRIs[3] and antipsychotics have, for the last several years, consistently ranked in the top ten of all drug classes by sales, and in 2003; the antidepressants Zyprexa and Zoloft alone garnered over $6 billion in sales.[4] When we add to these staggering figures that each year, dozens of drugs for the treatment of mental illness are in some stage of development (ninety-nine in 2002 for example)[5] at the cost of tens of billions of dollars in research and development, the picture emerges of either an incredible need for effective pharmacological treatment of medically based mental disorders, massive sales and marketing campaigns, or perhaps both. Regardless of which of these is the case, additional factors such as an increase in the duration of psychiatric conditions, increasing numbers of dispensed prescriptions, and the dramatic rise in the marketing and sales of brand name psychiatric drugs insure that there has, and will continue to be "gold in them thar pills."

Inherent but not immediately obvious in this simplification of the psychotropic phenomenon are some cardinal presumptions about mental illness, psychotropic drugs and the relationship between the two. One is that mental illness is equivalent to brain illness, which if true implies corollarily that treatment should be medical, or in this case, medicinal.[6] This presumption seems to be taken at face value by a culture preoccupied with one-stop shopping, lightening-fast communication and the quick fix of everything from mental illness to erectile dysfunction; so much so that there has been a wholesale embrace of the promise of "better living through chemistry"[7]

This dynamic rise in psychotropic drug creation and spending is due in large part to the combined success of the advertising, pharmaceutical and psychiatry industries in commodifying mental illness. Commodification refers to the transformation of a psychiatric phenomenon, in our case mental illness, into a marketable commodity. The machinery of medical science is, in a sense, re-tooled into a capital-driven and capital-producing engine. And, as competition for market shares increases in the highly competitive and lucrative arena of psychotropic medication,[8] "communication forms that abbreviate and truncate meaning systems into familiar signs and symbols," i.e., dramatic, eye-catching images and seductive text, ascend to the status of popular and powerful cultural icons.[9] Who is not familiar with Pfizer's promotional antidepressant campaign featuring a despondent anthropomorphized egg that is transformed through its close encounter of a Zoloft kind?

Another phenomenon at the root of the success of psychotropic marketing and sales is "medicalization." This refers to the blurring of boundaries between the states of everyday worry, fear and sadness into their pathological counterparts of anxiety and mood disorders. The public and medical professional are then made continually aware through every form of media, print advertising in our case, that either explicitly or implicitly exaggerate and pathologize these conditions.[10] Capitalizing on the turbulent effect of current events including terrorism, unemployment, and natural and economic disasters, as well as the disquieting influence of daily pressures including parenting, noise pollution, social gatherings and overcrowding, the alluring promises of psychotropic drug ads are often inescapable. People who struggle with the very common problems of shyness, sadness, nervousness, malaise and even suspiciousness are offered refuge under the umbrella of drug-assisted well-being. Exemplifying this point was a 2000 Bristol-Meyers-Squibb ad in *Reader's Digest* for the anxiety drug BuSpar. It depicted a smiling young woman triumphantly sitting atop a mountain of words that spell out daily complaints, e.g., "I can't sleep ... I'm always tired ... so anxious."

A Brief History of Print Psychotropic Drug Advertising

The first major push in print psychotropic drug advertising in this country came in the late 1940's to sell drugs that helped manage the rigors of daily life, as well as to assist a wounded population recovering from the collective trauma of war. Early ads in professional medical journals promised restful sleep, relief from the so-called psychoneurotic symptoms of depression and anxiety, an improved outlook and even aid to the unfortunate housewife managing both an ailing husband and returning war-veteran son who was "a drunkard too weak to support himself."[11] As was noted above, the introduction of the tranquilizer Thorazine ushered in the psychotropic era, contributed to deinstitionalization of the mentally ill, and most relevant to this discussion, the institutionalization of print psychotropic drug advertising. Importantly, up to that point, and for several decades to come, all print psychotropic drug advertising was to be found in medical journals, the audience solely being physicians.

Thorazine, along with its soon-to-arrive competitors Desbutal, Miltown, Serpasil, Sandil and Desoxyn, to name a few, picked up the pace with added promises of "counteracting the extremes of emotion, eliminating bizarre behavior problems, facilitating psychiatric treatment and dispelling shadows."[12] Throughout the rest of the 1950's, the push continued to advertise medications that were aimed not just at the everyday person, but also at those unfortunate previously hospitalized mental patients who were now trying to piece together lives outside of institutional walls. Images of contented former patients working productively were contrasted with those of their distraught, isolated and ostensibly deranged counterparts shown, for example, peering over the edge of a house of cards, shuffling aimlessly in vast (presumably institutional) courtyards, or as in a 1956 ad for the antidepressant Serpanry, turned away from the portal to an idyllic pastoral setting.

By the end of that first decade of advertising psychotropic drugs, families were depicted in various phases of reunion, men returned successfully to work, and women to their domestic responsibilities. Behavioral and emotional equilibrium were to be found in a jar. And so important was the content of the little jars that the pills took a preeminence in many of the subsequent drug advertisements. An early 1960's ad for Thorazine depicted a pill (in full color), rather than a person resting comfortably on the psychoanalyst's leather couch (in drab black and white). There wasn't even a psychiatrist in the traditional chair behind it to listen. This ad, and the powerful theme behind it, focused the spotlight on what was by that time a deep schism in the professional field between those who adamantly believed that the psychiatrist's role was to minister psychoanalysis, and those who increasingly relied on medication in treatment. The latter came to be cynically known in hospital circles as the drug doctor.

These drug doctors, and all others for that matter, were regularly bombarded by powerful and evocative advertisements for scores of psychotropic drugs that were being developed at an explosive rate. Black-and-white images of women returned to teaching careers were contrasted with their distraught domestic counterparts in before-and-after advertisements for antipsychotics such as Navane. In an advertisement for the enduringly popular sedative Valium, a 1960's image of shattered glass reflected the "severe psychic tension" of anxiety, while a centerfold, before-and-after, full-color advertisement for the antidepressant Deprol assured a full return to psychiatric health. Finally, the benign and smiling artistic image of eighteenth century physician and psychiatrist Philippe Pinel, known for his human treatment of the mentally ill, was evoked by a late 1960's advertisement for the antidepressant Elavil.

As a caveat, the Federal Trade Commission (FTC) gave the Food and Drug Administration (FDA) jurisdiction over drug advertising only a little over a decade before Thorazine and these other so-called wonder drugs came to market. However, it wouldn't be until 1981, by virtue of the successful regulation of drug package inserts, that the first over-the-counter drug would be advertised directly to the public.[13]

Since the inception of psychotropic print advertising, the advertising industry has honed its ability to capture if not direct popular and professional attention to the promises of psychotropic drugs. Capitalizing on the time-tested techniques of repetition, emotional evocation, simplification and the "picture superiority effect,"[14] the ads for psychiatric panaceas made bold statements, both explicit and implicit. For example, an early 1970's ad for the antipsychotic Stelazine made an implicit comparison between the philosophical and musical genius of Plato and Beethoven, and that of the drug, by featuring their busts above the advertising text of the drug. In another, a frightening African tribal mask was used to depict the primitive destructive nature of mental illness. Implied in the latter ad was that the advertised drug could re-socialize the sufferer, casting out the primitive demons of their mental illness.

Throughout the remainder of the 1970's and the 1980's, advertisements capitalized on the use of photographs, paintings, bold slogans, rich metaphors, catchy brand names and suggestive imagery to tout the benefits of psychotropic drugs. A male figure broke free of a plaster encasement in an ad for an antidepressant appropriately called Asendin, while the image of a (presumably) Stradivarius violin was used to market the antipsychotic Stelazine, a "classic," as the ad suggested. A visually shocking advertisement for the antipsychotic Navane depicted a frightened woman in a cage being terrorized by a bird many times her size, and a dove flitting over a shiny silver brain touted the benefit of Paxepam for treating anxiety. While most of the advertisements ostensibly capitalized on hope, many of their messages were lost in the attempt to shock, dazzle, mystify or entertain.

Pitching the Pill in the 1990's: Direct to Consumer Advertising

It is difficult to appreciate the magnitude and complexity of psychotropic print advertising over the last decade and a half without considering the cultural, economic and historical context[15] in which it has been embedded. As was noted earlier, 1981 was a watershed year, in which pharmaceutical advertising to the public began. Eight years later in 1989, $12 million was spent on direct-to-consumer (DTC) advertising.[16] By 2003, $25.3 billion was spent by pharmaceutical companies on drug promotion, $3.2 billion of which was allocated to direct-to-consumer advertising (with one sixth — $448 million) going to journal advertising.[17] While this latter figure represents only 16 percent of total DTC spending for the year, the amount of money spent in print advertising (which doesn't even include advertising in popular magazines) represented a full twenty-fold increase over the total DTC spending budget of 1989.

Bear in mind that print advertising extends far beyond magazines and medical journals, to encompass pamphlets and flyers sent to medical professionals, informational literature for patients, kiosks in malls and airports, newspaper ads and billboards. Add to these the amount spent on bringing psychotropic drug and mental health/illness awareness to the public through television, radio and the Internet, and what emerges is the fact that promotional spending on psychotropics is among the highest of all such expenditures. In 2004, promotional spending for antidepressants and antipsychotics ranked third and sixth ($1.5 and $.81 billion respectively).[18]

Not unsurprisingly, these two drug classes consistently rank in the top classes by sales ($11.2 and $6.7 billion respectively in 2003).[19] Further, it appears that there is a positive return on investment for over 90 percent of drugs that receive mass marketing nationally,[20] and that DTC advertised drugs receive a far greater return on investment than those drugs not associated with public marketing campaigns.

So successful is drug promotion, and DTC advertising in particular, that a recent Kaiser Family Foundation survey suggested that the most heavily marketed drugs are typically those that are highest in sales, and that six of ten out of those drugs that are the most heavily marketed were in the top twenty of all drugs sold.[21] This report also determined that the number of prescriptions written for the most heavily advertised drugs rose at the rate of 25 percent in 2004 alone, compared to all other drugs that did not receive such heavy marketing. While the specific impact of DTC marketing, and print advertisement in particular, on psychotropic drug sales has received far less statistical scrutiny, there is evidence to suggest that similar patterns are being established within this class of drugs. Specifically, of those sampled physicians favoring DTC advertising, psychiatrists ranked second out of 16 medical specialties.[22] When we consider that an estimated 70 percent of antidepressants and 90 percent of anxiolytics are prescribed by non-psychiatrists,[23] it is no surprise that among these doctors with positive attitudes towards DTC advertising, that SSRIs are the fourth most requested drugs by patients, with Paxil and Prozac being requested at a particularly high frequency.[24] When we add to this the findings that nine of ten consumers have either seen or heard an ad for drugs in the last year, and that 50 percent of those polled trust the accuracy of these ads,[25] and that in 2001 the number of patients who discussed a DTC ad with their doctors translated into $61.1 million in sales,[26] we realize the full power of direct-to-consumer advertising to influence both the patient and physician.

FDA Regulation of Drug Advertising

Within the FDA, the Center for Drug Evaluation and Research (CDER) has the responsibility of ensuring the quick progress of safe and effective drugs (prescription, over-the-counter, and generic) from research and development through clinical trials to market. Directly under the auspices of the CDER is the Division of Drug Marketing, Advertising and Communication (DDMAC), which continually monitors the pharmaceutical marketing environment. While the DDMAC is not itself an enforcement body, it reminds pharmaceutical companies through issuance of warning letters that the FDA has clear advertising guidelines that it believes are being violated in some manner. The FDA, as big brother, takes full advantage of its own power to remove drugs from the market, along with that of the Department of Justice and the court system to help the DDMAC get its message across.

Prior to 1997, advertisement, both print and broadcast, was required to carry at very least, a brief summary which highlights the drug's side effects, contraindications, and warnings, along of course with its indications. The brief summary, in essence, had to contain "fair balance," which provides the consumer a balanced picture of the drug's clinical attributes and limitations. After the issuance of its "Draft Guidance for Industry: Consumer-Directed Broadcast Advertisements" in 1997, which was finalized in 1999, the FDA lessened its restrictions on DTC advertising, which in turn affected what could and could not appear in print advertisement.

Three categories of advertisement emerged; product claim ads, help-seeking ads and reminder ads, each of which carried different levels of disclosure burdens with regard to the indications, contraindications, side effects and dangers of the drug. Reminder ads, which simply highlight the drug's name, and help-seeking ads, which address symptoms and encourage physician contact are freed of the twin burdens of "fair balance" and "brief summary." In contrast, "product claim" advertisements do just that: they make clear statements about what the particular drug can and can't do, what its dangers might be, and how to find additional information (typically through "800" numbers or directives to contact a physician directly). A glance through both professional journals and popular magazines will show that each of these has subsequently been used effectively and powerfully. It is not uncommon for a pharmaceutical company to let us know that something big is coming down the pipeline by launching a series of ads, each incrementally providing more and more information, usually in the form of reminder and help-seeking ads. By the time the full campaign has been launched with product claim ads, both the public and medical professionals know not only its use, but its full iconography.

Considering that billions of dollars are being spent annually to advertise drugs in hopes of elevating them to blockbuster status ($1 billion in sales per year), with a significant portion of that allocated to the marketing of psychotropics, it is not surprising that the DDMAC reviews thousands of pieces of promotional materials every year, with what is in essence a skeletal crew of under forty. In 2002, for example, over 6000 pieces of promotional material were submitted for review to 33 staff members.[27] Print and broadcast advertisement of all drugs must present fair balance, factual material, and cannot be false or misleading. Print-only advertisements, in addition, must at the very least describe the potential or known risks of the drug. In addition to the seemingly obvious ways that drug companies can err in advertising their product, they also are quite creative in getting their mis-messages across. The advertisements may contain language that is overly technical, or logic or research that is flawed, or they may overstate benefits or understate risks. These ads can also distract the reader through the use of overly dramatic imagery, or inflate the suggested prevalence or seriousness of the condition for which the drug is reportedly designed. This latter technique, a component of the process of medicalization, will be addressed at a later point, along with gender display, decontextualization and marginalization, are all powerful distorting influences in drug print advertising in general, and psychotropic advertising in particular.

The incidence of mis-advertising psychotropic drugs is purportedly low, with less than 5 percent of all DDMAC warning letters being sent to their manufacturers.[28] However, a qualitative analysis of these letters over the last seven years is quite telling of the underlying mechanisms being used by pharmaceutical companies to boost sales.[29] In 1997, Wyeth-Ayerst Laboratories was warned that its promotional materials for Effexor, an antidepressant, which included the slogan "broken hearts require special care," implied that the drug had received FDA approval for both depression and cardiovascular disease. A year later, Smithkline Beecham Pharmaceuticals was warned about a T-shirt distributed at a local health fair, containing the Paxil logo along with the slogan "multiple symptoms, one solution." DDMAC argued that presentation of the Paxil logo and slogan on the back of a T-shirt that advertised a children's advocacy center implied that the drug had been approved for use in children. They also argued that the slogan was too broad and misleading. In 1999, Janssen Research Foundation was warned that its promotional material, particularly its print material, misled consumers to believe that Risperdal, while not specifically tested on the elderly, was effective in treating hostility. Similarly, Organon was cited in the same year for stating that Remeron, an antidepressant, was effective in treating anxiety as well.

In 2000, Shire Richwood, the manufacturer of Adderall, came to the attention of the DDMAC for falsely claiming that its anti–ADHD (Attention Deficit Hyperactivity Disorder) drug was superior to Ritalin. While Richwood cited two laboratory studies demonstrating Adderall's relative efficacy over Ritalin, it was argued that these studies were seriously scientifically flawed. Two years later, Pfizer, Inc. was scrutinized because it was disseminating misleading promotional material at the annual meeting of the American Psychiatric Association about its antipsychotic Geodon. And finally, bringing this chronicle up to date, GlaxoSmithKline utilized a highly evocative TV and print campaign to market Paxil for the treatment of Social Anxiety Disorder (SAD). DDMAC argued that while the drug was indeed FDA approved for use with SAD patients, the advertisements which depicted downtrodden looking (very attractive) people wearing signs saying "self-conscious" or "nervous" implied that the drug was just as effective for people with these everyday, run-of-the-mill concerns.

Context and Decontext in Psychotropic Print Ads

The success of psychotropic advertising in assuring people that well-being is just a pill away has depended on effective utilization of cliché, metaphor, seductive images, and suggestive text capitalizing on binary oppositions such as "then-and-now" and "before-and-after." Four important advertising processes — marginalization, decontextualization, gender display and medicalization — have been and continue to be seminal factors in this effort. The process of marginalization involves simplifying the physician's role to that of a technician primed to dispense pills according to scripted cultural stereotypes. Decontextualization refers to the elimination of the personal, social and cultural contexts of peoples' lives from the explanatory equation, and the accompanying reduction of the complexities of living to predictable, manageable, and ultimately medically treatable symptoms. Gender display capitalizes on the use of entrenched gender stereotypes in advertising, while medicalization relies upon the reframing of everyday distress as illness.

Marginalization of the Physician

As was mentioned earlier, physicians had been the prime target for psychotropic drug ads up until 1997, when the FDA lessened its restrictions on the type of information that needed to be contained in direct-to-consumer advertising.[30] Ostensibly, the psychotropic drug ads educated and empowered physicians by undermining alternative treatments, entrenching the medicalization of non-medical problems, and promoting lack of confidence in personal health. This elevated the disease model of mental illness, and with it, the physician.[31] Early ads prominently featured well-clad officious professionals tending to distressed, disheveled and disoriented patients. A 1960's ad for the antipsychotic drug Trilafon depicted a beleaguered and despondent patient sitting across the desk from his psychiatrist; clearly, both were allies in the treatment.

How ironic that in a culture which has historically reified the medical professional, placing him in the central healing role, the very ads that rely on them for profitability eventually chipped away at that centrality. The ads of the 1950's were designed to show physicians how helpful these wonder drugs could be in freeing the mentally ill from institutional life. Drug and doctor were partners in liberation. Medicines were touted for their ability to "help keep more patients out of mental hospitals."[32] Wonderfully artistic and dramatic images reminded physicians that Thorazine and related drugs were the way to avoid the historically barbaric treatment of the mentally ill and, by association, to avoid the failures of his professional ancestors.

As deinstitutionalization of psychiatric patients progressed in the late 1950's and 1960's, psychotropic medicines were promoted as adjunctive aids to the physician who could now better reach his patient through psychotherapy. Nevertheless, those ads also made it quite clear that psychotherapy was not possible without the assistance of the medication that was being advertised. Poignant and emotionally evocative images with captions such as "the therapeutic alliance"[33] and "removing the bars between patient and psychiatrist"[34] reminded both patient and physician that they had a friend.

Insidiously, however, the physician became far less prominent in psychotropic drug advertisements, a mere bystander in this conflict for the collective soul of the suffering masses. In contrast to the ad for Trilafon mentioned above in which patient and physician are allies, in a more recent ad for the antipsychotic agent Zyprexa, a disheveled man reaches desperately upward to the outstretched hand of a physician. Upon closer inspection, the viewer notices that the likelihood that the two will reach each other is made possible only by virtue of the patient standing on a rock in the shape of the stylized "Z" associated with the name Zyprexa.

But the implied message was that they could no longer do their job alone. Few ads capture this process of physician marginalization better than a current one for the antipsychotic Geodon, in which a tangle of musical notes emerges from blackness into vivid color on a perfectly ordered musical staff. It features neither the patient nor the physician. It is the drug and the drug alone that retrieves the melody of life from the chaos of mental illness. Another ad, this time for the antidepressant Celexa, depicts a brilliantly colored flower sprouting victoriously from the parched and barren desert of depression.

There has been no apparent research into physicians' perceptions of the way in which they have been depicted in psychotropic (and other) drug advertisements. However, there has been considerable recent investigation of physician perception of the efficacy of DTC advertising. A survey of Midwestern physicians in both urban and rural settings[35] suggested that satisfaction with direct-to-consumer advertising is mixed, with greater perceived utility of these ads among younger and urban practitioners. Older and rural practitioners were more resistant to the idea of direct-to-consumer advertising and by association, to their own marginalization. A related survey of consumers in a Western metropolitan area[36] suggested that direct-to-consumer advertising could stimulate doctor-patient conversations about appropriate prescriptions. A survey of 199 physicians by *Psychiatric News* suggested that few physicians felt particularly pressured to prescribe medications suggested by their patients,[37] and that many regarded the phenomenon of DTC advertising to be at worst benign. In general, while their responses have clearly varied depending on the methodology and content of the survey procedure, those physicians favoring drug campaigning to the public indicate that it enhances treatment compliance, improves the therapeutic alliance, informs and educates the patient, and brings more people to treatment.[38]

Decontextualization

The central premise behind decontextualization is as follows: It isn't overcrowding, aging, parenting, terrorism, global warming, recession, unemployment or the pressure of being a man, woman or member of a minority group that is responsible for the epidemic of anxiety and depression in our culture. It is the individual's failure to adequately respond to these challenges for reasons of emotional or psychological inadequacy. Symptoms for which people seek relief through psychotropic medication and to which the pharmaceutical ads appeal are thus reinterpreted as personal failures and then recontextualized as illness. This in turn justifies the need for a solution that must be targeted at the individual rather than at the context in which the individual functions, i.e., their marriage, family, gender, culture and society. By localizing pathology within the person rather than in the external factors that give rise to them, decontextualization "serves to reinforce and legitimize social attitudes and relations [such as sexism and alienating working conditions] which may actually contribute to the problems these [medical] products target."[39] The promoted psychotropic agent may indeed help the harried housewife, disgruntled worker, disenfranchised teen or painfully shy salesperson muddle through their daily rigors. However, the seductive advertisements implicitly undermine self-help, alternative forms of treatment and the need to remedy the inequities, injustices and discomforts that gave rise to the problem in the first place.

By playing to and preying upon weakness, psychotropic drug advertisements make the moral assertion that people who struggle unsuccessfully under these pressures are of a lesser god, and as a result need the help of the psychiatric establishment. In a sense, the success of decontextualization rests in its power to victimize and dehumanize those who are ostensibly unsuccessful at living. This process was presaged in the early 1960's by psychiatrist Thomas Szasz, who in his treatise *The Myth of Mental Illness* suggested that "we don't expect everyone to be a competent swimmer, chess player or golfer, and we don't regard those who can't play as sick. Yet, we expect everyone to play at his own life game competently, and when they don't, we call them sick — mentally ill!"[40] In his later volume *Ideology and Insanity*, Szasz reflected on the ethics and morality inherent in calling people mentally ill, noting, "the notion of mental symptom is inextricably tied to the social and particularly ethical context in which it is made, just as the notion of bodily symptom is tied to an anatomical and genetic context."[41]

Consider a 1960's ad for the tranquilizer Prolixin that offered relief from the stresses of the day. The intentionally blurred image of the crowded metropolis literally and metaphorically shifted the reader's focus away from the relatively faceless denizens. We were not asked to consider the context, i.e., the opprobrious rat-race conditions of urban living that resulted in emotional stress. Nor were we asked to consider the humanity of the people caught in it. Instead, we were drawn to the oasis of clarity found in the promissory advertising text which zeroed in on the medicalized symptoms of the emotional stress.

Over the next several decades, this process of decontextualization played a significant role in the print advertising of psychotropic drugs. Gone from many of the ads were the doctors and patients, and even the drugs that were being ostensibly advertised. They were replaced by images from the laboratory, nature, or the artistic imagination of Fifth Avenue. A

1970's advertisement for Tranxene, an anxiolytic, featured a despondent women's face peering out from a water bubble at the end of a pipette. One can only wonder what it was that got her into that bubble in the first place! In that same decade, a very popular campaign for the antipsychotic Prolixin featured people walking across a bridge constructed in letters of the drug's name. The bridged connected a craggy peak with a bucolic pasture on the other side, but we have no idea why they needed to cross the bridge in the first place. A 1980's advertisement for the antidepressant Sinequan zoomed in on a budding plant at the end of a drew-draped twig — no reference at all, except metaphorically to human suffering and rejuvenation. And finally, a 1990's ad for the antidepressant Zyprexa featured a builder's level, implying that the drug represents a "tool for stabilization."

Fast forward to 2001 and the social, emotional and cultural upheaval following the attacks of September 11. In the 12-month period between October 2000 and October 2001, national sales for the top three antidepressants (Prozac, Paxil and Zoloft) rose 20 percent, or $499 million. Pfizer, maker of Zoloft, spent $5.6 million in TV and magazine advertisements in October of that year while Glaxo spent $16.5 million on their ads for Paxil in that same period, up significantly from spending in October of the previous year.[42] While these statistics don't speak directly to the issue of decontextualization as a driving force in the advertising of psychotropic drugs, the implication is that there was a dramatic need for psychotropic medication during that time period, even though the pharmaceutical companies very delicately avoided the connection between their increased marketing dollars and the events of 9/11.

Pfizer's advertisements for Zoloft during that painful period featured flags, candles, firemen, and referenced the $10 million spent by the company on relief funds. Advertising text such as "We wish we could make a medicine that could take away the heartache, but until we can, we will continue to do everything we can to help"[43] suggested that although they couldn't heal the nation from this tragic event, ultimately it would be their responsibility to do so. Here again as in the 1963 advertisement for Prolixin, it wasn't the sociopolitical antecedents of the stressor, which in this case is terrorism, that required attention; it was an otherwise helpless, anxiety ridden, victimized and psychologically impaired populace that required medical assistance. Context had been stripped from the event so that a wounded population could be sold on the merits of modern medication.

Gender Display

Common to all of the advertising campaigns has been their ability to capitalize, prey, some would argue, on deeply entrenched popular culture archetypes such as the beleaguered housewife, the struggling bread-winning husband, the lonely and disengaged senior citizen and the child isolated from family and friends by seemingly intractable behavioral and emotional disturbances. While it has been argued that the subsequent explosion of psychotropic drug advertising has fostered psychiatric stereotypes of men, women, children, minorities and the elderly, it can just as easily be argued that they have simply held up a mirror to a culture that already defines its population on the basis of these stereotypes.

No other single demographic in psychotropic print advertising has been researched as gender has been, so much so in fact that it has been acknowledged as a phenomenon in its own right: gender display.[44] These ads have been analyzed for their sheer relative quantity of men versus women, the ratio of women to men in various occupations, states of emotional well-being and illness, as well as for the depiction of the genders in medical roles within the ads.[45] Additionally, this research has been performed internationally, with most frequent reference to medical journals from Canada, Great Britain, Australia and New Zealand. This discussion, as well as the ones to follow, focuses only on American advertising, even though the trends appears to be quite similar across borders.

Over the years, the venue of print advertising has become infused with artistic and creative flair designed to evoke emotion and sympathy, drawing on the use of photo-realism and reference to classical art and music, along with complex imagery and metaphor. However, their messages consistently converge on two findings: that women suffer with mental illness to a far greater extent than do men, and are far higher frequency consumers of psychotropic medicines, particularly antidepressants and anxiolytics. Men, in consistent contrast, suffer primarily from work-related stress with situational (mental) disturbance. In these ads, women suffer predominantly from stress at home and in relationships, as opposed to the workplace, are far less frequently depicted in professional roles, and are usually consumers rather than providers of health care. Men are typically depicted as professionals, particularly as physicians in these ads, and appear as far less emotional overall.

Advertising companies have consistently taking full advantage of cultural expectations with regard to the gender imbalance inherent in psychiatric epidemiology rates. A 1960's antipsychotic ad for Navane featured a mother looking lovingly at her young son, who sat atop a kitchen counter amongst the groceries. It was Navane that brought her home to the bliss of domesticity and parenthood. Another depicted a young woman chatting with her female friend over breakfast, with a pastel colored early morning sky in the window behind them. A 1978 ad for Mellaril, an antidepressant, from the *American Journal of Psychiatry* depicted a woman boldly and happily striding with a bag of groceries, with the word "maintainability" above her head. A 1980's antidepressant ad for Asendin depicted a woman's face in a crumpled divorce decree, suggesting that the medication would liberate her from the decontextualized nightmare of divorce.

A more recent ad for Zoloft shows a mother in a business suit joyfully running through the park with her two young soccer-clad sons. The ad talks about the power of the medication to provide this joyful reconnection. Each of these suggests that relief from the stresses of parenting, domesticity and even divorce is just a pill away. Once liberated from the grips of disease rather than from the cultural dictates of their role, women are freed to return to that prescribed role or an idealized version of it. A current campaign for Paxil, another antidepressant, shows an athletic woman sitting atop a kayak, the oars balanced perfectly across her, with the caption "Power of Balance" emblazoned beneath.

With regard to the depiction of men in psychotropic drug ads, there has historically been a focus on the power of the pill to return the man to work by freeing him and those around him from the threat of his aggressive nature, by re-establishing the romantic bond with his partner or through removal of temporary barriers to well-being. This is, in comparison to ads featuring women, where there is an implication of permanence to the psychiatric condition, as opposed to the simple removal of transient, stress-induced disturbance. In these ways, the flaws of masculinity or at least the stereotypical limitations of the masculine role are reduced, as in the case of women, to treatable psychiatric symptoms.

As examples, a 1960's ad for Thorazine shows a man in mid-rage against a woman. The text talks about the control of agitation. A 1980's ad for an antipsychotic reveals the power of the drug to return sufferers to reality. It depicts a man whose image is cut in half. On the left is a robotic shell that is being reconstructed, square-by-square. On the right is the man fully restored, including hair and suit. A more recent ad for Remeron, an antidepressant, shows a 60-something couple embracing each other, with the man holding a brilliant bouquet of flowers behind her. As in the case of advertisements targeting women, the pharmaceutical industry is holding up a mirror to our entrenched cultural attitudes and expectations about men, i.e., their violent tendencies, their fulfillment through work, and their potential for grace and compassion (with medication).

Interestingly, the trends noted in this section appear to be experiencing somewhat of a reversal over the past five years, particularly in psychotropic advertisements that have appeared in popular magazines (as opposed to those that appear in medical journals). More men are depicted in family scenes in psychotropic ads, even though these seem to be restricted to promotions for ADHD medications for their children. More women are appearing in business suits, relieved by psychotropics of their stresses, much as their earlier counterparts were freed to return happily to home and hearth. Women are also more often being depicted in these ads as the physician, such as in the campaigns for Zyprexa. In these, it is not uncommon for a female physician (ostensibly a psychiatrist) to be walking supportively alongside her male patient (who is typically very composed, as compared to his deranged counterparts of decades past). As compelling as these trends may be, it is far too early to know whether this is an emerging (and enduring) trend, which will have the momentum to attack deeply engrained sociocultural stereotypes.

Medicalization

The introduction of Prozac in 1987 heralded the second coming of psychotropic medication, the first being the widespread acceptance of Thorazine thirty years before.[46] "Within two years, pharmacies were filling 65,000 prescriptions for Prozac per month, and within five years, 4.5 million Americans were taking it."[47] The first of a new class of antidepressants, the SSRIs (selective serotonin reuptake inhibitors), Prozac would be followed by many more, each aspiring to the status of blockbuster (more than $1 billion in sales annually). Sixteen years later in 2003, there were 142 million prescriptions written for SSRIs, which ranked third in the top ten _selling drug classes. Additionally, there were over a half-dozen SSRI antidepressants on the market, two of which alone garnered $6.4 billion in sales in 2003 (Zyprexa and Zoloft).[48] And this doesn't even include all other types of drugs being marketed and prescribed for all other psychiatric conditions. Add to this the estimate that between 1991 and 2001, there were upwards of 45 million office visits for depression, and the earlier stated finding that a large majority of antidepressants and anti-anxiety drugs are prescribed by non-psychiatric physicians, and we must ask whether so many Americans are depressed, anxious and psychotic, and thus in such great need of medication.

Almost as popular as Prozac was the 1994 runaway bestseller *Listening to Prozac* by psychiatrist Peter Kramer. In it was introduced the concept of "cosmetic psychopharmacology,"[49] which is the notion that many psychoactive drugs are prescribed and taken simply to enhance mood and to alleviate non-pathological states, such as sadness, worry, suspiciousness, self-doubt, fear, guilt ... the list could go on indefinitely. Cosmetic psychopharmacology is, as its name implies, a psychological face lift, designed as a lifestyle choice, rather than as a medical necessity. The notion of medical necessity in turn implies that either the physician determines that there is a medical problem or the patient complains of one (or both), which tautologically presumes that psychiatric problems are medical in nature. This gets back to the issue of whether mind indeed emanates in the brain, and as a result, mental problems necessitate alterations in brain chemistry, i.e., the use of psychotropic drugs.

Enter the notion of medicalization, the blurring of lines between (mentally) normal and (mentally) ill, so that the parameters of the otherwise everyday experience of sadness, anxiety and self-doubt can be expanded into the pathological range, thus necessitating medical treatment. This "disease mongering,"[50] as it has also been called, has been used to explain the explosive popularity of drugs to treat hair loss, erectile dysfunction and female sexual dysfunction. It has simultaneously been offered as way of understanding our national obsession with health and illness, as a way of obscuring the contexts in which (mental) health problems arise, and as a means of empowering drug manufacturers to wield self-serving drug campaigns. So much so, that in 1993, the World Health Organization (WHO) warned of the "inherent conflict of interest between the legitimate business goals of manufacturers and the social, medical and economic needs of providers and the public to select and use drugs in the most rational way."[51]

It continues to be the pharmaceutical industry that stands to profit most by medicalizing problems of daily living that have come to be called mental illness. Their vehicle for doing so is advertising and, in the context of this particular discussion, magazine and professional journals. Earlier in this discussion, the GlaxoSmithKline campaign for its blockbuster drug, Paxil, brought medicalization into bold relief. The FDA charged that through its evocative advertising using people wearing signs advertising that that were shy, self-conscious and worried, the drug manufacturer failed to clearly distinguish between normal and pathological states of sadness and self-consciousness on one hand, and Social Anxiety Disorder on the other. There are other equally compelling examples.

Most prominent among these has been the medicalization of the constellation of fear, sleeplessness, painful recollections and vigilance in the form of Post-Traumatic Stress Disorder (PTSD). As was earlier discussed, the advertising dollars spent and the retail return on antidepressants and anxiolytics after 9/11 was dramatic. It has been estimated that 13 percent of people taking psychotropics had dose increases in the twelve weeks following 9/11, and that in New York City, that number was closer to 17 percent, compared to 13 percent during the same period the year before.[52] The marketing campaigns capitalized on fear, anxiety and profound loss, all of which were grist for the psychotropic mill. PTSD became common parlance; seemingly a psychiatric illness perfectly crafted for the event. While initially popularized to better explain the psychiatric victimhood of soldiers returning from war, it came to "be associated with everything from childbirth to robbery to sexual harassment."[53]

The stories behind Generalized Anxiety Disorder (GAD) and Social Anxiety Disorder SAD are equally interesting. In 1998, GlaxoSmithKline received FDA approval to market Paxil, an SSRI antidepressant, for the treatment of (SAD), which is characterized by painful shyness and social withdrawal. The company produced promotional material suggesting that the incidence of SAD was far greater than was commonly accepted, and launched promotional campaigns highlighted by the slogans "It's Not Your Fault" and "Imagine Being Allergic to People." The very use of the term "allergic" implied disease, readily amenable to medication, as if it were poison ivy. This advertising effort coincided with an explosive proliferation of stories about SAD in the print and electronic media, powerful advertisement tools in their own right. Parenthetically, the SAD advertising campaign was voted Best PR Program of 1999 by the New York chapter of the Public Relations Society of America.[54]

During the spring of 2001, newspaper stories and testimonials began addressing a hidden disease, one that affected millions and was accompanied by symptoms of fatigue, irritability and restlessness. In April of that year, GlaxoSmithKline received FDA approval to market Paxil for the treatment of GAD. While there are no conclusive estimates of the prevalence of the disorder, large amounts of money and time were spent in getting the word out about the drug in the form of company-sponsored testimonials and workshops, advocacy efforts and advertisement.[55] Emotionally evocative print ad slogans such as "your life is waiting" helped to convince the American people that GAD was a disease to be reckoned with.

In the above scenarios, medicalization can be construed as an exploitative or opportunistic process. This may sound rather harsh, but when we stop to consider that there are numerous pharmaceutical companies vying for the same marketplace, it is no coincidence that there has been a "close parallel of slicing the taxonomic pie and the emergence of drugs for those conditions."[56] In other words, there has been, as some suggest, the emergence of an "ill for every pill" phenomenon. This has been addressed in the cases of Delusional Disorder, Panic Disorder and Obsessive-Compulsive Disorder, all of which have been made sufficiently distinct taxonomically from schizophrenia, general anxiety states and psychosis to warrant their own medications.[57] By the end of the 1990's, a popular magazine advertisement for Paxil could boast that its product relieved the symptoms of panic disorder, lifted depression and controlled OCD — a psychotropic hat-trick.

The last chapter in the story of medicalization is that of Female Sexual Dysfunction (FSD), which is not yet officially recognized by the American Psychiatric Association. It is not that female sexual dysfunction in its many forms does not affect women that is typically argued, but that it has been given a boost by the pharmaceutical industry in order to sell Viagra (sildenafil), and similar drugs. John Bancroft, director of the Kinsey Institute, believes that "the danger of portraying sexual difficulties as a dysfunction is that it is likely to encourage doctors to prescribe drugs to change sexual dysfunction."[58] While there have been numerous conferences, study groups and research studies involving FSD, there is little consensus as to the prevalence of the disorder, which varies widely and wildly. Nor is there consensus, as with its male counterpart, erectile dysfunction (ED), as to whether its origin is vascular, hormonal, neurological or psychogenic in origin. Nevertheless, and regardless of etiology, it, like SAD, GAD, and OCD, is being powerfully marketed as the women's lifestyle disease of the twenty-first century.

Making Drugs: Working the System

With so much at stake in the (psycho)pharmaceutical marketplace, it appears that old drugs, particularly profitable ones, never die; they just receive clever new marketing campaigns, get repackaged, re-patented, or re-applied to new niches. The question of why drugs cost so much is usually countered by the pharmaceutical industry with the argument that it takes a great deal of time and money to safely bring these life-saving agents to market. The consensus, albeit a hotly debated and reluctant one, in the pharmaceutical industry is that it costs over $800 million and takes 12 to 15 years to develop a new drug, and that research and development costs far outweigh marketing and advertising expenditures.[59] But there is the rest of the story.

In 1987, Prozac was approved, and soon after introduced for the treatment of depression. Over the next several years, Lilly received FDA approval to market its blockbuster drug for the treatments of Obsessive-Compulsive Disorder (1994), bulimia (1996), and for geriatric depression (1997). In 2001, Prozac was approved for the treatment of Premenstrual Dysphoric Disorder (PMDD), re-packaged from its familiar green and cream colors to pink and purple, and marketed as Serafem. In the same period of time,

GlaxoSmithKline, Pfizer and Forest Laboratories patented Paxil, Zoloft, Celexa and Lexapro, all for the treatment of depression. Threatened by the spate of competition, Lilly received patent extensions into 2004 for its block-buster by gaining approval for Prozac Weekly. Soon after Glaxo received a patent for Paxil in 1992, it launched a series of four lawsuits against competitor, Aponex, which was planning to develop knock-offs.[60] Each lawsuit garnered a 30-month delay in patent expiration, extending market control for at least another ten years. In the mid 1990's, Neurontin was approved for the treatment of epileptic seizures, and in 2003 garnered over $2.7 billion in sales. A year later, Pfizer, Neurontin's manufacturer, admitted to criminal wrongdoing in a whistleblower lawsuit by one its employees, and paid out over $430 million in fines.[61] Pfizer was charged with off-label marketing of Neurontin for the treatment of bipolar disorder. It had also become widely prescribed by psychiatrists, internists and general practitioners for PTSD and insomnia. How can these sort of things occur? This is where the advertising madness comes in.

The FDA requires only that a proposed drug be compared with a placebo during clinical trials. Inter-drug comparison is not necessary. This significantly cuts down on the amount of time that a drug falls under government review. The phenomenon of "me-too" drugs also comes into play, as the unregulated, free-market economy of the drug marketplace thrives on competition. A "me-too" drug is one that is a chemical copycat of an original and that has been tweaked in some minor way. In 2002, the FDA approved 78 drugs, only 17 of which were NMEs, or "new molecular entities." Seven of the seventy-eight drugs were considered improvements over existing drugs, while the remaining seventy-one were "me-too" drugs.[62] Each year, there are many drugs for all forms of mental illness in the pipeline, twenty-five for depression and eighteen for anxiety.[63]

The FDA also accepts clinical trial research that is not government sponsored. As a matter of fact, much of clinical testing takes place either in university or private laboratories sponsored by the pharmaceutical industry, called CRO's (contract research organizations). When this is considered along with the reality that pharmaceutical companies provide an extensive network of drug promotional meetings, contribute significantly to the American Psychiatric Association, offer continuing medical education training, and author numerous research outcome studies which are then signed off by others, the picture emerges of an industry that not only controls the price of drugs in America, but also plays a significant role in dissemination of information about those drugs.[64]

When we then combine the prevalence of the "me-too" phenomenon with the legal power of patent extension, the commercial clout of off-label marketing, and the major role that the pharmaceutical industry plays in drug research and print advertising, a very potent formula for financial success emerges. When we also consider that the cost of bringing a new drug to market may be closer to $100 million (compared with the oft-cited $800 million figure) and that marketing and advertisement costs typically exceed those of research and development, it is not surprising that in 2002, for example, the top ten drug companies made more in profits ($35.9 billion) than all other 490 Fortune 500 companies combined ($33.7 billion).[65] The print ads bear out the rest of the story, particularly in the realm of the most recent phenomenon in the pharmaceutical universe: extended release drugs.

A recent ad in the Journal of the American Psychiatric Association for Effexor, an antidepressant, made claims of proven effectiveness and tolerability, referencing scientific controlled studies. Upon closer inspection, the studies were not actually published in peer-reviewed journals, but presented at conferences (perhaps underwritten or contributed to by the drug company). A new spate of time-release and extended-release medications for anxiety (most prominently Xanax) and depression (most prominently Lexapro) utilize alluring hourglass and measurement imagery (and attractive women) to metaphorically depict time (and drug efficacy) elongation. Lilly's recent campaign for Stratera suggests that by taking the proven nonstimulant, the fun of the day can be extended well beyond school and into family time. A campaign for maintenance dosing with Lamictal to treat all phases of bipolar illness (depression, manic, hypomanic and mixed) cleverly utilizes satisfied customers in varying sitting and standing positions to reflect the drug's ability to support, maintain, and help to "stand up." Interestingly, drug manufacturers have become so cognizant of the ways that their advertisements can be scrutinized, and their research methods impugned, that it is not uncommon to find numerous footnotes in an ad. A recent advertisement for AstraZeneca's Seroquel (an antipsychotic) contained eight such references. Several of the referenced laboratory studies were done in conjunction with the pharmaceutical company (Seroquel study groups). While such fastidious ostensible accountability may satisfy the FDA and lay public, it is otherwise clear that these research studies are highly proprietary and self-interest driven. Finally, GlaxoSmithKline's newly released Welbutrin XL (extended release) notes that neither depression nor its treatment should come between people. Is it more likely that each of these extended release variants offer that much more, or that much better treatment than did their predecessors, or that they are simply examples of the latest use of me-too's, patent extension strategies, and flashy advertising campaigns to sell their products?

Conclusion

Psychotropic drug advertising debuted in medical journals shortly before the psychotropic era was inaugurated by the introduction of Thorazine in the mid 1950's. Over the years, drug manufacturers have successfully capitalized on advertising metaphors and dramatic images to lay the fruits of their labors at the doorstep of American consciousness. More recently and with the help of the FDA, psychotropic drug advertisements found their way a wide array of popular magazines (*Parents, Reader's Digest, TV Guide, Better Homes and Gardens, Time* and *Redbook*). It is no longer uncommon to hear references to Prozac in daily conversations, and expressions like "taking a Prozac Moment" have become idiomatic in our culture.

Several years ago, the books *Listening to Prozac* and *Prozac Nation* were runaway bestsellers that brought the battle between pharmaceutical companies for the American psyche and pocketbook into bold relief. Each year, an astronomical number of prescriptions are written for psychotropic medications by psychiatric and non-psychiatric physicians. Recent research suggests that "patients who request particular brands of drugs after seeing advertisements are nearly nine times more likely to get what they ask for than those who simply seek a doctor's advice."[66]

It is difficult to overstate the importance of an educated consumer, and DTC advertising by all credible accounts is having just that effect. But while the hard-sell is ostensibly on the merits of psychotropic medication, destigmatization of mental illness and consumer empowerment, the driving force behind that sell rests in the undeniable truth that (psychotropic) drugs sell, and sell big. Money and medical promises make for not only strange but also highly unlikely bedfellows, who toss and turn in attempts to win over a restless culture seemingly bent on self-stimulation, self-sedation or both. However, the most restless and those with the greatest stake in the "merchandising of mind mechanics"[67] is the pharmaceutical industry in its ongoing quest to create new niches to market their products.

At the height of height of Paxil's popularity several years ago, Barry Brand, Pfizer's product director, noted, "Every marketer's dream is to find an unidentified or unknown market and develop it. That's what we were able to do with social anxiety disorder."[68] Brand was referring to the marketing success behind the promotion of Paxil with its "Your life is waiting" campaign. Supporters argued (and still do) that social anxiety disorder, along with a host of other newcomers to the psychiatric landscape, are legitimate psychiatric conditions rooted in brain abnormalities, thus necessitating medical treatment. Detractors continue to contend that pharmaceutical companies medicalize shyness, just as they do sadness, guilt, fear and suspiciousness in order to sell drugs.

In addition to the metaphors, images and promises that have formed the foundation of these powerful and profitable print advertising campaigns, pharmaceutical companies have saturated the professional and popular landscape with a plethora of promotionals. The range of psychotropic pharmaceutical merchandise, e.g. pens, coffee mugs and clipboards, while breathtaking, is but a palpable manifestation of the promises found in psychotropic drug ads. It is not uncommon to find friends and colleagues drinking from a Zoloft mug, writing with a Seroquel pen, squeezing a Paxil sponge ball-brain, relaxing to a Prozac waterfall, eating popcorn and Poptarts in Risperdal packaging, wiping away tears with Librium tissues or telling time from a Geodon clock.

Bombardment is the more apt term for the psychotropic advertising campaigns that have colored our mental marketplace, in the attempt to remind stressed men, women and children that better living is within quick reach. And in a culture that turns to both superheroes and science, what could be a more fitting reminder of the power of the advertising industry than a recent promotional campaign for Metadate, a stimulant medication used to treat ADHD. With the promising power of its promotional Superman-like superhero Meta-Man, we are reminded that pills are as fast as speeding bullets and as powerful as locomotives in restoring mental well-being.

Notes

1. Edward Shorter, *A History of Psychiatry: From the Era of the Asylum to the Age of Prozac* (New York: John Wiley and Sons, 1997).

2. Source: NDCHealth, NDC Pharmaceutical Audit Suite, December 1999–October 2004. Data on file.

3. SSRI is "Selective Serotonin Reuptake Inhibitor." SNRI is "Selective Norepinephrine Reuptake Inhibitor."

4. In "IMS Reports 11.5 Percent Dollar Growth in '03 U.S. Prescription Sales." See <www.imshealth.com/ims/portal/front/articleC/0,2777,6599_3665_44771558,00.html> (viewed October 20, 2004). (archived)

5. From a 2002 Survey by PhRMA, "New Medicines in Development for Mental Illnesses," <http://www.phrma.org/newmedicines/newmedsdb/drugs.cfm> (viewed October 21, 2004). (archived)

6. For an extensive discussion on the erroneousness of these presumptions, see Elliot Valenstein, *Blaming the Brain* (New York: The Free Press, 1998).

7. In 1935, a corporate advertising campaign was launched promoting DuPont's role in improving daily life with the slogan "Better Things for Better Living ... Through Chemistry." The tag line "through chemistry" was removed from advertising in the 1980's. The slogan was replaced in 1999 with "The miracles of science(r)," capitalizing

on DuPont's heritage and strength as a science company. See <http://www.heritage. dupont.com/touchpoints/tp_1939/overview.html> (viewed November 14, 2004).

8. In 2003, the top ten drug companies, including Pfizer and Lilly, grossed $129 billion in sales. See <http://www.imshealth.com/ims/portal/front/articleC/0,2777,6599_ 3665_44771558,00.html> (viewed December 1, 2004). (archived)

9. In Robert Goldman and Michael Montagne, "Marketing Mind Mechanics: Decoding Antidepressant Drug Advertisements," *Social Science and Medicine* 22 (1986), pp. 1047–1058.

10. For a discussion of the relationship between psychotropic drug marketing and the proliferation of so-called mental illness, see Shankar Vedantam, "Drug Ads Helping Anxiety Make Some Uneasy," *The Washington Post,* July 16, 2001, p. A1.

11. Advertising text for Mebaral, Allonal, and Dexamyl appearing in the *American Journal of Psychiatry* between 1945 and 1954.

12. Taken from ads appearing in the *American Journal of Psychiatry* between 1954 and 1956.

13. See Francis Palumbo and C. Daniel Mullins, "The Development of Direct-to-Consumer Prescription Drug Advertising Regulation," *Food and Drug Law Journal* 57 (2002), pp. 422–443, for a detailed history of direct-to-consumer advertising (DTC) and its regulation.

14. Palumbo, et al., op. cit., 424.

15. See Palumbo et al., op. cit., p. 423. On a historical note, the 1906 Pure Food and Drug Act (the Wiley Act) was the first federal legislation that addressed the labeling of drugs, both over-the-counter and prescription.

16. Sing et al., op. cit., 423.

17. IMS Reports, op. cit.

18. For a detailed description of promotional expenditure in 2004, see <http://www. ndchealth.com/press_center/uspharmaIndustryData/top10therapeuticClassSales2003. htm> (viewed July 22, 2004).

19. See <http://www.imshealth.com/ims/portal/front/articleC/0,2777,6599_4969 5992_56378898,00.htm> (viewed December 11, 2003).

20. For a discussion about the controversy over direct-to-consumer advertising, see "DTC at the Crossroads: A Direct Hit," <http:// www.imshealth.com> (viewed December 3, 2004). (archived)

21. See "Impact of Direct-to-Consumer Advertising on Prescription Drug Sales, 2003," <http:www.kff.org> (viewed June 22, 2004).

22. Yilian Yuan and Nancy Duckwitz, "Doctors and DTC," *Pharmaceutical Executive,* August 2002, pp. 1–7.

23. James Strain, Niem MuChu, Kaiser Sultana, Anwarul Karim, Gina Caliendo, Shawkat Mustafa and Jay Strain, "Psychotropic Drug Versus Psychotropic Drug," *General Hospital Psychiatry* 26 (2004), pp. 87–105.

24. Yuan, op. cit., p. 38.

25. In Frank Auton, "The Advertising of Pharmaceuticals Direct to Consumers: A Critical Review of the Literature and Debate," *International Journal of Advertising* 23 (2004), pp. 5–52.

26. From the United States General Accounting Office (2002), "Prescription Drugs: FDA Oversight of Direct-to-Consumer Advertising Has Limitations," <http://www. gao.gov> (viewed May 5, 2003).

27. In Kimberly Kaphingst and William DeJong, "The Educational Potential of Direct-to-Consumer Prescription Drug Advertising," Online *Health Affairs* 23, no. 4 (2004), <http://content.healthaffairs.org/cgi/content/abstract/23/4/143.com> (viewed November 2, 2004).

28. For an analysi s of FDA warning letters to pharmaceutical manufacturers, see Kim Bartel Sheehan, "Balancing Acts: An Analysis of Food and Drug Administration Letters About Direct-to-Consumer Advertising Violations," *Journal of Public Policy and Marketing* 22 (2003), pp. 159–169.

29. The misleading slogans and advertising errors in warning letters from the DDMAC can be found at <http://www.fda.gov/foi/warning.htm> (viewed November 22, 2004).

30. Palumbo, op. cit., p. 430.

31. See Charles Medawar, "Because You're Worth It," *Health Matters* 21, no. 43 (2000/2001); and Barbara Mintzes, Ariminee Kazanjian, Ken Bassett, Robert Evans and Steve Morgan, "An Assessment of the Health System Impacts of DTC Advertising of Prescription Medicines (DTCA)," *Centre for Health Services and Policy Research — University of British Columbia*, February 2002.

32. Taken from a 1955 ad for Thorazine in the *American Journal of Psychiatry.*

33. Taken from a 1970's ad for Haldol in the *American Journal of Psychiatry.*

34. Taken from a 1960's ad for Trilafon in the *American Journal of Psychiatry.*

35. See Susan Petroshius, Phillip Titus and Kathryn Hatch, "Physician Attitudes Toward Pharmaceutical Drug Advertising," *Journal of Advertising Research* 35, no. 6 (1995), pp. 35–41.

36. Stephen Everett, "Lay Audience Responses to Prescription Drug Advertising," *Journal of Advertising Research* 31, no. 2 (1991), pp. 43–50.

37. Anonymous, "Direct to Consumer Ads Have Their Positive Side," *Psychiatric News*, February 4, 2000, pp. 1–3.

38. Auton, op. cit.

39. Quoted in Daniel Kleinman and Lawrence Cohen, "The Decontextualization of Mental Illness: The Portrayal of Work in Psychiatric Drug Ads," *Social Science and Medicine* 32 (1991), pp. 867–874.

40. In Thomas Szasz, *The Myth of Mental Illness* (New York: Anchor Books, 1961), p. 14.

41. In Thomas Szasz, *Ideology and Insanity* (New York: Anchor Books, 1970), p. 35.

42. See "U.S. Physicians' Response to Patient Requests for Brand Name Drugs," *IMS Health*, 2002, <http://www.imshealth.com/public/structure/dispcontent/1,2779,1203–1203–144020,00.html> (viewed October 12, 2002). (archived)

43. Quoted in Eleftheria Parpis, "Fear Factor," *Adweek*, November 12, 2001, p. 2.

44. "Gender Display" is defined as "portrayal of culturally established correlates of sex in commercial advertising," and can be found in Erving Goffman, *Gender Advertisement* (New York: Free Press, 1967), cited in Joellen Hawkins and Cynthia Aber, "Women in Advertisements in Medical Journals," *Online Sex Roles: A Journal of Research* 28, no. 3–4 (1993), pp. 233–242.

45. For detailed discussions of gender depiction in psychotropic print advertising, see the works of Arthur Nidelly, "Drug Advertising and the Medicalization of Unipolar Depression," *Healthcare for Women International* 16 (1995), pp. 229–242; Finy Hansen and Dawn Osborne, "Portrayal of Women and the Elderly in Psychotropic Drug Ads," *Women and Therapy* 16, no. 1 (1995), pp. 129–141; and Sarah Munce, Emma Robertson, Stephanie Sansom and Donna Stewart, "Who Is Portrayed in Psychotropic Drug Advertisements?" *The Journal of Nervous and Mental Disease* 192 (2004), pp. 284–288.

46. For a compete discussion of the first coming of psychotropics, see Melvin Sabshin, "Turning Points in Twentieth-Century American Psychiatry," *American Journal of Psychiatry* 147 (2003), pp. 1267–1279. In it, the author addresses the "rise from the ashes" of psychotherapeutics against a backdrop of ideological and clinical tensions in the field.

47. Quoted in "A Science Odyssey: People and Discoveries—Prozac Introduced in 1987," <http://www.pbs.org>, 1998 (viewed September 11, 2004). (archived)

48. Referenced in "Bruised but Triumphant," Medical Marketing and Media (2003), <http://www.imshealth.com> (viewed January 12, 2005). (archived)

49. See Peter Kramer, *Listening to Prozac* (New York: Penguin Books, 1994).

50. See Ray Moynahan, Iona Heath, David Henry, and Peter Gotzsche, "Selling Sickness: The Pharmaceutical Industry and Disease Mongering/ Commentary," *British Medical Journal* 324 (2002), pp. 886–891.

51. Quoted in Barbara Mintzes, Sylvia Bonaccoroso and Jeffrey Sturchio, "For and Against: Direct to Consumer Advertising Is Medicalising Normal Human Experience," *British Medical Journal* 324 (2002), pp. 908–909.

52. See Benjamin Druss and Steven Marcus, "Use of Psychotropic Medications Before and After September 11, 2001," *The American Journal of Psychiatry* 161 (2002), pp. 1377–1383.

53. Derek Summerfield, "A Critique of Seven Assumptions Behind Psychological Trauma Programs in War Affected Areas," *Social Science and Medicine* 99, no. 48 (2001), pp. 1449–1462.

54. See Brendan Koerner, "Disorders Made to Order," *Mother Jones* 27 (2002), pp. 58–64.

55. Ibid., p. 59.

56. "The Other Drug Wars," <http://www.pbs.org> (viewed December 25, 2004). (archived)

57. In David Healey, *The Antidepressant Era* (Cambridge: Harvard University Press, 1997), the author discusses the history of psychotropic medicine and its role in reshaping psychiatric taxonomy.

58. Quoted in R. Moynihan, "The making of a disease: female sexual dysfunction," *The British Medical Journal* 326, issue 1379 (2003), pp. 45–57.

59. This figure of $800 million derives from a series of independent studies conducted at Tufts University Center for the Study of Drug Development and by the Boston Consulting Group (2001 and 2000 respectively). They were referenced in a series of interviews with pharmaceutical and medical experts titled "The Other Drug Wars" which aired on PBS in 2004. See <http:/www.pbs.org> (viewed December 25, 2004). (archived)

60. Marcia Angell, *The Truth About the Drug Companies: How They Deceive Us and What to do About It* (New York: Random House, 2004).

61. From an interview titled "Analysis: Fine of $430 Million Levied Against Pfizer for Illegal Marketing Practices," <http://www.npr.org/templates/story/story.php?story Id=920362.htm> (viewed December 23, 2005). (archived)

62. See Alan Holmer, "New Medicines in Development for Mental Illness, a 2002 PhRMA Survey," <http://www.phrma.org> (viewed January 9, 2005).

63. Holmer, ibid.

64. Angell, op. cit.

65. Angell, op. cit.

66. Quoted in Carol Lewis, "Selling Your Cure on the Telly," *New Statesman*, June 24, 2002, p. R20.

67. See Goldman and Montagne, op. cit., for a complete description of this concept.

68. Quoted in Shankar Vedantam, op. cit.

5 Psychotropics, It's What's for Dinner!

Technologies of Sex, Gender, Body, and the Mind in the Medicalization of Food

PHILLIP VANNINI

> For the majority of us, food is far more than a bunch of nutrients that provide energy, build bones, make muscles, or improve the immune system. Food can also be used as a drug to numb or stuff down feelings of anxiety, anger, sadness, boredom or loneliness. When we are stressed out, food is our good friend, always giving without asking for anything back. But eventually food can become our worst enemy in the form of weight or health problems. And even if we manage to lose the excess weight, if we don't resolve our underlying emotional or behavioral issues, the lost pounds and the newly found problems are likely to return.
>
> — Anonymous, paraphrased from Internet Web site

> Throughout history, whether food worked for you or against you usually was a matter of luck or choice. Things have changed today. Thanks to our knowledge about the food/mind/mood connection you can now choose food that will energize your brain, change your moods, and make you a more effective, motivated, and perhaps even more contented individual.
>
> — Paraphrased from Judith J. Wurtman

"A pill for every ill," as it has been suggested, might very well be the official slogan of our contemporary psychotropic culture.[1] "A pill for every ill" connotes not only the endless availability of pharmaceutical goods in our capitalistic market, but also the unabated rise of consumer demand for such goods. Indeed, in our pharmaceutical culture not only is psychotropic drug use widespread, but so are the numerous disorders that need to be continuously cured. But upon a closer look "a pill for every ill" is even more deeply revealing of the American *Zeitgeist*. A consumer-driven economy must not only meet existing demand, but also generate new ones. This is, simply put, the expansionary logic of capitalism: while resources and productive capabilities are endless (at least such is the utopia of capitalistic ideology), human needs are not (such being the dystopian component of this ideology). "A pill for every ill," therefore, turns into a simultaneously utopian and dystopian call to action: there are never enough disorders, and therefore we must continuously generate new ones. The process whereby logic and ideology expands by generating new ills and new pills in order to colonize the life-world of inmates of the new mental asylum is what I call *psychotropization*, the object of this chapter.

Psychotropia — as a metaphor — refers to an imaginary and surreal place, and yet its real-life referent is painfully real. Psychotropia refers to our constantly disordered and over-medicalized Western society, which exists as our mental asylum, our total institution, our collective home. Psychotropia is a metaphor in this chapter, but it is also real in the sense that we build it every day through our beliefs and values, our conduct, our moods, our disorders, and our cures. In this sense, then, Psychotropia becomes a metaphor for our culture and society, our entire way of living, and more precisely for our schizophrenic disposition which manifests itself in the simultaneous cultural production of social malaises and endless consumption of illusory cures, i.e., psychotropization.

Psychotropization, more precisely, refers to the process whereby (a) the conditions for the emergence of sociocultural and psychological malaises are rhetorically constructed — "the social construction of disorder"; (b) individual and collective subjects are seduced into becoming "ill" and subsequently into defining themselves as such — "victimization"; and (c) new cures for such ills are provided — "seduction into psychotropic consumption" — and new ills are subsequently created, thus beginning the process anew in a continuous loop.

We find a clear example of the psychotropization process by focusing on the practice of food consumption. In the mental asylum of Psychotropia we are all patients, and all of our practices are potentially indicative of mental disorder and therefore subject to the surveillance and control of the asylum's wardens. Consequently, many of our objects of consumption are psychotropized, i.e. imbued with the so-called healing power of psychotropic drugs. In our society, even natural physiological functions such as hunger and appetite — as argued in the following pages— have been turned into a socio-cultural and psychological disorder through the promotion of contradictory dispositions toward food. Eating has therefore become a purely instrumental activity in a psychotropic society. We eat psychotropized foods in order to cure conditions defined as pathological by the ideological currency of the times. Food and eating therefore function primarily as medical techniques— or technologies of the body and mind— that inmates embrace in order to temporarily cure their minds and bodies until a new disorder appears, which then in turn becomes the object of new cure.

In what follows, I describe in detail how this process takes place. I begin by laying out the framework of my metaphor: the social architecture of Psychotropia. I then turn to a descriptive analysis of the process of psychotropization by first looking at the social construction of eating as malaise, then by focusing on the processes through which subjects are seduced into victimization, and finally by reflecting on how the wardens of Psychotropia claim to cure their inmates. As an empirical validation for my arguments in this chapter I use instances of discourse on food and eating selected from magazines, actual conversations, and Internet Web sites.

A Schizophrenic and Synoptic Psychotropia

Schizophrenia and Culture

The doors to the psychotropic asylum are now open — as Rubin has remarked — and new inmates are flocking in.[2] As the ideology of a psychotropic society expands, so do the walls of the total institution we now all live within. As a total institution, however, ours is a radically different one from those envisioned by Goffman.[3] Rather than an asylum based solely on lack and deprivation (as mental institutions, prisons, convents are), Psychotropia is also based on forced consumption, or better yet on the continuous generation and reproduction of schizophrenic desire. Furthermore, our wardens are not merely in charge of supervising inmates and imposing punishment. Rather, the wardens of Psychotropia — generally identifiable as the members of psychotropic pharmaceutical industry as well as all those who officially or unofficially promote their discourses— *seduce* inmates into learning to supervise themselves and into administering their own medication.

By referring to schizophrenic desire, culture, capitalism, or society, I do not mean to diagnose the entire population of Western society with the psychiatric condition of schizophrenia. Within our society, schizophrenia becomes a metaphor as well; a metaphor for our self-antagonistic and contradictory existence.

My metaphor draws upon the philosophy of Gilles Deleuze and Felix Guattari.[4] In *A Thousand Plateaus: Capitalism and Schizophrenia,* Deleuze and Guattari argue that contemporary capitalism is a schizophrenic system in that it is constructed around the individual as a unit of revenue and profit. In constructing the individual as an atomized consumer, the capitalistic system de-territorializes subjects from their original collective referents, but at the same time re-territorializes them into new consuming units and collectives. The existence of any such schizophrenic system is thus at the same time both constantly collapsing and under restructure. This happens because schizophrenic capitalism works by transforming desire into schizophrenic desire. Let us clarify further.

In any total institution, desire is perceived by inmates as lack or repression. For example, deprivation of the self, as Goffman found, led asylum inmates to crave affirmations of the self that were both symbolic and material.[5] Inmates, for example, desired independence as much as they desired possessions. Much like other wardens, those of schizophrenic capitalism constantly ensure that desire is perceived as lack with their total institution. Within our society, however, desire is not only perceived as lack or repression, but also as productive.

Desire is schizophrenic within the walls of Psychotropia because it is at one time a manifestation of production and repression. Much like the notion of productive desire embraced by Deleuze and Guattari,[6] desire in this system is both a form of will-to-power (e.g., will to health and happiness) and a form of will-to-repression (e.g., will to illness and misery). And it is precisely through the character of schizophrenic desire that the wardens of Psychotropia ensure that its inmates are trapped in it forever. The logic is relatively simple: for as long as there is lack there will be desire. For as long as there are pills inmates will seek them to cure their ills. And for as long as there is profit in the selling of pills there will be new ills for inmates to adopt and to cure. In sum, the metaphor of schizophrenia sensitizes us to the contradictory simultaneous presence of will to healing and will to disorder.

From a Panoptic to a Synoptic Total Institution

Up to this point, I have operated under the unquestioned assumption that Psychotropia, the new mental asylum, operates under the relatively simple structure of a master-slave relationship (warden-inmate). If this were truly the case, we could imagine the architecture of our society to resemble that of a common (i.e., panoptic) prison where wardens gaze on inmates to ensure they will conduct themselves properly. But because we are dealing with a schizophrenic total institution, our social architecture is radically different as it is deeply shaped by the contradictory nature of inmates, who, to a great extent, are prone to enslaving themselves as well as other inmates. As explained below, Psychotropia, therefore, is not a panoptic total institution, but instead a synoptic one. The difference between the two is relatively simple: whereas each inmate in a panoptic institution supervises and controls himself/herself, each inmate in a synoptic institution controls himself or herself as well as other inmates, and is in turn also supervised by these others.

Total institutions of the panoptic kind generally impose harsh limits on communication flows of all kinds. In part, this allows wardens to repress inmates' desires. But within synoptic institutions, desires must be continuously stimulated and therefore communication flows must abound. Indeed, within Psychotropia madness and cure are most often merchandized through mass mediated communication. As various chapters of this volume suggest, messages that contribute to the social construction of disorder and the seduction of cure are distributed through widely circulated magazines, newspapers, songs, movies, Internet Web sites, and television commercials. And as Rubin has argued, what these messages achieve is a twofold effect, marginalization and decontextualization:

> The process of marginalization involves simplifying the physician's role to that of a technician primed to dispense pills according to scripted cultural stereotypes. Decontextualization refers to elimination of the personal, social, and cultural contexts of peoples' lives from the explanatory equation, and by doing so, reducing the complexities of living to predictable, manageable, and ultimately medically treatable symptoms.[7]

While marginalization and decontextualization are more or less what Deleuze and Guattari would identify as de-territorialization, how does re-territorialization take place? In other words, once a social agent is turned into a disordered consumer unattached to either significant others (e.g., physicians, counselors, analysts) or one's self and biography, who will ensure that such consumers will fall to the seduction of the possibilities offered by "a pill for every ill"? Strangely enough inmates will, and they will do so by controlling themselves within their synoptic, schizophrenic asylum. Indeed, not only are Psychotropia's inmates schizophrenic in that they manifest both productive and repressive desire at the same time, but they are also schizophrenic in that they manage at the same time to be the victimizers, the victims, and the healers of their own conditions. Let us proceed in reverse order.

The processes of marginalization and decontextualization make it possible for the inmates of Psychotropia to become their own healers. As reigning consumers in a free market they have a vast array of choices available to cure their own illnesses. All it takes to get a hold of a pharmaceutical solution to their problem is a short trip to the drugstore or an even shorter trip to their personal computers for some online pharmacy shopping. The potential for self-actualization is in this sense purely mesmerizing: why worry when you have the solution for your problems at your fingertip? And consequently: why stop after just one disorder when you can collect more than one, and even as many as you can afford to pay for? This is possible because the sovereign consumer is also the sovereign medical patient operating within a similar ideology: "get as many disorders and cures as you can afford, it's your freedom!" and "shop till you drop!" As a matter of fact what we have is something radically different from what Goffman observed. In his observations on ways of life within mental asylums, Goffman found that inmates would engage in "release binge-fantasies"[8] — or daydreams about what they would do to treat themselves upon release. In Psychotropia, instead, we have reverse release-binge fantasies: daydreams of splurging into psychotropic drug consumption upon admission into the world of mental disorder.

Of course, before having this kind of release at the drugstore, one needs to become a victim to illness. In order to become a victim one must work at it. As sociologists James Holstein and Gale Miller have remarked, a victim is one who effectively undergoes the process of victimization.[9] Victimization is a rhetorical project, a practical accomplishment of social actors engaged in discursively constructing and interpreting the conditions under which one can convincingly argue that he or she has been victimized. Rubin provides us with many clear examples of the rhetorical work of victimization. For instance:

> Consider a 1960s ad for the tranquilizer Prolixin that offers relief from the stresses of the day. The intentionally blurred image of the crowded metropolis literally and metaphorically shifts the reader's focus away from the relatively faceless denizens. We are not asked to consider the context (i.e., the opprobrious rat-race conditions of urban living that results in emotional stress), nor are we asked to consider the humanity of the people caught in it. Instead, we are drawn to the oasis of clarity found in the promissory advertising text that zeroes in on the medicalized symptoms of the emotional stress.[10]

By identifying herself as "stressed out" the consumer will then have the discursive resources necessary to perceive herself as a victim: a victim in need, and a victim deserving of immediate relief from the pathological *symptoms* (rather than from the *cause*, as Rubin rightly points out), and therefore a victim/consumer with the spending power and freedom to cure herself.

We are finally back at square one: the victimizer. From what the paragraph above suggests, the answer should now be a bit clearer: inmates are their own victimizers, albeit with the help of their wardens—the pharmaceutical industry. Let us reflect on the dynamics by which inmates victimize themselves, and in order to do so, let us begin by introducing the concept of the Panopticon. The Panopticon is a blueprint for a prison designed by Jeremy Bentham in the late 1700's.[11] The Panopticon was never actually built, but Bentham's idea achieved great popularity in large part through the later writings of Michel Foucault who argued that the Panopticon is a great metaphor for our contemporary society at large.[12] A panoptic prison can best be described as a cylindrical structure made of several stories. Each story, shaped like a circle, houses prison cells visible in their entirety from a tower-like structure erected high above the prison atrium. Inside the top of the tower reside the wardens, whose great surveillance power is ensured by the fact that without moving they can easily supervise each inmate in his/her cell. The true power of the Panopticon, however, resides in the fact that whereas the inmates can be seen by the wardens at all times, the wardens remain invisible to the inmates. As a consequence, inmates begin to assume they are constantly under watch and therefore begin to watch themselves. By doing so, they internalize the gaze of their controllers. It is precisely through this mechanism that consumers aid pharmaceutical companies in the process of self-victimization and therefore become, at least in part, their own victimizers.

The process of internalization of the gaze of one's oppressors was quite familiar to Goffman. In *Asylums*, Goffman found that a common "mode of adaptation to the setting of a total institution is that of 'conversion': the inmate appears to take over the official or staff view of himself and tries to act out the role of the perfect inmate."[13] It should be noted that a similar phenomenon also occurred in concentration camps, where some long-time prisoners adopted the vocabulary, disposition, countenance, and ideology of the Gestapo.[14] Such process of internalization was necessary for the routine maintenance of such total institutions, and it is equally necessary for the continued existence of our schizophrenic society. It is only by accepting the rhetorical truth of socially constructed mental disorder and by therefore internalizing it, that an illness becomes putatively real to its victim. And it is only by accepting the rhetorical truths about socially constructed psychotropized substances that subjects turn non-drugs into psychotropic drugs.

Such process of conversion and internalization constitutes the basic difference between a panoptic and a synoptic structure.[15] Such difference lies in the fact that most inmates who undergo the process of "conversion" become rule-enforcers not only toward themselves, but also toward others.[16] Such inmates regularly refer all instances of rule-infraction of their fellow inmates to the authorities, and even intervene by themselves in preventing violations and in administering punishment. Psychotropia, the new mental asylum, is teeming with such subjects. These are the coworkers, friends, and family members who enforce the schizophrenic ideology of health and the use of psychotropic drugs to dear ones—instead of providing the solidarity, sympathy, and support that as members of the same community they could provide.[17] These are, therefore, the victims and self-victimizers who seduce others into the asylum.

Take the example of a woman who, fatigued and stressed with the competing demands of work and family, turns to psychotropic drugs in search of comfort and tranquility. By internalizing the ideology promoted by the pharmaceutical industry, and by continuing over time to cure the symptoms rather than the causes of her "disorder," this woman is a victim of psychotropic culture. But let us imagine that this woman is also mother to a young child. A child who—like many children these days—is keen on consuming junk foods, junk drinks, junk games, and also a child who suffers from "junk" family relations (possibly due to the same causes that her mother ignores as social causes of her condition). Alarmed by her child's vivaciousness, the woman deliberates that her daughter is a victim of Attention Deficit Hyperactivity Disorder and therefore in dire need of psychotropic drugs. The mother, in sum, has victimized herself first, and secondly her daughter, and by doing so she has not only internalized the ideology of a panoptic, psychotropic culture, but she has also enforced an unhealthy ideology on others, in the name of health.

Because of the common presence of victims converted into victimizers who gaze upon themselves and others—thus ensuring that all inmates properly internalize the gaze of the wardens—rather than a panoptic Psychotropia, what we have is a synoptic Psychotropia. It is an asylum marked by a health ideology so contradictory that it can be safely argued to be schizophrenic. Let us now examine how these dynamics work in the case of food and eating.

The Psychotropization Process

The Social Construction of Disorder

The process of psychotropization begins with the discursive construction of disorder. The social construction of disorder is a rhetorical process whereby certain beliefs or practices become associated with illness, impurity, unwholesomeness, risk, danger, moral and aesthetic impropriety, and lack of concern for one's self and health. In our society, there is an abundance of everyday-life practices that have been recently imputed to be unhealthy or disordered, and eating is one of these. Over the past two decades or so, the public culture of eating has been inundated with instances of discourse promoting healthy eating and condemning unhealthy foods (however defined given the fads of the moment). Numerous exposés have denounced the declining health of North Americans, so much so that their corrosive eating habits led to the regulations of food preparation in restaurants and public schools — amongst other places — and to the promotion of healthy eating in households across the continent. A fat nation is a nation at risk of heart attack, liver disease, and moral and aesthetic decay. And an unhealthy nation is a nation at risk of becoming its own mortal enemy; a particularly resounding theme at a time when Westerners have come to come to feel ever so anxious about enemies from both outside and within. As a result, the rhetorical promotion of healthy eating has been conflated with the usual themes of individual and collective responsibility, independence, achievement, and freedom, and also with currently "hot" themes and issues such as positive self-body image and sexual performance. Eating, in sum, has become a potentially dangerous activity and food consumption is now subject to the logic of risk-management.

Over the past few decades, the medicalization of food and eating has been accompanied by the rise of the medical field known as nutrition science. Even though the roots of nutrition science are to be found in the mid-1800's in Europe, nutrition science has only begun to assume more visibility with the rise of the modern welfare state[18] and the control and regulation of citizens' bodies that such a state demands.[19] While nutrition science was born to face the problems arising from food scarcity, ill-health, and food-preservation and transportation, over time nutrition scientists have gradually replaced earlier concerns with modern-day problems — such as obesity and related health problems — due to the overabundance of food and the public's lack of education about food properties. Nutrition scientists these days make it a primary objective to raise public awareness about what constitutes "good food" and what eating "good food" and "bad food" can do for us. Their public health campaigns have resulted in the U.S. in the publication of such documents as the *Dietary Guidelines,* issued by the National Health Institute, and the *Recommended Daily Allowances,* set by the National Research Council. Other Western nations have adopted similar measures.

Parallel to the rise of nutrition science and the diffusion of nutrition discourse across all spaces of public culture has been the increase in the symbolic value attached to food and food consumption. People attach symbolic value to the foods they consume to express their sense of identity and also to maximize the physical capital of their body appearance.[20] If there is one characteristic of our so-called postmodern culture that most people will agree upon, it is the preoccupation that people have with their appearances, and in this sense it is common to view eating as a strategic activity undertaken to look fit for postmodern selfhood. Within the psychotropic synopticon, therefore, food and "proper eating" become technologies of the body[21]—i.e., techniques that the dwellers of Psychotropia internalize in order to cure putative disorders and to look good for their scopophiliac fellow-inmates.

The most common technology of the body is the diet. The four-letter word "diet" is now not only as common in everyday parlance as other less-polite four-letter words, but it is also just as likely to evoke strong emotions in speakers and addresses. To go on a diet is to bend to internal and external pressure to conform to health and body-appearance ideals, and to internalize the notion that improper eating is a serious disorder. As an example of the synopticism I discussed earlier, consider the following excerpt from a conversation I overheard as I walked into a classroom:

A: You're eating that greasy pizza from the cafeteria again?
B: I know. I just didn't bring any lunch today.
A: So much for your workout earlier this morning.
B: Yeah, this is gonna go right on my ass.
A: Seriously, you should go on a real diet. You're always complaining of feeling moody and depressed; you should eat less fats and less carbs. Get some fruits in your diet. I always have fruit as my lunch and I feel great in the afternoon.
B: You're right. You're making me feel guilty...
A: Good, you should be!

There are now as many diets as there are people who create and follow them, and fad diets never go unnoticed. Consider for example just a small sample of the latest fad diets: the cabbage soup diet, the South Beach diet, the Atkins diet, the Scarsdale diet, the three day diet, the one good meal diet, the metabolism diet, the grapefruit diet, the Slim Fast jump start diet, and my favorite: the seven-day all-you-can-eat diet. Not to mention the ever so austere Russian Air Force diet.

The combined effects of the growing political power of nutrition science and the popularity of what I call pseudo-nutrition science and scientists (e.g., the people who gave us the Russian Air Force diet and those who published it in their magazines) have resulted in the existence of disordered eating as a social malaise. By disordered eating, I do not refer to known eating disorders such as anorexia nervosa and bulimia, but more in general to the sense of uncertainty and chaos that many people experience when they face the signals of hunger. Indeed "to eat that, or not to eat that?"— might very well be the existential question that Hamlet would ask today. Such cultural disposition toward self-doubt, at least when it comes to eating, is at the very root of the formation of a schizophrenic food culture to which we are all potential victims.

Take for example *any* women's magazine (for that matter even *any* mainstream national magazine will do) and count the advertisements that will ask you to indulge your cravings for junk or gourmet foods as well as those advertisements (and articles as well) that will ask you to scrupulously control what you eat. The average Westerner is so often bombarded with contradictory (i.e., schizophrenic) messages about food that eating becomes tough everyday work. And not work as in food-preparation or gathering, but as in decision-making process. For example, as I type on my keyboard it is precisely noon: time to take a break and eat something, but what? Here on my university campus, our students have been successfully fighting tooth and nail for the last five years to increase their access to healthy foods, so I should have no problem finding something to eat that is good for me. But what do I really want and what do I really need? Well, my body and mind need energy for the rest of the day so I need carbohydrates. But wait ... carbs? The whole continent has practically banned carbs from their diet as if it was mortal sin, and I am looking for carbs? By eating carbs, I am told, I am getting nothing but fatter. And maybe I am a little chubby, after all. I guess I should work out more. Yeah, I will go to the gym later. But to work out I need energy, carbs. But too much energy will make my hyperactive, though. Do I want to feel hyperactive when all I need to do today is focus on this chapter in order to beat my editor's deadline? Maybe I should get no carbs and all meat, but maybe get some caffeine to perk up. But coffee can stain my teeth and make me look ugly, and that would upset my wife. Not to mention that drinking coffee would mean eating at least some sugar, which is carbs! Ok, you get the picture; not only do we live in highly reflexive state of modernity,[22] but our reflexivity is causing us to be schizophrenic and obsessed with food.

Foods, as my dysfunctional moment above testifies, have gone from means to achieve ends of survival to means to achieve ends higher on a scale of reflexivity. As inmates of Psychotropia turn to foods to cure putative mental disorders they exact more precision, more efficiency, in order to make wiser decisions. Hence, both nutrition science and pseudo-nutrition science are here to help by turning foods into carefully measured sources of microbiological, biochemical, and biophysiological entities. A meal turns into a mathematical function of calories, lipids, proteins, carbohydrates, vitamins, sodium, and fiber, and consequently, eating turns into a medical practice. Consider for example the role played by "functional drinks" in people's diets. Functional drinks are drinks such as sports drinks, energy drinks, vitamin and mineral enriched drinks, nutraceutical drinks, and wellness drinks that are consumed primarily not to quench thirst or because they taste particularly good, but instead for such goals as invigoration, mood-lifting, and sexual excitation. Some functional drinks are even consumed for their alleged "negative-calorie" properties, or in other words for their supposed capability of causing the digestive system to burn a higher amount of calories than the one taken in by consuming that product. Reflect, if you will, on a typical day in the life of a Russian Air Force fighter ... er ... dieter:

Breakfast
½ cup of decaf black coffee + 1 toast or 3 saltines
Lunch
7 ounces of red meat + 1 tomato or 2 eggs + 1 mandarin
Dinner
3½ ounces of ham + 8 ounces of banana-less fruit salad + 1 plain yogurt
Throughout the Day
Drink at least 4 pints of water or diet soda and feel free to add some Worcestershire sauce or vinegar to your meal.

Inmates of Psychotropia, afflicted by uncertainty and lack of scientific education, become easy prey to the latest fad disorders and the fad diets meant to prevent them or combat them. In all fairness, let it be clear that there may be some objective truth to the discourses of nutrition science, but what is more important and even more interesting is the rhetorical and ideological force that these discourses assume in a culture with schizophrenic tendencies toward food.

At least in part, the reasons behind our schizophrenic attitudes toward food consumption may have to do with the dialectic of body and identity in postmodern society. As sociologist Mike Featherstone has pointed out, the difficulties connected with disciplining our own body practices arise from the contradictions inherent in the asceticism that practices such as dieting and exercise demand, and in the hedonistic nature of the ends to which such practices are means.[23] In simpler words, while food consumption demands sacrifice, our ultimate goals (fitness, beauty, happiness, well-being, etc.) are entrenched in the philosophy of pleasure, indulgence, and enjoyment typical of an affluent consumer society. Within Psychotropia desire for food is therefore subject to temptation, repression, and affirmation of desire at the same time.

The contradictions inherent in consumer culture in relation to eating are further complicated by more profound connections between the body and the mind. Western Judeo-Christian culture is marked by a philosophical current known as dualism, an idea that manifests itself in such beliefs as the separation of mind and body. It is precisely such sources of dualism that aggravates the process of psychotropization. As explained in the next two sections, dualism makes it possible for the dwellers of the Panopticon to treat food and the embodied practice of food consumption as an activity instrumental to the achievement of goals such as mental well-being, as in the case of "mood-food."

Seduction into Illness and Victimization

Up to this point, I have reflected on rather broad cultural characteristics of our contemporary schizophrenic disposition toward food and eating. The process of psychotropization of food and eating is based on the macro-discursive foundations just examined, but it also takes hold at the practical and micro-level of experience and interaction. Inside Psychotropia, inmates use certain types of foods as psychotropic drugs in order to alleviate themselves of depression, anxiety, psychosis, and other kinds of disorders. But in order for consumer objects other than psychotropic drugs to be used as psychotropic drugs, consumers must first internalize the belief that they are indeed mental patients in need of medical treatment. I refer to this process as seduction into mental illness and victimization.

Victimization and seduction into mental illness are inseparable components of the process of psychotropization, for victimization always occurs by means of seduction. Seduction here does not have any sexual connotation (though it may take sexual form); rather, seduction refers more broadly to charm, allure, enticement, and will-to-belief. Seduction here also refers to the simultaneous production of both repressive and productive desire. Members of our consumer culture are seduced to believe that psychotropic drug consumption is just like any other form of consumption — empowering, harmless, leisurely, and instrumental — through a twofold process of de-territorialization and re-territorialization, as (a) health and happiness are *always* constructed as lacking in everyday life and *always* desirable; and (b) psychotropized drugs are always constructed as capable of bringing the health and happiness that one lacks.

Let us begin to take a close look at texts selected from various magazines, conversations, and Internet Web sites in order to demonstrate how subjects are seduced to believe they lack happiness and health. The following text, paraphrased from *Chatelaine*, constructs a season of the year (winter) as a source of ill and sadness:

> BEAT THE WINTER BLUES BY KNOCKING DOWN CARBS!
> During the winter, maintaining your healthy lifestyle is hard. So beat those seasonal blues with our delicious, comforting carb-conscious recipes.

Here we can clearly see the process of seduction into illness and victimization at work. The text addresses the reader as an ill individual, someone who is weak enough to be incapable of adapting to the normal course of the year and the passing of seasons. There is nothing abnormal about the succession of seasons: summer follows spring, and is followed by fall and winter. This happens every year, everywhere in the world, with quite a degree of regularity. Generally, species tolerate this. Some hibernate, some reduce their levels of activity, some migrate south, and some eat up more calories to combat the cold. None of this requires much pain or effort. But in a schizophrenic capitalistic society every source of discomfort, no matter how mild, must be prevented and solved in highly reflexive ways. Hence the reader's sense of discomfort-turned-illness (the "blues," or SAD — seasonal affective disorder) is justifiable and deserving of immediate psychotropic intervention. By granting sympathy to the reader ("maintaining your lifestyle is hard," the text bemoans) and by positing constant cheerfulness and an upbeat disposition as an unquestionably desirable and possible state of mind, the reader can easily simultaneously feel ill (as lacking health and happiness) and a victim of circumstances (the winter).

Victimization, as Holstein and Miller explain, is a procedure whereby responsibility is deflected, causes are assigned, responses and remedies are specified, and failure is accounted for.[24] Victimization, therefore, is a practical achievement of discursive interaction. Take for example the advice below, paraphrased from an Internet site for men's health and fitness:

> TIRED? STRESSED? MOODY? DOWN ON YOURSELF?
> Feeling "out of it" is a normal experience for many men in today's fast-paced world. It can be hard to maintain a healthy eating plan, a regular workout schedule, or even get enough sleep when you have so many commitments and responsibilities. But don't give up on your goals! Get jacked today with this energy-raising, mood-perking, fast and easy-to-prepare, protein-packed power lunch. Hey, you never know, you might actually manage to *impress* that good-looking girl working out at the gym today!

In this text we can clearly see all of the components of the discursive process of victimization. The text assumes that the reader has failed at keeping up regularly with healthy eating, exercise, and rest. Failure manifests itself in fatigue, stress, "bad" moods, and depression or loss of self-esteem ("down on yourself?"). Failure, however, is accounted for by reference to the fast-paced life to which the reader is seemingly a victim. Because of the hurried pace of everyday life it is okay — the text suggests— to feel "out if it." As matter of fact, not only is it not the reader's own fault, but feeling "out of it" is a common experience for many men — the text tells us. "You are a victim"— the text seems to suggest — "of circumstances well outside your control, so don't be too hard on yourself: simply adopt the remedies that we recommend!" The remedies, of course, entail the use of food-turned-psychotropic: protein, fruit, and some quick sugar that not only will alleviate anxiety, depression, and fatigue, but also stimulate the reader into making a sexual pass at that hot little number exercising at the coed gym.

De-territorialization and re-territorialization work by decontextualizing subjects from their normal experiences of mind and body and by recontextualizing such experiences into unachievable, utopian circumstances. Men's fitness magazines provide particularly clear examples of this. It is quite common for a men's magazine to boldly express goals that readers are supposed to share (as in a message like "Get her!" — juxtaposed with a photograph of a scantily clad female fitness model), accompanied by victimization strategies like the one presented above or even more high-flung ones like the one paraphrased below:

> GOT NO ABS AND NO GUTS?
> Eat these power foods and make them [women] beg for you!

In a message like this, disorder — in the form of lack of sexual appeal and self-confidence — is deeply intertwined with discourses of heterosexuality and hyper-masculinity, and connected to food as a psychotropic stimulant to achieving the goals inherent in such discourses. Things are quite similar in women's magazines, if not in style or terminology certainly in the connection between victimization and seduction into self-insufficiency and in the inevitable consequent discursive transformation of food into psychotropic technologies of the body, gender, and sex.

Seduction into Psychotropic Consumption

The third and final component of the process of psychotropization is what I refer to as seduction into psychotropic food consumption. Whereas the first two aspects of the process have served to create new ills and new patients, seduction into psychotropic consumption refers to the actual process of constructing and consuming new "pills."

Foods may be used to achieve a great variety of goals. In a consumer culture, desire is perceived as lack, but as suggested earlier, Psychotropia is a rather unique total institution: here desire is both oppressive and productive at the same time. The schizophrenic structure of Psychotropia in fact ensures that while states and feelings of lack are common among all inmates, so are the material tools to address such feeling of lack, at least momentarily. This is of course the consumerist philosophy of "a pill for every ill." Here, I describe what pills are used to control inmates' moods.

The last few years have witnessed an explosion of the mood-food phenomenon in public health culture. Mood-food is food consumed in order to regulate and control one's affective disposition rather than in order to satisfy hunger or cater to one's appetite. Mood-food is believed to have antidepressive, anti-anxiety, antipsychotic, tranquilizing, and even mild hallucinogenic functions (in the case of erogenous stimulation). Magazines and Web sites that promote mood-foods abound and their messages are generally similar. Consider for example the following message, paraphrased from a science-oriented Web site:

WHO DO YOU WANT TO BE TODAY?
Foods are similar in many ways to subtle drugs. The distinction between the two categories is not at all clear-cut. Boundaries between the two are even further blurred by the recent creation and rapid growth of functional foods or nutraceuticals. These designer-foods combine nutritional value with disease-preventive and medicinal benefits. Nevertheless, let us not forget that all the constituents of food are psychoactive. Therefore, in choosing to eat this food or that food, one literally determines who and what one is going to become.

Eating right is important because the best way to lead a long and healthy life is to eat as little as is prudently possible. The anti-ageing effects of being *under-* but not *mal-*nourished have been demonstrated in all species researched so far. A diet that is low in calories and balanced will boost the immune function, preserve memory and keep blood pressure low. Caloric-restriction can give all those who practice it the chance to extend life-expectancy by up to 50 percent; and to feel and look younger for longer.

Nutrition is not everything there is, however. After you have ensured that your diet and lifestyle are just about right, then you will reach a genetically constrained plateau of well-being beyond which there's nowhere else to go. From that point on, only psychopharmacology, genetic therapy and then nano-level hedonic engineering are going to make your life significantly better.

It is altogether uninteresting to me to attempt to dispute or even to merely consider the validity of the positive physiological claim that foods have essential psychotropic properties. As a critic of our psychotropic culture, what is interesting to me, instead, is to consider the rhetorical force that a claim such as the one excerpted above has on its audiences and therefore to consider psychotropization as a sociological and communicative process.

Let me explain further. Foods are objects with variable nutritional value. But within a specific cultural context, food — like all objects — also assumes symbolic values that people attach to it.[25] As a consequence, people will act toward food on the basis of the meanings it has for them. For example, the excerpt above shows that people may select food on the basis of the potential it has to allow them to live longer, maintain a youthful appearance and disposition, preserve memory, feel happier, and develop a particular self-identity. All of these symbolic meanings are highly relevant in a society that values youth, self-actualization, hedonism, individuality, physical appearance, and so forth. It is in this sense that food becomes psychotropized and it is in this sense that the psychotropization of foods is a social process. In sum, when we act toward food in relation to the psychotropic value we believe it has, we are seduced by its symbolic and instrumental value as a "pill."

The paraphrased excerpt reported above is also interesting for another set of reasons. As the anonymous author of the piece points out, the boundaries between food and drugs have now become blurred, and to all intents and purposes such boundaries are altogether collapsed in a psychotropic society. All things that consumers ingest, therefore, are consumed on the basis of their putative psychotropic power. When food and drugs become members of the same dietary group, the only difference between the two happens to be their quantitative power to cause certain desired psychic effects. Thus, for example, if we find that chocolate fails to alleviate depression, then we will possibly opt to consume more powerful psychotropics in order to achieve the illusion of immortality and well-being.

Within Psychotropia, the pleasure of consuming food is non-existent because instrumentality precedes and overrides pleasure for the sake of pleasure. At the same time ultimate goals such as longevity and health are never subject to scrutiny, even though we ought to seriously consider whether a long life deprived of some of the somatic pleasures that food consumption gives us is worth living. Furthermore, in Psychotropia the achievement of such goals as health, happiness, and longevity demands the adoption of technologies of the body and mind that firmly deny the possibility of enjoying a healthy and happy life. Consider the following paraphrased excerpt from an article widely distributed through network television channels and their Web sites:

The Mood-Food Connection

Food is linked to your emotions, something that can lead to serious weight problems. For instance, many people eat when they are happy, or sad, or under stress. These emotional triggers can become patterns that are very difficult to break. The cycle of eating out of frustration, anxiety, loneliness or boredom can be attacked, however. What you need to do is be very aware of the events, feelings and situations occurring before, during and after eating. By thinking about the events that trigger eating, you can learn ways to disrupt eating patterns. The strategies we list below should help you.

Separate eating from other activities. Do not sit in your chair, watch TV, or read the morning paper while you eat. If you do so you will feel like eating anytime you engage in these activities, whether you are hungry or not.

Consider eating as a pure experience. Don't do anything while eating. Concentrate on chewing. Do not chew too fast: measure the rate and speed of biting and chewing. Taste every bite. Other activities become a distraction from eating. When you are distracted you get all the calories you need and more, but only part of the pleasure. Therefore you are wasting calories—calories you have wasted, not tasted.

Follow an eating schedule. Plan well in advance the number of times you will eat, what you will eat, at what times, and where.

Limit the places where you eat. Certain places can be associated with eating, and that is a problem. Some people can eat anywhere. They eat standing up, sitting down, at the kitchen counter, in an easy chair, lying in bed, or driving a car. But if you cannot do that because it causes distractions and the emergence of patterns select one place in your home where you will eat. Do all your eating there, but do nothing else (not playing chess nor paying bills, etc.). Do not eat anywhere else.

There are at least five behavioral techniques can break unhealthy mood/food patterns and help you lose weight and maintain your weight loss.

1. *Set realistic goals* to prevent disappointment and a sense of failure that could lead to breaking your diet. Your goals must be achievable. If they are not, you could become depressed, disappointed, and as a consequence you could deviate from your eating plans and gain weight.

2. *Make intermittent goals.* Don't make an unrealistic goal, like walking six miles. Instead, make a quarter of a mile your goal and once you've walked that far do try walking a bit longer.

3. *Keep a record of all you eat and drink.* Make a journal and record everything. Write everything in detail: as when, where, and what you're doing while eating. This will allow you to keep track of how many calories you have in your food account.

4. *Avoid a chain reaction.* Some people eat because of a behavior we're used to doing and continue to repeat. For example, whenever we get stressed we eat ice cream. This will make you abandon your weight loss plan and stress you out even more, and even cause you to fall into a depression, which can then lead to eating more ice cream and so forth. Break the chain with a nonfood reward. Instead of ice cream, take a bath.

5. *Reward yourself for achieving your goals along the way.* But food should not be a reward. Instead of eating tortilla chips reward yourself with a shopping spree.

By medicalizing the practice of eating as the article above suggests we do, food consumption becomes but a step within a patient's psychiatric biography. By internalizing the advice of pseudo–food experts, nutritionists, and psychiatrists, eating turns into a goal-oriented practice: eating must be done exclusively in order to achieve health, balance, and longevity and therefore it must be closely monitored, controlled, measured, and made predictable. Whether such surveillance is necessary in order to break a nefarious food-mood connection, or in order to generate a positive one, what is sure is that the practice of eating is now identical to the medical administration of drugs.

At this point, the reader may wonder what specific foods are used as psychotropic drugs, and what their functions are. In a partial attempt to satisfy my reader's curiosity I report below a collage of excerpts from columns of dietary advice published in magazines or on the Internet. I find it impossible to resist the urge to insert snide remarks (I do so within square brackets) and the reader is asked to bear with my sarcasm and skepticism. Please note that information contained within round brackets is instead obtained from actual sources.

- ILL: DEPRESSION

Pills

- SAMe (pronounced "Sammy": an over-the-counter nutritional supplement designed by Dr. Richard Brown and Teodoro Bottiglieri that you can buy in supermarkets, vitamin shops, and health-food stores);
- Orange juice, leafy greens, beans, and bananas;
- Breakfast cereal;
- Spinach;
- Whole-grain bread, crackers;
- Salmon, albacore tuna, sardines, and mackerel;
- Chocolate, and all sugar combined with fat [which can obviously make you feel depressed on the scale];
- Coffee;

Avoid

- coffee [no, it's not an editorial mistake], chips, salami, pepperoni, and pastrami [and boloney].

- ILL: LACKADAISICAL SEXUAL PERFORMANCE

Pills

- Caviar (its properties nourish nerve cells which can heighten romantic instincts. Best consumed with *plenty of,* but not *too much,* Vodka [I could have told you *that!*]);
- Red chili pepper flakes;

- Chocolate (legend has it that Montezuma drank 50 cups of chocolate every day to boost his virility before visiting his harem of 600 women [Ever heard of Montezuma's revenge? Perhaps it should be known as Montezuma's *harem* revenge!]);
- Oysters (oysters have plenty of zinc, which is necessary for sperm production [which is seemingly a necessary and sufficient condition for romance?]);
- Truffles (the fact that truffles are rare and expensive adds to their mysterious and romantic reputation [and the fact that sows sniff them out from underground because they find their smell inviting goes to demonstrate that men are pigs?]);
- Asparagus (the magazine *Chatelaine* suggests preparing asparagus by wrapping them inside a pocket of fleshy pink salmon and by spreading a creamy sauce on the tips of the asparagus);
- Coffee;
- Garlic [makes people wanna kiss ya];
- Radishes (which used to excite ancient Egyptians as well);
- Tomatoes (called "the apple of love" by the French).

- ILL: ANXIETY, HOSTILITY, IRRITABILITY, STRESS

Pills
- Brazilian nuts, sunflower seeds, whole grain cereals;
- Swordfish sandwiches [did somebody say McDonald's?];
- All carbohydrates (breads, pasta, rice, potatoes, fruits);
- Chocolate;
- Alcohol.

Avoid
- Alcohol and chocolate [once again, not a mistake], coffee, tea, and cola.

- ILL: LACK OF CONCENTRATION, REDUCED MEMORY

Pills
- Coffee;
- Eggs;
- Animal liver, fish, poultry, meat;
- Beans, peas, cheese, milk, tofu.

Avoid
- Carbohydrates (they may make you fall asleep).

If we agree on the possibility of a placebo effect, potentially any food may work as a psychotropic. In common language, placebo foods are generally referred to as "comfort foods": foods generally consumed under condition of stress in an attempt to gain control over a situation. Comfort foods common to a lot of people include ice cream, tea, and soup. While comfort foods and psychotropized foods are not the same — since the latter are generally shared by more people and undergo a different definitional process — both testify to the connection between mental order or disorder and food consumption in a psychotropic society. In sum, psychotropic and psychotropized foods are common and widely used.

As a final note on psychotropic foods, it is interesting to remark on the schizophrenic disposition that we, as a society, have toward certain foods and drinks like coffee and chocolate. The list I presented above shows that chocolate and coffee have as many positive effects as negative, while also working positively and negatively *simultaneously*. Chocolate is particularly fascinating to me. As one of a small global minority who dislikes most kinds of chocolate, I am perplexed by the contradictory reactions that most people present when faced with chocolate. Chocolate connotes richness, lushness, refinement, and luxury, as much as it evokes images of fatness, surrender, irrationality, and immoral decadence. As the ultimate sin of our schizophrenic society, chocolate can romance, comfort, and seduce while inspiring sentiments of guilt, shame, and loss of acceptance. As a postmodern Adam and Eve's apple, chocolate seduces us into feelings of lack and temptation, but it also surrounds us with its ubiquitous presence — always accompanied by the feeling that temptation is both prohibited and yet obligatory, and that surrender is both inevitable and positive as well as avoidable and the cause of more disorder. With every bite of chocolate, and any psychotropic food, ill is cured and yet reborn — the very condition of regeneration of schizophrenic capitalism.

Conclusion: The New Asylum

Throughout the pages of this chapter, I have argued that a common tendency in a psychotropic society is to generate the conditions for new ills in order to merchandise new pills. I have referred to this tendency as psychotropization, which I have defined as the process whereby subjects are seduced into self-victimization and psychotropic consumption in order to cure socially constructed disorders. By focusing on food I have examined how the inmates of Psychotropia turn non-drugs into psychotropic drugs. But as suggested earlier, the process of psychotropization goes well beyond the symbolic and material arena of food consumption.

Within Psychotropia — a product of the more general condition of schizophrenic capitalism — psychotropization exists in relation to practices as varied as aromatherapy, sun-therapy, tourism, exercise, spirituality (especially of the "new age" kind), book-reading, and more. Take tourism, for example. It is not uncommon for a resort or even an entire geographical region to market itself as a blessing for the mind and the body. Such advertising campaigns might claim to offer holiday-goers products, services, and practices which can provide ecstasy of the senses, rejuvenate, alleviate stress and fatigue, heal from seasonal affective disorder, restore self-confidence and a sense of serenity, and more. In all these contexts the process of psychotropization takes a standard and generic form, which can be understood as a particular case of the phenomenon Erving Goffman labeled "looping."[26]

Goffman argued that looping occurs when "an agency that creates a defensive response on the part of the inmate takes this very response as the target of its next attack."[27] In other words, looping occurs whenever a subject suffers punishment for breaking a rule he or she was pushed to break. Looping is at the very core of Psychotropia's social structure: "messing up"[28] is expected within the new mental asylum because inmates are constantly seduced into breaking rules, so that they can be profitably cured by their wardens. Food, as argued throughout this chapter, provides an excellent example of looping. Inmates will inevitably wind up eat something they have been lured into eating; only to later acknowledge it is bad for them. Thus, in order to cure a new feeling of disorder they will need to take psychotropized foods and become obsessed about them, only to find out that such obsession will bring about new disorders and the need to take new cures. And on and on will this dialectic of territorialization and re-territorialization continue, thus ensuring the existence of a schizophrenic order.

What is particularly alarming about this system is the continuous violation of the "territories of the self"[29] (one's body, actions, thoughts, feelings, and possessions) that ensues. Within the public culture of postmodernity, health (in its schizophrenic ideology) has become such a moral, logical, and aesthetic imperative that it is now unfathomable to be unhealthy for anyone who can help themselves.[30] Indeed, for anyone to be unhealthy — or worse yet to merely *look* unhealthy — means having to remain on the outside of Psychotropia; to be marginalized and ostracized from the rest of society on the inside. And it also means having to sooner or later publicly acknowledge that one is unfit and inexorably guilty for being so. It is only until one "cries uncle" — to borrow from Goffman[31] — or until one publicly confesses one's sins — to borrow from Foucault[32] that one can finally be admitted into the total institution of contemporary health only to find out once within it, that "new mortifications of the self by way of the body"[33] and therefore new violations of territories of the self will continue ad infinitum.

Notes

1. Lawrence Rubin, "Merchandising Madness: Pills, Promises, and Better Living Through Chemistry," *The Journal of Popular Culture*, vol. 38 (2), 2004, pp. 369–383.

2. Rubin, op. cit.

3. Erving Goffman, *Asylums: Essays on the Social Situation of Mental Patients and Other Inmates* (Garden City, N.Y.: Anchor Books, 1961).

4. Gilles Deleuze and Felix Guattari, *A Thousand Plateaus: Capitalism and Schizophrenia* (Minneapolis: University of Minnesota Press, 1987).

5. Goffman, op. cit.

6. Deleuze and Guattari, op. cit.

7. Rubin, op. cit., p. 373.

8. Goffman, op. cit., p. 50.

9. James Holstein and Gale Miller, "Rethinking Victimization: An Interactional Approach to Victimology," *Symbolic Interaction*, vol. 13 (2), 1990, pp. 101–120.

10. Rubin, op. cit., p. 376.

11. Jeremy Bentham, *The Panopticon Writings* (London: Verso, 1995).

12. Michel Foucault, *Discipline and Punish: The Birth of the Prison* (New York: Vintage Random House, 1979).

13. Erving Goffman, op. cit., p. 63.

14. Bruno Bettelheim, *Surviving, and Other Essays* (New York: Knopf, 1979).

15. On the concept of synopticism see Roy Boyne, "Post-Panopticism," *Economy and Society*, vol. 29 (2), 2000, pp. 285–307; Thomas Mathiesen, "The Viewer's Society: Michel Foucault's 'Panopticon' Revisited," *Theoretical Criminology* vol. 1 (2), 1997, pp. 215–234.

16. Goffman, op. cit., p. 63.

17. Charles Edgley and Dennis Brissett, "Health Nazis and the Cult of the Perfect Body: Some Polemical Observations," *Symbolic Interaction*, vol. 13 (3), 1990, pp. 257–279.

18. Stephen Mennell, Anne Murcott, and Anneke vanOtterloo, *The Sociology of Food* (London: Sage, 1992).

19. Bryan Turner, *The Body and Society* (Oxford: Blackwell, 1984).

20. Deborah Lupton, *Food, the Body, and the Self* (London: n.p., 1996), pp. 94–130.

21. Michel Foucault, "Technologies of the Self," in *Technologies of the Self: A Seminar with Michel Foucault*, eds. L.H. Martin, H. Gutman, and P.H. Hutton (London: Tavistock, 1987).

22. Ulrich Beck, Anthony Giddens, and Scott Lash, *Reflexive Modernization* (Stanford: Stanford University Press, 1994).

23. Mike Featherstone, "The Body in Consumer Culture," in *The Body: Social Processes and Cultural Theory*, eds. M. Featherstone, M. Hepworth, and B. Turner (Newbury Park, California: Sage, 1991).

24. Holstein and Miller, op. cit.

25. Herbert Blumer, *Symbolic Interactionism: Perspective and Method* (Berkeley: University of California Press, 1969).

26. Goffman, op. cit., p. 35.
27. Goffman, op. cit., pp. 35–36.
28. Goffman, op. cit., p. 53.
29. Goffman, op. cit., p. 23.
30. Edgley and Brissett, op. cit., p. 260.
31. Goffman, op. cit., p. 17.
32. Michel Foucault, *The History of Sexuality, Volume One: An Introduction* (New York: Pantheon, 1978).
33. Goffman, op. cit., p. 21.

6 Rappers, Ravers, and Rock Stars

The Deviantizing Hand of Music in Psychotropia

ROBERT KELLER

Modern music is as dangerous as narcotics.
— Pietro Mascagni

Whoever controls the media controls the mind.
— Jim Morrison

Music is your own experience, your own thoughts, your wisdom. If you don't live it, it won't come out of your horn. They teach you there's a boundary line to music. But, man, there's no boundary line to art.
— Charlie "YardBird" Parker

Enter Psychotropia

Psychotropic drugs—drugs once designed specifically to modify the behavior of the mentally ill—have become a not so silent epidemic. Since their conception, though most dramatically in recent years, the number of children, teens, and adults using psychotropic substances such as Xanax, Prozac, Adderall, and Ritalin has rapidly increased.[1] In addition to the exodus to doctors' offices to legally acquire these drugs is an equal or greater movement toward acquiring them illegally either for the purpose of either self-medication or, more commonly, for recreational use and abuse.

Today, whether or not we realize or choose to accept it, we live in a backwards society in which the use of psychotropic drugs has become so ingrained into our culture that it has become a normal way of life. It is a society whose members readily ingest a medicated solution to life's problems and who often consume these same substances for entertainment without afterthought, and in its most extreme form, a society in which the use of psychotropic drugs has even become desirable. As a result, it has become increasingly difficult in psychotropic society to firmly distinguish the barrier between its mentally healthy and mentally ill occupants.

A common fallacy shared among many, and perhaps responsible on some level for the inception of such a society, is that there exists such a thing as intrinsically good and bad drugs. As Richard DeGrandpre writes in his book *Ritalin Nation,*

> Part of the confusion here stems from the fact that there is tendency in our culture to view a psychoactive drug categorically, as either an angel (for example, Prozac) or a demon (for example, crack). Because of this cultural prejudice of treating drugs as inherently good or bad, we do not realize that the nature of the drug can be greatly altered simply by changing the manner in which it is used. As we should know from narcotics used to kill our pain in the hospital, whether a drug is an angel or a demon is really more a question of context and personal perspective than one of pharmacological destiny.[2]

It is obvious that most people would not consider crack to be an angel, and due to the positive effects of certain psychotropic drugs such as Ritalin, for example, most would not consider them to be devils. Sadly, because of the positive effects, many abusing these drugs feel that they are safe when they can in fact be dangerous and addictive. As DeGrandpre later points out, "Because Ritalin is a recreational stimulant that can be obtained with relative ease and with less criminal charges, it stands out as a real option for many who are interested in having 'a good time' with drugs. And, as greater numbers of children continue to take the drug in high school, greater quantities get into circulation."[3]

Though this quote focuses on Ritalin, it would remain true for a myriad of other psychotropic drugs. The fact remains that these substances are often cheaper to acquire than their illicit counterparts. Put simply, these medications originally designed to treat the mentally ill now treat the masses, ill or not. Along with marijuana and hallucinogens, Ritalin has become the number three abused drug on college campuses,[4] where other psychotropics such as Xanax and Ambien are also commonly abused.

What could be the catalysts behind this movement? What are the major considerations behind the progression of these drugs as they descend categorically from angel to devil? How could the use of psychotropic drugs move from the status of taboo to an almost glorified state? Perhaps a good place to point the finger would be at the various forms of mass media that are omnipresent in our culture. Slowly over time, the ideas encountered in mass media such as movies, television, and music have seeped into and now pervade our collective consciousness.[5]

Music is one of the strongest, if not the strongest, form of media through which to communicate with the masses (especially with the youth — the music industry's top consumer group) and its role in Psychotropia is both unique and complex. This essay traces drug references implicit and explicit in rock, hip-hop, and club music to show how the music industry has contributed to the rise of psychotropic society.

The Pills Are Alive...

Though music has in no way acted alone in the creation of Psychotropia, it has certainly helped pave the way for it by warping the perception of the masses with regard to the acceptance of drugs— psychotropic and otherwise. To get a better idea of how music relates to and operates in Psychotropia, we must first understand music on its own. On a global level, many cultures are defined by the music they produce, and on the local level, groups within these cultures are often defined through smaller subdivisions of their music. Perhaps most interesting is that on some level yet smaller than the last, people within these subgroups attempt to define their very moods and behaviors through the music they listen to. This discussion on the effects of music dates at least as far back as Plato in his discussion of musical ethos, where he asserted that certain intervalic structures could influence their listener's behavior.

In this manner, music can be used as a personal soundtrack for virtually every occasion. For instance, many couples have songs that are distinctly "theirs"; songs that not only bring them back to when they originally fell in love but even help them to experience those same feelings of love anew. On the flip side, many people remember the songs that were popular when they were rejected by their first love, songs that easily create a feeling of sadness. Everyone has music that can psych them up and music that relaxes them. In a recent movie, *Blade: Trinity*,[6] one character even created personalized MP3 soundtracks to kill vampires to.

Another recent example of this occurred on VH1, a popular music based station, whose "Soundtrack to War"[7] series depicted soldiers stationed in Iraq speaking candidly about the music they listened to while fighting insurgents. The music mentioned, while quite diverse in style, was used to psych the soldiers up. Popular songs included "Bodies," by Drowning Pool[8] and "Bombs Over Baghdad," by Outkast.[9]

Before long and without even trying, one can build a case that music itself, with its ability to enhance or modify our behavior, can act in many ways similar to psychotropic and even psychoactive drugs. To go a step further, music is commonly studied for its therapeutic merit and put to use in therapies such as GIM (Guided Imagery and Music). Here, a therapist guides a patient through an altered state of consciousness induced by music.

The natural synergy existing between music and mind altering drugs should come as no surprise, then. Indeed, while GIM therapy was born out of current research, it existed thousands of years before our understanding of it. The therapeutic practitioner here was the shaman, using drums, rattles, or digeridos (usually but not always) in conjunction with hallucinogens to heal the afflicted or to gain insight and guidance from the spirit world.

DeGrandpre writes, "It is not abnormal to seek changes in one's state of consciousness, whether from mind-altering drugs, meditation, or other forms of stimulus change."[10] That music can alter our state of consciousness solely through the experience of it is not an insignificant point. On the contrary, it is this facet that has made music as prevalent in our culture as it is, and that has created the symbiotic relationship with drugs.

Though few would expect it, drug references in music are nothing new. The influence of drugs in music can be witnessed in classic compositions such as Hector Berlioz's *Symphonie Fantastique* (1830), in which the music reflects an account of an opium trip gone awry. The influence is also felt in our contemporary classical music, for example, in compositions such as Terry Riley's piece titled *Mescaline Mix*. It is not surprising, then, that this influence is still felt strongly. In fact, as we will soon see, much of our popular music was actually born out of the influence of various drugs.

Walking a Fine Line

As previously mentioned, the difference between considering a drug to be psychotropic and helpful or psychoactive and harmful is often simply a difference of context, rather than any characteristic intrinsic to the substance. Clearly, the boundary between these two classifications— psychotropic and psychoactive — begins to blur upon close consideration. Ritalin is a prime example of this. While the drug was originally used as a psychotropic to calm hyperactive children, it is now frequently abused recreationally for its psychoactive properties.

There are many drugs, in fact, that fall into this blurred boundary separating psychoactive and psychotropic drugs. The drug MDMA (methylene dioxymethamphetamine), commonly referred to as Ecstasy, was originally designed shortly before World War I and has been alternately used as an appetite suppressant, a "truth" drug, and an antidepressant. As Reynolds points out, "Used in marriage therapy and psychoanalysis, the drug proved highly beneficial."[11]

Despite protests from numerous therapists proclaiming that the drug's use and study could greatly enhance our understanding of psychotherapy, it was banned in 1986 due to its use in the dance club scene. Ironically, the controversy surrounding the federal hearings to classify the drug as Schedule I created a media frenzy that attracted national attention and actually led to the rise in its popularity.[12] This drug, once considered a helpful psychotropic in psychotherapy, is now considered a hazardous psychoactive because of its use in the context of the dance club.

Cocaine, a drug referenced widely across many genres of music, was also originally used as a psychotropic agent. Torgoff writes, "When newspapers began extolling its virtues, cocaine became increasingly popular among doctors and patent-medicine makers as a local anesthetic and antidote to low energy and depression; entrepreneurs were soon packaging it for rich and poor and people of all ages, putting it in tea, soda pop, and wine."[13] Interesting once again in this quote is the role of the media influencing the rise in popularity of cocaine.

As in the case of MDMA, cocaine was once used for its psychotropic properties but its abuse led to its banning. Though the legal issues surrounding cocaine cannot be blamed as much on music as MDMA, this now illicit substance is still one of the most referenced drugs in song lyrics and even more explicitly in song titles — the most famous of course being Eric Clapton's remake of J. J. Cales' "Cocaine."[14]

This short survey outlines a progression of drugs and music that should leave no surprise about the proliferation of drug references in the popular music of today. The multimillion dollar question is how the music of today contributes to the edifice of psychotropic society. Before we begin to untangle this question we must briefly study the factors contributing to the rise of such a society.

The Need for Speed

One would have to try hard to refute the fact that the pace of life in our culture has steadily accelerated since the 1950's. Though most would agree, few take into consideration exactly how much it has sped up and the repercussions resulting from such a change. Sensory addictions resulting from this acceleration are defined by DeGrandpre as, "whether in the child or adult, a disturbance of conscious experience in which the person suffers from the inability to cope with *slowness*."[15] While DeGrandpre is focusing on culture in general, music is a big part of our culture.

To keep up, music over time has also become faster, louder, and bigger — one need only turn on the radio to observe this. But something deeper has happened that most are unaware of. Though music can be conceived as a reflection of this cultural acceleration, the relationship is reciprocal. In other words, while the speeding up of culture results in faster and louder music, this music then perpetuates and even propels the culture that gave birth to it. Even the manner in which we tune our classical instruments has been affected by this. The standard tuning pitch for a musical instrument is A440. This designation represents the pitch, A, that vibrates at a frequency of 440 hertz. Slowly, this frequency is creeping up to where now it is common to observe solo performers and orchestras tuning to 444 hertz or higher.

Perhaps Maverick said it best in the 1986 box-office hit *Top Gun*[16] when he confided to Goose, "I feel the need ... the need for speed." Though obviously speaking of his F14 Tomcat, Maverick's statement reflects the philosophy of much of our popular culture. As DeGrandpre asserts, "Within this hurried sphere of motion, both the pace of life and the intensity of the stimulus world around us continue to intensify, largely because of ongoing transformations taking place in modes of human experience."[17] He later continues, agreeing with Maverick, "We're not just moving through our lives faster; we're also acquiring a heightened need for speed."[18] Speed in this context can be taken really more as a metaphor for new stimulus. As music grows out of and directly enhances this need, we can see yet another aspect of the music industry helping to build and perpetuate Psychotropia. While DeGrandpre is primarily concerned with stimulant drugs, particularly Ritalin, there is no reason to think that this need for new stimulus would be limited to any one drug.

Music of Today

There are a variety of ways in which music contributes to the edifice of psychotropic society. The most obvious are the direct references to psychotropic substances by way of lyrics. The music industry also contributes in countless more indirect ways. As we will see, be it intentional or not, the business of selling music, particularly hip-hop and club music, has become one with the business of promoting drugs.

For many, music offers identity to its supporters who often feel compelled to dress, talk, and behave in a style similar to the specific musical artist they are attempting to emulate. This trend is not new. In 1962, famous bebop saxophonist Charlie "Bird" Parker spoke the famous words quoted at the beginning of this essay. He proclaimed that if you did not live the music, you would not be able to perform the music. As Torgoff writes, "If musicians became willing to indulge in [Parker's] vices because they thought it might make them *play* like Bird, many would now pursue them because they thought it might make them *feel* like Bird."[19] In this quote, the vice that Torgoff is specifically referencing is heroin. We can see here the direct influence that musicians had and still have on their fans. Unfortunately, emulating the lifestyles of musicians, particularly those in the hip-hop movement, carries with it negative connotations such as crime, violence, and drugs.

What are prescription drugs like Adderall or Ritalin to students in light of rappers rhyming about harder drugs like crack or heroin? What would make students try harder in class when there is a drug that might help do it for them? I once knew a kid who sold his Ritalin to friends who would eagerly ingest it for recreation. In college, I had a roommate who would purchase Ritalin (his source would deposit it in an envelope in his mailbox through the inter-campus mail system) if he had a paper that would require him to be up all night to write. As a graduate student I knew other students who would take Adderall as a study aid.[20]

These are all too common scenarios throughout the educational system today. An interesting parallel helps bring things into perspective. Jack Kerouac, while writing his famous 1957 book *On the Road*, exhibited similar behavior. As Torgoff relates, "He took Benzedrine constantly, sleeping and eating very little, existing only on pea soup and coffee and cigarettes, sweating so much that he soaked through T-shirt after T-shirt, getting up to change the shirts and hang them out to dry as he changed the music he listened to."[21]

It is becoming more and more normative for students to use these substances in order to enhance performance both inside and outside the classroom. The difference of course is that in the 1950's, the people who cracked open Benzedrine inhalers to ingest the drug (frequently with coffee) were thought of as deviants. This practice of ingesting drugs to aid concentration for study and work is now considered standard for many students. Perhaps even more common, however, is the presence of these drugs at parties. Ritalin is typically snorted at college parties, frequently used in conjunction with marijuana and alcohol.

The myriad of non-psychotropic drugs (prescription, illegal, controlled, and otherwise) referenced in the lyrics and encountered in the lives of music stars also contribute to psychotropic drug use. The music industry has become so saturated with drug use of every type that it has helped to desensitize the populace and make drugs more acceptable. At times, as we will see, music can actually create the desire to experiment with the drugs that these musical artists sing or rap of. Worse still perhaps is that this ideology has helped make it more of a standard practice to be on any type of drug including psychotropics–legitimately obtained or otherwise.

Below is a brief survey of the deviantizing effects surrounding hip-hop, rock music, and club music. One will find that the relationship between drugs and music often extends further than the surface level lyrical references to the point where learning more about the music tends to involve learning more about drugs. It should be noted that due to the legal issues surrounding intellectual property, lyrics will not appear in this paper. Readers are encouraged access the lyrics via the Internet through any of the numerous Web sites available.[22]

Rock Music

The term "rock music" is a blanket term that covers possibly more subgenres than any other form of popular music. Included in this long list are subgenres such as country rock, Christian rock, cock rock, pop-rock, classic rock, grunge rock, garage rock, punk rock, prog-rock, indie rock, alternative rock, acid rock, emo, electro-clash, hardcore, and straight-edge. An entire paper could easily be devoted to untangling the boundaries between these styles and defining them. Suffice it say, for the purpose of our current discussion and to borrow a popular phrase, "they are all rock and roll to us."

Rock music, when considered along side club and hip-hop music, has a lengthy history and with this history, of course, comes change. While the music referred to collectively as rock has transformed over time, its association with drugs has not. After all, the original king of rock and roll, Elvis Presley, died a much publicized death due to an amphetamine overdose. As it was in the beginning, as is now — the "sex, drugs, and rock 'n' roll" attitudes expressed in many rock songs that were criticized for their deviantizing messages are still being criticized today.

Rock music enticed many people to try drugs. Director Oliver Stone became interested in LSD through music while stationed in Vietnam. In an interview with Torgoff he relates,

And then when the Doors' album came over, I just thought, My God, who *are* these guys? If they're making that kind of music, this is a breakthrough — what are they on? The guys said, "Acid." We just knew it was a thing you could get on the streets of Australia. I felt that if it was producing this kind of music, it would be good for me, too.[23]

The Velvet Underground is another band that is said to have had this effect on its listeners, but in this case the drug reference was heroin in songs like "I'm Waiting for the Man,"[24] and the aptly titled "Heroin."[25] Listeners in both cases not knowing much if anything about the drug beforehand became interested through the references in the music.

Drugs and rock music became so integrated that direct lyrical references were not necessary to inspire drug use. Concerning the Beatles' release of their album *Sgt. Pepper's Lonely Heart Club Band*[26] in 1967, John Philips wrote, "Now there was an album that proved to the masses what musicians had believed for years: that music and drugs work wonders together. The nation-wide hunt for rock-enhancing psychedelics had begun."[27] Although we have touched upon the predominance of heroin in the jazz scene, never before had music been so explicitly tied to drugs.

One of the largest and most public displays of the relationship between drugs and rock music took place shortly after the Beatles' release of *Sgt. Pepper's*. In 1969, hundreds of thousands of people flocked to the musical event known as Woodstock. Schowalter writes, "The Woodstock music festival and its half million attendees has traditionally been viewed as a portrait of Aquarius— a manifestation of a cosmic consciousness more profound than the same year's moon landing."[28] Perhaps even more profound than the music at this rock festival was the presence of mind altering substances— a presence encountered both within the people and the music that can scarcely be exaggerated.

Interestingly, Torgoff later writes of subsequent generations, "Having missed out on Woodstock, they felt robbed, as if the party had passed them by, and so they had a lot of catching up to do. Hippies, happenings, and great causes had vanished like the great buffalo herds; what was bequeathed to them were the drugs."[29] This is perhaps responsible for a change in attitude towards drugs in music. The previous quote by Philips mentioned a search for drugs to enhance the music. As the newer generations have grown increasingly familiar with these drugs, the search has become one for music to enhance the drugs. These drug-oriented generations seem to have shifted away from the "consciousness expanding" drug culture of the 1960's in favor of a culture oriented more toward just getting high whatever way possible.

While psychoactive drugs are referenced frequently in rock music, there also exist several references to psychotropic substances. At times these substances are referenced in a negative light. For example, Duran Duran's track "Lady Xanax,"[30] deals metaphorically with a female (Lady Xanax) who is beginning to crumble under the stress of her addiction to the drug Xanax. Taking on a slightly different angle, in Bad Religion's track "21st Century Digital Boy,"[31] we find a statement about today's upbringing of youth. The lyrics tell the story of a boy who has many toys but has not learned how to read or survive through daily life due to his parent's lack of caring. Blamed for this is the mother's use of the drug Valium. Interestingly, this song is actually a play on King Crimson's earlier track titled "21st Century Schizoid Man,"[32] depicting a man attempting to cope with the world around him.

Also, contained in Bad Religion's title are undertones of another finger pointing the blame on technology. Technology, as we will see, is a common theme among songs referencing psychotropic drugs in rock music. This occurrence highlights the movement away from family values towards technology and drugs. Another example of technology and psychotropic drug use can be found in a track off Green Day's latest album called "Jesus of Suburbia."[33] In the lyrics of this song we meet a character (Jesus of Suburbia) who is addicted to television and consumes only soda pop and Ritalin. Despite his poor dietary practices and shunning of the rest of the world, he feels there is nothing wrong with him. This statement is not uncommon among medicated and depressed adolescents. This apathetic attitude reflects the many children who are prescribed drugs like Ritalin, but sell it because they feel they do not need it.

In the Barenaked Ladies track "This Is Where It Ends,"[34] the narrative of the lyrics is of a character who is faced with depression, yet still shuns the use of drugs to fix it. These lyrics are in opposition to many song lyrics' positive references to psychotropic drugs. In Grandpaboy's track "Psychopharmacology,"[35] we meet a character who is suffering from a myriad of problems (drug abuse, malnutrition, psychosis) who is ready, despite his extensive list of problems, to resolve his issues with more drugs—this time of the psychotropic type. The attitude here is that no matter how many problems someone has, there are drugs available to fix them.

U2's track "Xanax and Wine,"[36] is another reference to technology and drug use, however, this time drugs are painted in a positive light. In the lyrics, we meet a character who is dealing with depression by obsessively watching television to escape. He, through metaphor, attributes the retention of his sanity and possibly his existence to the drugs Xanax and wine. Further positive lyrical references can be found in Sting's song "Lithium Sunrise."[37] Here we see a character, much like the one in "Xanax and Wine," who is fighting through a lonesome depression. Rather than Xanax, however, this time the character depends on the drug Lithium to get him through another night and even to heal his very soul.

Lou Reed's track "Walk on the Wild Side,"[38] takes us through very short encounters with various characters. One these characters, a girl named Jackie, is suffering from an addiction to speed. Like any addiction to speed, the user's body and mind will crash from the fatigue of chronic drug use. In this case, Reed suggests that Valium could have been used to soften the effects of this crash and to calm Jackie down. This is a reference to Valium and other like psychotropic substances that are prescribed to quell the symptoms of detoxification from other substances.

Perhaps one of the most positive depictions of a psychotropic drug in a rock song comes from the Smashing Pumpkins re-release of King Crimson's "Girl Named Sandoz."[39] Here, the antipsychotic drug Sandoz is represented as a girl whose life is dramatically changed. She learns many things from Sandoz and asserts that everyone has something to learn from her as well.

More neutral references to psychotropic drugs are also common. In David Bowie's "All the Madmen,"[40] we meet a character living and being medicated with Librium and treated with EST, in a mental institution that he does not want to leave. This is a more neutral reference because, presumably, due to the character's living situation, he is mentally ill. Another similar depiction is found in Aerosmith's track "The Farm."[41] Here, the farm is a metaphorical reference to a mental institution that the character says he needs to go to. He is taking Prozac to keep his emotions in check. Nirvana's "Lithium,"[42] is an interesting track. The lyrics, like many other of Kurt Cobain's, are enigmatic. However, due to the name of the song and its clashing sections of loud and soft, we begin to grasp these lyrics as a musical representation of bipolar disorder, where Lithium is the drug of choice to overcome it.

The classification of these references of positive, negative, or neutral seem inconsequential. As we have seen, any reference, good or bad, has the power to attract attention and potentially lead to drug use. As such, even without the rock concert atmosphere that deviantizes on its own, we see that the lyrics have the potential to accomplish the same end.

Hip-hop

Hip-hop is an umbrella term that covers many subgenres including freestyle rap, crunk, and screw. We can view hip-hop as a genre, in a progression evolving from preceding musical genres. Harry Shapiro writes,

It seems that every ten years or so after a form of black music has been tamed and co-opted into the American mainstream, the next generation of innovators come forward with a new style to recapture the identity of black music and the communities in which it was born. In succession soul, funk and disco were absorbed; by the late eighties it was time for something different. From this background emerged rap — embedded in a new young urban black lifestyle known as hip-hop. Initially as least, rap took black music away from corporate rock and created a whole new environment of home made music involving sampling, mixing, and remixing.[43]

Much of the music to come out this era was indeed a reflection of the community from which it was born — the inner city. Imbued with crime and drug references from the start, it is no wonder there exist so many of these references today. As Shapiro later puts into perspective, "Many rock stars have stated that it was music which saved them from a life of crime; within rap, the two have often co-existed side by side. This is hardly surprising given that many rap artists came from areas of incredible social and economic deprivation."[44] This still holds true two decades later although many rappers today are sometimes accused of lying about their rough past in order to attain the crucial street credibility needed to make it in the business. Over the years, the hardships endured by these rappers have become the model for success.

As such, hip-hop is perhaps the most notorious musical genre in the popular music repertoire for its glorified references to drugs. Heard as frequently as the drug references are those to a barrage of other sorts of deviant behavior including (but definitely not limited to) crime, gang violence, and prostitution.

Despite hip-hop's initial and continued orientation around life in the inner city ghetto, it has grown to be among the most popular genres in contemporary popular music. One need only reference the current top fifty Billboard chart,[45] tunes in to the latest music award ceremony, or simply listen to the majority of music audible when driving around town. The overwhelming popularity of hip-hop, of course, is not limited to its original black audience. This crossing of audiences is nothing new. Concerning the jazz scene in the 1950's, Torgoff writes, "The hallowed school of hipness handed down through a whole generation of jazz musicians [was now] being incorporated into the lives of white middle-class exiles seeking new identities. It was a complete role reversal as [whites] tried to take on the speech, dress, attributes, and mores of the black musical culture of the time."[46]

A similar situation exists today; however, the attributes of these musicians have changed much in the past fifty years. Though we saw Charlie Parker's influence on the use of heroin in the 1950's, people attempting to emulate the lives of the hip-hop musicians of today do so by reportedly engaging in a variety of drugs as well as criminal activities. This is not to say that all hip-hop fans and rappers are or will become criminals, nor that all hip-hop music depicts thug life — that would highly inaccurate. However, this deviantizing effect we have seen before is difficult to ignore.

In hip-hop, we find rappers rhyming about ingesting everything from liquor to crack and heroin. Sizzurp, also referred to as Drank, is a volatile cocktail derived from the mixture of cough syrup (desired for its codeine and dextromethorphan) for those who cannot afford the more expensive alternative, crushed pills (usually pain killers but Xanax frequently substitutes), soda, vodka or rum, and sometimes milk of magnesia to counter the constipating effects of promethazine with codeine.[47] As the mix is meant to be sipped over time, it is frequently served in a baby bottle that is passed around a group of people. Ironically, the cough suppressant quality of this bizarre amalgamation also enables the user to smoke larger quantities of marijuana without coughing.

If this practice sounds somewhat obscure if not outright bizarre, one might be shocked to learn of the subgenre of hip-hop known as Screw. Started by the infamous DJ Screw, the inventor of Sizzurp (who is coincidentally said to have also died from an overdose of it), this subgenre is devoted to enhancing the effects experienced through the ingestion of this cocktail. The music is characterized by its slowed beats mimicking the slowed down effects one experiences from the drink.

According to a popular hip-hop Web site, screw music was born out of Houston's alternative hip-hop scene, fueled by the use of codeine as a recreational drug — aka "syrup sippin.'" Screw simulates the drug's trademark hallucinatory effects, producing an "innovative, trance-like new hip-hop groove, a slower pace crafted by pitching down the mix until a lumbering, often eerie, tone is achieved."[48] As one can tell through this quote, as well as the rather extensive discussion on how to make Sizzurp above, this music has created quite an interest in the use of drugs.

If the originally obscure references to drugs like Sizzurp have become common knowledge, then certainly the more direct ones are understood as well. While Sizzurp (if made from pain killers), just like many other drugs referenced in hip-hop (marijuana and crack, for example) are non-psychotropic, there exist numerous references that do pertain specifically to psychotropic drugs. In hip-hop, however, we will see that the line between psychotropic and non-psychotropic drugs is entirely meaningless as the emphasis is quite frequently solely on getting high — often by any means available or necessary.

Drug references in hip-hop music typically do not reflect occasional recreational use. Frequently, multitudes of drugs consumed in gargantuan proportions are incorporated into the lyrics reflecting a perfectly normal way of life (or at least a great party). To go a step further, many hip-hop lyrics depict this lifestyle as ideal, often creating a desire in the listeners to emulate it. Common sense would argue that those who can actually can keep up with this lifestyle stand a great chance of becoming addicted to drugs and inflicting serious damage on themselves and others.

Another frequent theme in hip-hop music besides drug abuse is money. The successful hip-hop artists cannot seem to spend their money fast enough. And of course what good is having everything if no one knows about it? Present in hip-hop videos and lyrics are testaments of pride in the material possessions owned by the artist. Whether it be twenty-inch chrome rims, the big house, or a pimped out ride, references run rampant.

This is all to the chagrin of the people attempting to emulate the lifestyle. Many fans spend more money than they have on gold chains, diamond earrings, cars, and of course, drugs, to help complete the "look." This shortage of money undoubtedly leads to depression and potentially to a prescription for antidepressants which, with all the references to these drugs in the music, is often viewed as a positive — or at least an acceptable consolation prize for not having the hip-hop mansion.

Rappers are known for telling it how it is. But for those outside the urban ghettos that many of these rappers come from, the situations made explicit in many hip-hop songs would not be otherwise known. For example, in the mid 1980's there was a crack epidemic in the urban centers of America. In an interview with Torgoff, Craig Reinarman recounts,

> [Crack] was not something that you found on your average street in even a medium sized city; in fact, it was only known in certain circles within certain neighborhoods of those cities. In the summer of 1986 there had been several network shows on crack, and by the time they were done, there wasn't a farm kid in Idaho who didn't know what it was. If you really look at the causal arrow between stories and use, the stories preceded the mass use of crack.[49]

While this quote reflects how the television media influenced the crack epidemic, music acts in the same way. In fact, the television coverage of crack was meant specifically to deter people from trying it. Imagine the ramifications possible in music — a medium in which drugs are often represented as a positive thing. Hip-hop lyrics have clearly affected our perception of drugs, psychotropic and otherwise, making them seem like a normal everyday occurrence.

Three 6 Mafia's track titled "Sippin' on Some Syrup"[50] is a representative of the attitudes mentioned above. First off, there is little doubt that the "syrup" mentioned in the title of the song is indeed some configuration of Sizzurp. Further drug references ensue. Throughout this song there are references to marijuana, ecstasy, alcohol, and cocaine in addition to a rather explicit description of the defilement of an impaired female. The tone of the lyrics reflects that the listeners are not living well if they do not share in these experiences. From the first verse, the listener is made to feel inferior as Pimp C, living the thug highlife, burps (presumably from his Sizzurp) at those that cannot afford the twenty-inch chrome rims on their cars that he has on his "ride."

Continuing along the same lines are drug references in D-12's track "Purple Pills."[51] In this song, along with references to sex and violence, comes a profusion of non-psychotropic drug references including psychedelic mushrooms, Marijuana, Cocaine, Ecstasy, speed, LSD, mescaline, crack, heroin, and (perhaps somewhat out of place) gin and tonic. Though astounding, it is not just the quantity of drug references in the song that is detrimental, but also the quantity in which these drugs are ingested. One does not even need to read the lyrics to comprehend the potential effect on listeners. In the beginning of the song, rapper Eminem remarks that his demeanor is calm, similar to that of his mother on the psychotropic drug Valium. Here we see no delineation between psychotropic and non-psychotropic drugs. Instead, the above songs chronicle drug use at its most extreme as a normal way of life — a life based on getting high on any drug you can get your hands on.

Lil' Wyte's track "Oxy Cotton,"[52] takes a slightly different approach. While mentioning non-psychotropic drugs such as Oxycontin, Lortab, Ecstasy, morphine, marijuana, Percocet, alcohol, and even nicotine patches, he also makes mention of taking psychotropic drugs as well. This list includes Xanax, Valium, and Seroquel. Lil' Wyte makes mention of how some people melt down Oxycontin in order to inject it, but asserts that he prefers to take it orally in conjunction with the Seroquel. Once again, the sheer number of references and amounts of these drugs consumed, as well as the specificity pertaining to how these drugs are to be taken, has served to normalize and even glorify drug use. This song even includes directions on how to make the drug hit harder through injection.

Two other of D-12's tracks, "American Psycho"[53] and "Shit Can Happen,"[54] are of further interest in our discussion of hip-hop. In the first, in addition to a reference to Sizzurp, we find a rapper blaming his life of crime on Ritalin. In the latter, we find a reference to Prozac in the context that some of the more violent types should be on it. A track named "Happy Pillz" by Murs[55] is an example of a hip-hop song poking fun at Prozac use, likening it to brain surgery in a shed. However, other drugs such as Klonopin seem to be reflected in a more positive light, keeping the rapper calm.

It would appear, at least from the sampling above, that drug references in hip-hop music are possibly more deviantizing than those found in rock music. This is primarily due to the proliferation of drug references in hip-hop music. Many times, the music takes us a step past desensitizing drug use to the point where it becomes desirable. In light of this all, however, one must concede the following argument made by Shapiro:

> Generally, the attacks in America on rap for its apparent glorification of violence are a bit rich coming from a society where the National Rifle Association has such political power and Hollywood's coffers overflow from the proceeds of Rambo, and all of its shoot-em-up film and computer game offspring, not forgetting the whole Tarantino oeuvre.[56]

However much hip-hop music does contribute to the change in attitudes creating Psychotropia, it is not acting alone. As we learned, this music began as a reflection of a process already in action. Due to mass distribution, however, this process, originally contained in small areas, has spread to the masses and is now considered normal.

The Club Scene

Though some sources refer to rave as a subgenre of electronic dance music,[57] more commonly the term refers to a large all-night (and often all-morning) musical event drawing people in sometimes by the thousands.[58] The music that one would expect to encounter at a rave can be classified as "sampladelia." Reynolds defines this as a term "covering a vast range of contemporary *Hallucinogenres*— techno, hip-hop, house, jungle, electronica, swingbeat, post-rock, and more. 'Sampladelic' refers to the disorienting, perception-warping music created using the sampler[59] and other forms of digital technology."[60] This music, while typifying raves, is also commonly encountered in significantly smaller venues such as clubs and bars that play it on certain specified nights.

Possibly nowhere are drugs more imbedded into our popular musical culture than in the rave and dance club scene. Though any number of drugs can be found at raves, the drug of choice to accompany the music is frequently Ecstasy. Shapiro writes,

> Dance music and ecstasy stood astride this new culture beyond the stimulant effects and empathogenesis even to the point of a palpable synergy between the rhythm of the music and the effect of ecstasy on the brain whereby the drug stimulates certain receptors which encourage the user to engage in repetitive acts without necessarily being aware of them. A combination of the repetitive 4/4 house music beat and ecstasy consumption produced dancers who entirely synchronized their bodies to the music.[61]

This natural synergy is no secret to the producers of this music. In fact, the music has eventually become geared toward people on drugs frequently by people on drugs. Reynolds writes,

> Over the years, rave music has gradually evolved into a self-conscious science of intensifying MDMA's sensations. House and techno producers have developed a drug-determined repertoire of effects, textures, and riffs that are expressly designed to trigger the tingly rushes that traverse the Ecstatic body. Processes like EQ-ing, phasing, panning, and filtering are used to tweak frequencies, harmonics, and stereo imaging of different sounds, making them leap out of the mix with an eerie three-dimensionality or glisten with hallucinatory vividness.... Drug determined forms of rave music are really "understood" (in a physical, nonintellectual sense) only by the drugged.[62]

Ravers unable to obtain Ecstasy, or not willing to deal with the morning after effects common to high doses of the drug, often substitute other easier-to-find drugs such as Ritalin, caffeine pills, and even over-the-counter fat burners such as Metabolife for their speedy effects. The urge to consume these stimulant drugs is fueled by the desire to keep up with the all-night relentless dancing one encounters at a rave or dance club.

Many consider the experience of dance music itself to be drug-like for its intense regular rhythmic pounding. Hutson writes, "Due to the sensory overload of throbbing music, exotic lighting, exhaustive dance, and sensation-stimulating drugs, the rave becomes a mega-surface that gratifies a relentless and intense desire for pleasure."[63] He later continues that these "prominent features at raves, may physiologically produce altered states of consciousness."[64] Because of this relentless and intense desire that Hutson writes of, it is not hard to see why many club-goers choose to supplement and enhance the altered state of consciousness achieved solely through their experience by ingesting drugs. Unfortunately, this practice often produces a state where many ravers become unable or not content just experience the music and the atmosphere without the drugs.

Although Ecstasy was originally used as a psychotropic, it has become one of the most abused illegal substances in the club scene. Taken occasionally, the drug brings about an intense euphoria that is felt throughout the mind and body. Taken frequently, the user builds up tolerance and will have to take higher doses to achieve the same effect as before. Not only are users more prone to become depressed about not being able to experience the same euphoric feelings, but over time excess Ecstasy abuse can result in depression, paranoia, mood swings, and eventually even mental breakdown. In the scene, this is considered a faux pas, and people reaching this state via Ecstasy abuse are commonly referred to as "E-tards."

Despite the numerous legitimate problems associated with Ecstasy, many psychiatrists are still against the banning of MDMA because they feel the drug could have a positive therapeutic result if used in a proper context. Reynolds writes, "Advocates claimed that a five-hour MDMA trip could help the patient work through emotional blockages that would otherwise have taken five months of weekly sessions."[65] From this it is no wonder why, as Reynolds continues, "at a rave the emotional outpouring and huggy demonstrativeness is still a major part of the MDMA experience."[66]

Rave culture is fascinating and we must remember, as Reynolds points out, "rave is more than just music and drugs; it's a matrix of lifestyle, ritualized behavior, and beliefs. To the participant, it feels like a religion; to the mainstream observer, it looks more like a sinister cult."[67] Though Ecstasy has had many negative effects, one can witness positive effects as well. As Hutson writes, "ravers claim to find a world of harmony, equality, and communality; a place similar to humanity at its early tribal stage."[68] A common mantra amongst ravers is the acronym PLUR, which stands for Peace, Love, Unity, and Respect. Many ravers deliberately attempt to live by this mantra. At raves, one will notice more of a balance of people of different races and of both sexes—especially when compared with the predominantly black hip-hop following and the predominantly white rock following.

Ecstasy, whether known or not to its users, is taken as a psychotropic drug. I knew a girl who was prescribed Prozac for her depression very close to the time she discovered Ecstasy. Because of the complications that would result from taking the two substances simultaneously she chose to go off the Prozac in favor of Ecstasy. The therapeutic value of Ecstasy and raves proved greater than that of its more commonly accepted alternative. This therapeutic effect of raves is sometimes referred to as technoshamanism.

Ironically, even though the club scene is a breeding ground for drug use, because dance music is primarily focused on dance beats, it is usually without words so there are few lyrical references. Even in the absence of words, however, songs such as "Halcyon and On and On," by Orbital,[69] manage to reference drugs, albeit within the title. In this case the word Halcyon, a word meaning peaceful or serene, is a double play on words as it is also a reference to the sedative sleep-inducing drug by the same name. Of no coincidence, then, is this track's notably sedate character in a genre characterized by a more energetic feel.

Dance music also frequently contains short samples of people talking. As with the double play on words above, these samples are often taken out of their original context in order to imply something different. For example, you can have a sample of an airline attendant telling someone to "enjoy the trip." Heard in dance music, this is a clear drug reference where the word "trip" refers to the trip associated with a journey to an altered state of consciousness caused by ingesting a drug of some sort.

Another example would be words such as "control." Repeating the word "control" sounds innocent enough, but when the last part of this word — "rol" — is repeated, it is a reference to Ecstasy. A roll is another word for a hit of ecstasy and rolling is the word used to denote someone under the influence of the drug. This descriptor originated from one of Ecstasy's side effects — temporarily making the user's eyes roll back with larger doses. Hearing the sample of the word "control" chopped up so the emphasis is on the last part, repeating several times at a climactic part in a song, is practically a command for the dancers to ingest the drug. Another of these devices is simply the double play of the word Ecstasy in the lyrics of a song.

The effects of the rave and dance club scenes are interesting. While related to the use of stimulant drugs such as Ritalin and Ecstasy, they have reportedly proven to be a form of therapy in and of themselves — sometimes even preventing drug use. While this may be true for some, the overwhelming drug references in the music likely promote more illicit drug use than they prevent.

When the Music's Over

It is not my intent to suggest that music, or any other single media force for that matter, is solely responsible for the conception, propagation, or perpetuation of our pervasive drug use. As evidenced earlier, the urge to alter our states of consciousness through diverse methods ranging from quiet meditation to intense dancing to psychotropic drugs appears intrinsic to our human experience. What makes music unique from other forms of media is its innate consciousness altering ability. This ability is not only a large part of the reason for the ubiquity of music in our everyday lives, but is also a major link in the chain between music and drugs.

Rock, hip-hop, and club music, three significant genres from our current repertoire of popular music, have been discussed above in considerable detail with regard to their deviantizing effects. For many adolescents, the biggest consumer group for the music industry, the initial seed of curiosity over drugs may be planted through music. Ironically, this creates the potential to transform consumers of music into consumers of pharmaceutical products (psychotropic and otherwise). Though one must acknowledge the proliferation of drug references encountered in other forms of mass media, these references seem eclipsed by the fact that certain subgenres of music are specifically engineered to enhance a drug experience —

most notably, as outlined above, screw, which caters to the use of Sizzurp, and certain forms of dance music linked to Ecstasy ingestion.

To be sure, while the deviantizing force of music extends below the surface lyrical references to drugs, the latter references clearly also contribute. As we have seen, whether or not the references to drugs contained in music can be considered positive or negative does not seem to influence the overall effect on society. References to psychotropic drugs in a positive light make these drugs more acceptable. Negative references still brace the foundation of this society by referencing drugs and other deviant activity that might not otherwise have been immediately obvious.

These days, it is not an infrequent occurrence for musical artists to be hailed as demigods—their words becoming living testaments and their fans, their worshippers. One of the result of this exaltation is attempts by the consumers to emulate these artists. Thus, due to the proliferation of songs containing drug references, drugs have not only become part of a normal way of life, but even a desired path.

As the message of many songs is to get high by any means necessary, the lines between psychotropic and psychoactive—angel drug and devil drug—and even mentally healthy and mentally ill, have blurred to the point of insignificance. As psychotropic drugs are often more easily attainable than illicit drugs, they have become the recreational drug of choice for many. Also, because of the normalization of psychotropic drugs in our society, the urge to acquire prescriptions for these drugs through doctors has grown. Though psychotropic drugs were originally designed to aid the mentally ill, the idea of a solution in pill form has also become normalized, if not appealing.

Allen Ginsberg, a prominent beat writer in the 1950's whose works contained several controversial drug references for the time, commented in an interview with Torgoff after his 1956 publication of his poem *Howl*, that the use of drugs, was going to be "one the fundamental ways we would define ourselves as a people in the second half of the twentieth century."[70] Ginsberg, if not right on, was not far from the mark if we consider music as another way in which we define ourselves, and the fact that the roots of all three of the musical genres discussed above are historically and continually entwined with drug use. The prevalence of LSD in rock from the 1960's, crack in early rap from the 1980's, and Ecstasy in the clubs of the 1990's can scarcely be exaggerated.

Though it is too early to pair a specific genre of music with a drug of choice for the first generation of the twenty-first century, it is not surprising that some refer to this generation in which psychotropic drugs have become pervasive as Generation Rx. As psychotropic drug use (licit and illicit) grows in popularity, the music industry's references to these drugs likely contribute to the popular demand they ironically helped to create.

Notes

1. For further details on Ritalin's increased presence, please reference <http://www.add-adhd.org/ritalin.html.

2. Richard DeGrandpre, *Ritalin Nation* (New York: W.W. Norton and Company, 1999), p. 178.

3. Ibid., p. 180.

4. Ibid.

5. Of course, one must concede that the ideas related to the masses by the various media forms are echoes of what is already happening in some parts of our society. We shall see, however, that the media is responsible for bringing these ideas to the masses.

6. *Blade: Trinity*, David Goyer. director, Marvel, 2004, videocassette.

7. Information concerning this show can be viewed at <http://www.vh1.com/shows>. (archived)

8. Drowning Pool, "Bodies," *Sinner,* LP, Wind-up, 2001.

9. Outkast, "Bombs Over Baghdad," *Stankonia.* LP, La Face, 2000.

10. DeGrandpre, op. cit., p. 164.

11. Simon Reynolds, *Generation Ecstasy: Into the World of Techno and Rave Culture* (New York: Routledge, 1999), p. 82.

12. For more information see <http://www.erowid.org/chemicals/mdma/mdma_info6.shtml>.

13. Martin Torgoff, *Can't Find My Way Home: America in the Great Stoned Age, 1945– 2000* (New York: Simon and Schuster, 2004), p. 317.

14. Eric Clapton, "Cocaine," *Slow Hand,* LP, Polydor, 1996.

15. DeGrandpre, op. cit., pp. 29–30.

16. *Top Gun*, Tony Scott, director, Paramount Pictures, 1986, videocassette.

17. Degrandpre, op. cit., p. 22.

18. Ibid., p. 24.

19. Torgoff, op. cit., p. 27.

20. The humorous thing about this is that my roommate was far more content getting caught up in unimportant conversations with me while I was trying to sleep while the one on Adderall would stop studying to discuss at length the intricacies of Pokemon.

21. Torgoff, op. cit., p. 45.

22. One such Web site can be viewed at <http://www.songmeanings.net>.

23. Torgoff, op. cit., p. 179.

24. The Velvet Underground, "I'm Waiting for the Man," *The Velvet Underground and Nico,* LP, Verve, 1967.

25. The Velvet Underground, "Heroin," *The Velvet Underground and Nico,* LP, Verve, 1967.

26. The Beatles, *Sgt. Pepper's Lonely Hearts Club Band,* LP, Parlophone, 1967.

27. John Philips, *Papa John: An Autobiography* (Garden City, New York: Dolphin Books, 1986), p. 173.

28. Daniel F. Schowalter, "Remembering the dangers of rock and roll: Toward a historical narrative of the rock festival," *Critical Studies in Media Communication* 17, no. 1 (March 2000), pp. 86–102, especially p. 90.

29. Torgoff, op. cit., p. 340.

30. Duran Duran, "Lady Xanax," *Pop Trash*, LP, Hollywood Records, 2000.

31. Bad Religion, "21st Century Digital Boy," *Stranger Than Fiction*, LP, Atlantic, 1994.

32. King Crimson, "21st Century Schizoid Man," *In the Court of the Crimson King*, Rec. EG, 1969.

33. Green Day, "Jesus of Suburbia," *American Idiot*, LP, Warner Brothers, 2004.

34. Barenaked Ladies, "This Is Where it Ends," *Born on a Pirate Ship*, LP, Warner Bros., 1996.

35. Grandpaboy, "Psychopharmacology," *Grandpaboy*, LP, Soundproof/Monolyth, 1997.

36. U2, "Xanax and Wine," *The Complete U2*, iTunes, 2005.

37. Sting, "Lithium Sunrise," *Mercury Falling*, LP, A&M Records, 1996.

38. Lou Reed, "Walk on the Wild Side," *Transformer*, LP, RCA, 1972.

39. Smashing Pumpkins, "Girl Named Sandoz," *Pisces Iscariot*, LP, Virgin Records, 1994.

40. David Bowie, "All the Madmen," *The Man Who Sold the World*, Rec. 1971, EMI, 1999.

41. Aerosmith, "The Farm," *Nine Lives*, LP, Sony/Columbia, 1997.

42. Nirvana, "Lithium," *Nevermind*, LP, Geffen Records, 1991.

43. Harry Shapiro, *Waiting for the Man: The Story of Drugs and Popular Music* (London: Helter Skelter Publishing, 1999), p. 170.

44. Ibid., p. 171.

45. <http://www.billboard.com/bb/charts/hot100.jsp>.

46. Torgoff, op. cit., p. 133.

47. For a rather humorous and sometimes cryptic yet in depth discussion from the experts themselves of the intricacies of sizzurp, see <http://www.faqs.org/qa/qa-1140.html>. (archived)

48. Anon., "New Set Hits the Street February 8th," <http://hiphopfoundry.com/news.php> (March 18, 2005). (archived)

49. Torgoff, op. cit., p. 351.

50. Three 6 Mafia, "Sippin' on Some Syrup," *When the Smoke Clears*, LP, Loud/Hypnotize Minds/SRC, 2000.

51. D12, "Purple Pills," *Devil's Night*, LP, Shady Records, 2001. Presumably, the "Purple Pill" mentioned several times throughout the song is a purple pill other than Nexium.

52. Lil Wyte, "Oxy Cotton," *Doubt Me Now*, LP, Hypnotize Minds, 2003.

53. D12, "Shit Can Happen," *Devil's Night*, LP, Shady Records, 2001.

54. D12, "American Psycho," *Devil's Night*, LP, Shady Records, 2001.

55. Murs, "Happy Pills," *End of the Beginning*, LP, Definitive Jux, 2003.

56. Shapiro, op. cit., p. 173.

57. "Rave," *Groves Music Online*, <http://80-www.grovemusic.com.libezp.lib.lsu.edu> (viewed March 18, 2005). (university access required)

58. For general information about raves please see <http://www.hyperreal.org/~mike/pub/altraveFAQ.html> or for an example of a recent rave explore <http://www.ultramusicfestival.us/>.

59. The sampler is a device that enables its user to create brief recordings (samples) of prerecorded music and manipulate them in any number of ways.

60. Reynolds, op. cit., p. 41.

61. Shapiro, op. cit., p. 182.

62. Reynolds, op. cit., p. 85.

63. Scott R. Hutson, "The rave: Spiritual healing in modern Western subcultures," *Anthropological Quarterly* 73, no. 1 (January 2000): 35–49, p. 4.

64. Ibid., p. 6.
65. Reynolds, op. cit., p. 82.
66. Ibid., p. 84.
67. Ibid., p. 9.
68. Hutson, op. cit., p. 12.
69. Orbital, "Halcyon and On and On," *Orbital 2,* LP, Sire/Wea, 1992.
70. Torgoff, op. cit., p. 65.

7 From Playground to Pharmacy
Medicating Childhood
Dr. Michael Brody

> I keep picturing all these little kids in this big field of rye.... If
> they're running and they don't look where they're going I have
> to come out from somewhere and catch them. That's all I'd do
> all day. I'd just be the catcher in the rye and all. I know it's crazy.
> — J.D. Salinger, The Catcher in the Rye (1951)

The FDA has directed manufacturers of all antidepressant drugs to include the following new section at the beginning of the package insert in boldfaced type and enclosed in a black box:

> Suicidality in Children and Adolescents: Antidepressants increase the risk
> of suicidal thinking and behavior (suicidality) in children and adolescents
> with major depressive disorder (MDD) and other psychiatric disorders.
> Anyone considering the use of [Drug Name] or any other antidepressant
> in a child or adolescent must balance this risk with the clinical need.
> Patients who are started on therapy should be observed closely for clinical
> worsening, suicidality, or unusual changes in behavior. Families and care-
> givers should be advised of the need for close observation and communi-
> cation with the prescriber. [Drug Name] is not approved for use in
> pediatric patients except for patients with [Any approved pediatric claims
> here]. (See Warnings and Precautions: Pediatric Use)[1]

Even months before the above warning, I met Jen, who was presented to me as a seven-year-old girl who had been placed on Zoloft and Ritalin by her pediatrician for the last three months. This resulted in a sleep disorder and weight loss. Thin to begin with, Jen appeared physically frail, depressed and sick. Speaking to her parents, who argued through the entire first meeting, revealed that Jen was the focus of a nasty divorce settlement over visitation. Her symptoms appeared to be more consistent with a child who was always trying to make peace between her parents and failing. With little prodding, Jen began playing out her family's conflicts using my cloth puppets. After taking further history and asking for an academic evaluation, psychotherapy with Jen continued and her parents began regular meetings with a family counselor who served as a mediator on visitation and other issues related to Jen's development. Medication was stopped.

This was not the case with Robert, an attractive nine year old, who came to see me for problems related to sleeping (staying awake most of the night) poor appetite and difficulty making friends. His parents were concerned about days missed in school due to "stomach aches and head pain," although Robert seemed to be an excellent, committed student. While happy about his academic progress, his parents were also aware of Robert's worried demeanor and lack of interest in age-appropriate fun. Robbie, as his parents called him, was the youngest of three children. The oldest, a girl, was off at college "doing quite well as usual." The middle child, a junior in high school, was "focused" on his SATs and the wrestling team. Robert's siblings had "no problems." In taking a complete history from the parents, it was revealed that Robert had been taking Ritalin for the past two years, prescribed by his pediatrician to help him concentrate in class. It was clear early on that, like his siblings, Robbie was expected to excel and that the Ritalin he was taking was like "magic" and necessary to help him keep up his fourth grade marks. On completion of my evaluation with the recommendations of family counseling and a trial of seeing how Robert would do without the medication, I was told, "Thanks for my time but they will work it out themselves with the Ritalin."

The Black Box

The possible suicidal potential of antidepressants, along with the published research demonstrating that SSRIs (Selective Serotonin Reuptake Inhibitors—a class of antidepressant medication) for children are at best only minimally effective, has fueled a media frenzy. Doctors, drug companies and the FDA have all been blamed for a lack of oversight.[2] A blizzard of regulatory activity has erupted, matched by new FDA warnings, advisory committee meetings and public hearings evaluating the safety of SSRIs for kids.[3] Most of the pediatric antidepressant use is still "off label," in other words, not FDA approved specifically for depression, while benefit of a drug for depression in this young population has only been proven for fluoxetine (Prozac) and even then, not that strongly. As a memo from the FDA on Prozac for children revealed: "The evidence for efficacy based treatment on pre-specified endpoints is not convincing."[4]

Yet, in the last 10 years there has been a prescription explosion in the use of psychotropic medications for children. *The Washington Post* reported an increase of 3 to 10-fold between 1987 and 1996 in the number of antidepressant "scripts" written for children, with a further 50 percent rise between 1998 and 2002, with the largest increase in children younger than six.[5] In 2002, about 2.7 million prescriptions for SSRIs and other antidepressants were given to children aged one to eleven, and another 8 million for children twelve to seventeen.[6] Meanwhile, prescriptions for CNS (Central Nervous System) stimulants have increased (23.8 to 30.0 per 1000) over the five-year period from 1995 to 1999,[7] led by a three-fold increase in the use of Ritalin in children ages two to four,[8] pushing the actual production of methylphenidate (generic name of Ritalin) up over 740 percent and amphetamines by a factor of 25 in the years 1991–2000.[9] Add to this the world wide surge in the use of psychoactive drugs for youth particularly in Latin America and the United Kingdom, and we see what is transpiring in our country as merely a reflection of this global phenomena.[10]

For many in the mental health field, the fact that approximately one to two million children per year receive one or more prescriptions for these mind drugs is being heralded as a victory for child health, as childhood depression and learning disorders are connected to adult morbidity and even increased risk of suicide.[11] We have seen the enemies— depression and Attention Deficit Hyperactive Disorder — and have effectively intervened with medication. The value of better available diagnosis and treatment with drugs has created a drop in the overall suicide rate, and decreased learning disabilities.[12] But for other child specialists who are interested in the long term well-being and psychological development of kids, one wonders if this avalanche of pills is nothing more than a sinister mirage, producing an illusion of well-being while concealing not only more dollars for the psychiatric profession and the pharmaceutical and health insurance industries, but possible serious long term risks for our children.

This debate heated up early in 2004, when Great Britain banned the use of paroxetine (Paxil) for children, and issued new labeling instructions, urging that young patients be watched for deepening depression, suicide ideation, agitation and manic symptoms. This action was a direct result of the British Journal *Lancet's* study of four antidepressants (Paxil, Zoloft,

Effexor and Celexa) given to children.[13] The medication, according to the *Lancet*, showed not only no benefit, but presented a risk of causing suicidal behavior. The investigation, done as a meta-analysis of all available trials of antidepressants use in children, was the first to be done in a peer-reviewed journal.

The primary consequence of the *Lancet* study was to expose the routine policy of suppression of clinical trials unfavorable to a drug's efficacy by the pharmaceutical companies. And if the bad publicity in the popular press as well as the scorn of professional organizations and peer-review journals[14] wasn't bad enough, the drug industry found itself with even more serious problems when the courts became interested, as the New York State attorney general, a rising political star, sued GlaxoSmithKline for hiding information that demonstrated the potential danger of giving Paxil to depressed children.[15]

With over 50,000 drug clinical trials going on in this country at any given time, the American Medical Association became just one of several medical groups demanding a centralized government database through which these research efforts would be registered at the onset of every study.[16] "Transparency" of trials was now demanded, even if the results were negative, as individual drug giants including Eli Lilly and GlaxoSmithKline promised new disclosure policies.[17]

The FDA, reeling from their own lack of competence in the handling of this issue, finally got the message and released what has been termed a "black box warning," the strongest warning short of a ban for the selective serotonin reuptake inhibitor antidepressants prescribed for children.[18] This warning will be placed on the drug's label and more importantly in all direct to consumer advertising (DTC) such as TV, magazine and radio drug ads. The black box warning also has many monitoring and malpractice implications for all physicians prescribing these drugs.[19]

At the time of this writing the effectiveness vs. safety controversy as applied to the pediatric use of antidepressants is far from over, but the dialogue has led to soul searching by all professional and lay parties involved in the psychiatric treatment of children. Unfortunately this huge influx of publicity may have also led to a loss of the public's trust in the medical community, which has not been helped by my own professional organization's quick "warning about the warnings." Both the American Psychiatric Association (APA) and the American Academy of Child and Adolescent Psychiatry (AACAP) immediately issued what could only be perceived as self serving statements, stressing the value of medication and the importance of monitoring.[21] But, already, the negative media surrounding this controversy has led to a drop in antidepressant prescriptions for kids by as much as 18 percent.[22]

The debate has also raised a number of related questions: Is the FDA's action positive? With a limited number of child psychiatrists, who will treat depressed youngsters? Are pediatricians who treat depressed kids more vulnerable to malpractice? Are drugs out as part of a therapist's armamentarium?

These are all questions I will attempt to answer, beginning with this: How did it happen, that as a society, we came to rely on large quantities of chemicals to fix our kids? When did the pacifier get replaced with a pill?

Make Believe Culture

In my clinical work with families as a child psychiatrist, I have observed a highly accelerated pace of life accompanied by a general lack of parental availability. These factors are linked together by more than the usual economic pressures, the soaring divorce rate and the increased numbers of both parents now in the workplace. As a result, children are seeking entertainment, nurturance, stimulation, status and identity through material popular culture, the new (postmodern) parent. The real basis of this new time obsessed materialistic culture is the influence of a "Rich and Famous" celebrity-preoccupied media that screams for more: more possessions, more sexual pleasure, more meaning, and, most of all, more fantasy (consider *Reality TV*, Internet porno, credit card debt) that allows us to venture into the realm of the artificial. Since we require the time to both pay for (work) and enjoy (leisure) these options, the kids get left behind in a void all too readily filled by their own commercially driven popular culture. Television, and now the Internet, act as detached but powerful parents, as they replace being read to and played with by real moms and dads. Parents have long realized that electronic images can act as a form of social control (baby-sitter) and are therefore not very critical of the media's impact on their kids. They use the TV, videos and now DVDs to gain some free time. Using up to 5 hours a day of screen time, these media images have become real to kids. Whether cartoon or human, they begin to serve as idealized family members who are always available, always fair and consistently heroic.

As a result, children today not only want to watch or listen to their favorite media icon/baby sitter, they also want to buy what they are seeing, whether a multi-functioning toy, cereal or shoe emblazoned with a favorite TV or sports character. They want a share of celebrity, a piece of the personality whose name or picture is on their purchase, and by association, on them. This celebrity glow is promoted not only by the networks and cable stations, which interrupt and dominate narrative content with at least 15 commercials per hour, but are made more attractive by the lack of a parental presence. This celebrity driven narcissistic atmosphere also has kids taking on the new role of status symbol.

In a "parent narcissistic media world," a child's success is more than a source of parental pride, it is essential to it. For self absorbed parents, children do not exist on their own or even as part of a family. Who kids are becomes merged and fused with unrealistic expectations, usually based on the parents' feelings of inadequacy. Children become mere objects to mold and pressure. The main role of kids is to make up for the adult parents' failures and deficiencies. Unfortunately, the gap between these unrealistic or excessive expectations and reality is often filled with depression, for both child and parent. The media's stress on people like Donald Trump or *American Idol* stars fosters these unattainable goals. Make-overs, the red carpet and *Entertainment Tonight* threaten to create constant dissatisfaction with one's own life. But, since it may be too hard for us to change things, let the focus fall on our kids. This is more than the need to have our children lead a better life than ours. We have become stage parents and, like *Gypsy*'s mom, only enhanced by our child's success.

The increased number of child and teen beauty pageants, plus the stresses of spelling and math competitions, as well as the legitimized violence of organized kid sports, are all evidence of the destruction of the innocence of childhood. The reader just has to witness a children's swimming meet to understand how fun, sportsmanship, and pride have all but disappeared from what was once a healthy child activity. Parents scream at the refs, boo the other team and berate their own kids for forgetting their form. One understands the frustration and exhaustion of driving one's child to early morning practices and having to endure the sweaty confines and endless waiting at poolside. Whether it is swimming, dramatics, math team or choir, children have to excel, to develop their resume, early on, for the ultimate parental quest, college acceptance at Prestige U, whose costs as well as suicide rates have escalated.[23]

As our kids become more objectified by status and credentialing, they feel alone and lost. Parents become overly intrusive and lose empathy for their young, while pushing private college counselors and college preparation courses on them. Although most students apply to the same 50 colleges, parents become guarded and secretive about their child's choices. The college selection preoccupation intensifies in the junior year of high school to such an extent that one parent recovering from a life threatening illness remarked to me in a serious tone, "Wouldn't it have been sad, if I died before I knew what school Sarah got into?" It is therefore not really surprising that stimulants prescribed for ADHD are now being used to give some students an extra edge for success on the all important SATs.[24] Childhood has become hyper-competitive and driven as demographics create a Darwinian competition for survival of the smartest or highest-scoring. Children have many more demands placed on them with extra lessons and activities, fears of terrorism and unfortunately less emotional support, as their harried, cell-phone-wearing parents try to get them into the best pre-school.

What happened to childhood? Where's the fun? When is the down-time? And what happens if the child succumbs ("breaks") to the pressures of all they have to do? They need to be fixed quickly, much like an athlete in a big game. Give them a pill to get them right back into the race or to even promote their performance. Kids line up daily outside the school nurse's office, as medication (stimulants) is all too freely given out to help with focus. And while reluctant at first to give pills to their youngsters, lack of school success creates such a fear of failure in a parent that the discussion soon changes to "fixing a chemical imbalance" with the possible use of multiple psychotropics. This ready acceptance of a medicinal fix is also the consequence of a marked societal change in attitude about the stigma of mental illness. Today a psychiatric diagnosis seems to be an advantage, as everyone wants to be included. A movie or TV show can't be produced without at least one character suffering from an alphabet disorder: OCD (Obsessive-Compulsive Disorder), ADHD (Attention Deficit Hyperactivity Disorder), ODD (Oppositional Defiant Disorder) or PTSD (Post-Traumatic Stress Disorder). Mental disability has not only become entertaining, but for anxious parents an academic plus for your child to receive more test time, note takers, and "resource classes." Psychologists who do educational testing can't seem to charge enough for the diagnostic labels that they too readily dispense at the conclusion of their evaluations. Limiting TV or video gaming, providing a quiet space or a truce on marital fighting in front of Bobby, takes too much time and effort. Giving Bobby a prescription for Ritalin, rather than a social or educational intervention, is then validated at school. There, teachers and administrators have little time and patience for students as they pray at the altar of standardized testing, and devote all of their energy to assuring that there will be "no child left behind."

The Impossible Profession

As a sub-specialty of medicine, psychiatry has always been considered more social science and philosophy than "real medicine." Steeped in the theory and enduring legacy of psychoanalysis, the profession has historically sought legitimacy by aligning itself with scientific notions. Abstractions such as the unconscious mind and libidinal energy seemed nebulous and immeasurable. Peter Gay in his book *Freud, A Life for Our Time*[25] describes how even Freud understood this as he tried to provide a concrete quantitative biological basis for his psychology with his so-called Scientific Project. Practical interventions, based on reliable diagnosis, were needed instead of vague, time consuming "talk treatment." A biological, brain-chemistry, evidence based scientific approach became the wish of clinicians who were, in part, thinking of legitimacy in the eyes of government and private insurance administrators. This chemical agenda also fit the academic community and the pharmaceutical industries, which were always looking for increased research dollars. The biological path appealed to the self-help and parent alliances as well, who advocated for both the removal of guilt and possible entitlement of special education, under the Individuals with Disabilities Act (IDEA).

A major breakthrough in this direction came in the form of a guide which formalized diagnosis within the context of a biological framework. The *DSM, Diagnostic and Statistic Manual,*[26] the holy bible of contemporary psychiatry which was and continues to be authored primarily by medical (psychiatric) professionals, offered an ostensibly biological basis for different disorders related to the mind. Sophie Dziegielewski discusses how the *DSM* attempted to combine the psychological and the biological into a more unified and scientific system of diagnosis in her book *DSM-IV-TR in Action.*[27] Criticism and accusations of the *DSM* based on its marginalization of other mental health fields, over-emphasis on the medical model, its "masculine bias," and pejorative labeling of patients accompanied its publication. Supportive research, based on clinical field trials with the publication of *DSM III*, did little to contain questions relating to the guide's reliability and misuse, as did *DSM-III-R.*[28] Even the later and currently used *DSM IV,*[29] based on more than 500 field trials supplying cultural, gender and age-based information, did little to eliminate these concerns. Of course, the primary problem that therapists still have with the *DSM* is the lack of diagnostic reliability, which makes it difficult to initiate appropriate treatment. Simply tallying lists of a child's symptoms is often not enough for consistent diagnosis, without clinical experience and attention to one's own subjective feelings while interacting with the child during the evaluation process. It is interesting that an article in a recent edition of *The New Yorker,* usually the number one magazine found in a psychiatrist's waiting room, states how "reliability [referring to regular diagnosis in the *DSM*] is probably lowest in the place where most diagnoses are made: the therapist's office."[30]

Despite these reliability and territorial problems, the *DSM* does make diagnosis uniform, promoting professional communication and education. It has also become a huge money maker, since its initial publication in 1952. The perennially evolving *DSM* has generated more than 106 million dollars for the American Psychiatric Association,[31] while many more dollars reach the pockets of its individual members, as both government and private insurance companies demand *DSM* diagnosis for reimbursement.

The *DSM* has codified the profession of psychiatry while at the same time creating new included pathologies. The *DSM*, through its almost constant revision, creates disorders that are not only more diagnosable but also require medication. For example, the *DSM IV* changed the requirements from *DSM-III-R* for the diagnosis of ADHD by lowering the requisite number of symptoms from eight to six. For young females, staying out too late or intimidating others on a regular basis were now added to the symptom list of childhood conduct disorders. Even Pervasive Mental Disorder has become more inclusive, as pediatricians and primary care physicians must include new syndromes in this category such as Rett's Disorder (found only in females from 5 to 24 months old with deceleration of head growth, loss of hand and language skills and associated with mental retardation), Asperger's Disorder (autistic-like symptoms with no language impairment), Childhood Disintegrative Disorder (normal development for 2 years followed by a drastic developmental decline into autistic-like states). The end result of these changes to the criteria for these *DSM* childhood disorders has been a larger of number of children who may qualify as patients, and a larger potential need for psychotropic drugs.

HMOs: Revenge of the Primary Care Providers

The authors of *Beyond Managed Care* discuss the historical roots of health maintenance organizations (HMOs), dating to the late 1800s in the United States, when physicians charged lodges and unions a flat fee for prepaid care.[32] Henry Kaiser, a West Coast industrialist, accepted such a health plan from Sidney Garfield, a California physician, for his employees.

In the mid–twentieth century HMOs like Kaiser Permanente and HIP in New York slowly evolved, as the cost of health care and its percentage of the gross national product soared. Psychiatric care contributed to these costs, as mental illness became less stigmatized and treatment became more available. Popular culture, through the love of all things Freudian, helped foster an increase in therapist income, and insurance reimbursement became money in the bank.

This medical boom lasted until the 1980's, when a threatening globalization forced American corporations to look at their bottom line, high fee-for-service health costs, often a non-issue for their international competitors. HMOs, now run by powerful insurance companies protected against law suits by a loophole in the existing Employee Retirement Income Security Act (ERISA), a complicated law that had more to do with pension protection than medical care, offered a cheap answer.[33]

Effective marketing, selective patient pools (only the young and healthy), and a focus on profits created a business strategy that forced the HMOs to focus away from health and well-being to illness. Costly psychiatric treatment became an immediate "managed care" target, especially psychodynamic psychotherapy that often took years and was difficult to evaluate. The HMOs considered only short-term, bottom-line consequences of treatment, as their insured clients often moved from one insurance health plan to the next. There was no consumer or corporate loyalty. Why should health insurance continue paying for "play with clay," special schools, long-term residential care and family sessions? Paying for medication was far less expensive and treatment success from drugs perceived as more immediate. The expensive fee-for-service psychotherapy model was quickly replaced by a cheaper pharmacy promoted by managed care.

HMOs quickly instituted peer review, monthly phone or mail monitoring, and other complex gate keeping that created enough obstacles to turn psycho-dynamically oriented psychiatrists away from this new system of care and bury them in paper work. Medication became the treatment of choice as psychiatrists started seeing a high volume (several clients an hour, instead of one for a "fifty minute" hour) of patients, prescribing meds, and thus pleasing "managed care" companies.

Most importantly, HMOs affected therapist credentialing as insurance companies, now owners of HMOs that previously fought to keep social workers and counselors off their panels (lists of providers), now included them and their cheaper fees. Marginalized and ignored for many years by specialists, the primary care doctors also became very powerful, as they alone under the HMO model, controlled all referrals to specialists, including psychiatrists. With capitation (one flat fee), the primary care physician actually has an economic incentive to deny tests and procedures, as the money comes out of his pocket.

We also see why the basic message of the pharmaceutical companies' pitches and perks, to just write a prescription, is so seductive to the primary care doctor, given the reality of their limited training in psychiatry, let alone child psychiatry. It is a frightening fact that 75 percent of all prescriptions for antidepressants and 30 percent of antipsychotic meds are written by physicians who are not psychiatrists, and who usually treat a high volume of patients in less time than is needed to do a complete psychiatric evaluation.[34] The drug companies love the primary care physicians, some of whom are willing to try newly marketed drugs after attending brief continuing education courses given over a weekend at a nice resort. These vacation packages, of course, are not adequate in dealing with complex illnesses like bipolar disorder and schizophrenia.

The use of pediatric psychotropic drugs requires even more developmentally sophisticated, well trained, and experienced specialists. Ironically, the ratio of psychiatrists to primary care physicians now stands at 1:7 and the field of child psychiatry continues to shrink to less than 7000 in the U.S. Training programs produce a paltry 300 of these specialists a year, and even then, it is hard to know how many of these will simply be converted into pill dispensers. Demand for their services, on the other hand, continues to skyrocket while their "non-recruiting" fee structure doesn't. Waiting periods to see a child psychiatrist are measured in months even for serious problems such as eating and schizophrenic disorders. Psychotherapy becomes almost a luxury, as time constraints foster the use of more and more pills, even though the best therapeutic outcomes are the result of a combination of psychotherapy and medication. It is problematic that only a child psychiatrist can appreciate that severe depression may affect only 3–5 percent of children and adolescents and may exist at extreme ends of a spectrum. Depression can be part of a bipolar disorder at one extreme, and a situational/adjustment reaction (death, failure, separation) at the other. Not every unhappy kid coming to see his or her primary care doctor should get a pill. The proper treatment needs to be prescribed for the right illness. Primary care physicians and pediatricians have to be educated to understand that one intervention or drug does not fit all.

This was seen clearly in the case of Jeffery, a nine-year-old boy who was brought in by his parents at the recommendation of his school for being disruptive in class and refusing to leave the classroom for recess. Born two months prematurely, Jeffery was the third of three children. He spoke at thirteen months and walked at almost two years. His parents were high-level political appointees who spent limited time with their children. The only consistent time was on weekends at their second home near the beach. This house was also the tragic setting for the near drowning of Jeffery's older sister when he was five. The sister did suffer brain injury as a result of the incident and attends a private school for students with learning issues. Jeff suffered from sleep and eating problems after the event but the parents were reassured by their pediatrician that "this would pass," unfortunately an all too common intervention on the part of physicians in regards to behavioral or psychological problems in children.

After several weeks, Jeffrey did begin to eat and sleep better, but showed other symptoms. He was anxious, frightened of loud noises, had no interest in other kids and had difficulty learning. Not only school but simple tasks like tying his shoes became challenging. His family doctor now put him on an antidepressant and a long acting CNS stimulant.

On evaluation it was clear that Jeffrey was regressed, with little eye contact and limited speech. The parents, whose emotions about him were confusing, did not seem to know their child and used the time with me to discuss their guilty feelings about their "damaged" daughter. It was clear that while both psychotherapy and medication were needed to control some of Jeffrey's symptoms, particularly his anxiety, the parents needed both guidance and psychotherapy of their own to deal with several important familial losses.

Howard, a ten-year-old overweight boy, illustrates the importance of a detailed evaluation and taking the necessary time to do this type of exam even in a crisis. Howie, as his parents called him, was brought to see me for aggressive behavior toward his mother and baby brother. Two months previously, Howard was put on an SSRI antidepressant by his family physician due to his lack of activity, enthusiasm, or interest in friends. Staying in his room watching TV, Howard demanded snacks, leaving the house only to attend school, where he was failing and isolated. Soon after the start of medication, Howard did come out of his room, but in an angry, aggressive and uncontrolled manner, often physically attacking both his brother and mom. Upon calling the family doctor about this unsettling turn of events, the parents were immediately referred to a psychiatrist who asked me to see them. My evaluation revealed that Howard was not the only family member with problems. His father was diagnosed with a bipolar disorder and two grandparents had drinking problems. Subsequent visits demonstrated Howard's hyperactivity and pressured speech. He was taken off all medications, calmed down and then placed on a mood stabilizer for a bipolar disorder. He continues to do well. Taken together, the cases of Howie and Jeffery illustrate that with appropriate informed evaluation and the care of a child specialist, medication may indeed help. Without these, the converse may be true.

The Pharmaceuticals: Pushing Pills

Banners proclaiming "Welcome to the American Psychiatric Association" greeted visitors entering the huge annex of New York City's enormous convention center. Plasma TVs, free calculators, and attractive representatives all screamed out that "technology rules."

"Dissolving the Mind-Brain Barrier" was the theme of this international meeting that brought mental health workers from all over the world. The convention also included a large number of global pharmaceutical companies who have done their part in "dissolving and reducing the mind" to a simplistic chemical organ. A quick survey of the exhibit area revealed the ratio of drug marketing space to books, dominated by the *DSM*, and other related services (computer programs, employment opportunities, insurance) at about 10:1. Some of the pharmaceutical exhibits were the size of small towns, colorful and attractive. Pfizer, Zoloft, Effexor, Abbott, Bristol-Myers Squibb, Eli Lilly, Shire, and GalxoSmithKline had a large share of the hall's real estate. "Sign in." "Have you tried our drug for Major Depressive Disorder?" "It works with kids." I was casually told this falsehood, as if giving a powerful psychoactive medication was the same as giving a child, a sick child, some candy. "Here, take this brochure on our unpublished study of 56 patients." Only 56 children and I was supposed to feel good about its safety. But hold it, right there on a big TV, children were playing ball and riding bikes. Was this intended to reassure me? As I turned away from these happy images, yet another pen was thrust into my hand.

Pharmaceutical companies saw not only the clinical value of these medications, but, according to Elliot Valenstein in his book *Blaming the Brain*,[35] lots of money. Using a targeted (to psychiatrists) marketing campaign that utilized an increased sales force, a huge media blitz, legislative lobbying, speakers programs, conferences and "bridges" to hospital-based psychiatrists, Smith, Klein and French (the drug company) had over 2 million patients receiving Thorazine regularly, just 8 months after their new "miracle anti-psychotic" was introduced. This market success created a steady stream — more of a river — of drug reps visiting psychiatrists' offices with pens, pads and free samples. Teleconferences, free dinners, golf outings, tickets to concerts and even trips to Vegas became part of "continuing medical education." Attend a free dinner and receive a "stipend," plus education credits.

As these activities ballooned out of control, they gained the attention of government agencies and patient advocacy groups. To avoid regulation, drug companies decreased their doctor courting practices and in a new-market strategy, put their cash into direct advertising to patients. Using a blitz of TV ads showing the benefits of quick, easy chemical cures for depression, with fast talking barely understandable and illegible end qualifiers presenting adverse side effects, has been a sensational success as measured by increased profits for the drug industry. Television advertising for drugs went from 13 percent to over 60 percent in the nineties, as spending for DTC advertising increased from 266 million dollars in 1994 to 2.5 billion dollars in 2000.[36] Ads in magazines like *Good Housekeeping*, *GQ*, *People* and *Sports Illustrated* are effective. *Parade* Magazine now contains full page spreads declaring a parent's pleasure of "now seeing Mat rather than just his ADHD," because of the magic of a new long acting psychostimulant. Phrases such as "clinically proven," and "effective," sound right to consumers, but may mean little when compared to a placebo. Unfortunately, the FDA, the regulatory agency responsible for testing the truth of these ads, is too overwhelmed to evaluate these claims.[37]

Revenues for the pharmaceuticals do increase in proportion to direct-to-consumer advertising, which in large part is also a function of the new "patient empowerment." Anyone can now go on-line to gain information and support in chat rooms about their afflictions in order to make demands about their treatment to their own physicians. Web sites devoted to medical issues on the Internet continue to grow exponentially. While supportive and helpful to most, the immediacy and seemingly credible cyberspace with cable modems and DSL reinforces the cultural idea of quick, painless, true results. Importantly, the European Union has placed a ban on direct-to-consumer prescription drug advertising, thus not only lowering health care costs, but also maintaining higher life expectancy rates.[38]

Since patients have became "Internet informed" health consumers, they are further influenced by hospitals and physicians who also sell their services in popular magazines and on TV. But they are bombarded even more by pharmaceutical ads, where the number one advertised group of drugs, in terms of sales, in proportion to advertising dollars spent, are antidepressants.[39]

One must also consider the more covert use of product placements on TV that promote the use of drugs for kids. Popular culture resonates while it reflects society; even an episode of *The Simpsons* devoted to the negative impact on Bart of taking a CNS medication validates stimulant use. The same can be said of an ongoing theme of *Desperate Housewives*, where a mother abuses her son's stimulant meds to gain more energy. Psychiatric medication has become highly visible in shows like *The Sopranos* (Prozac), and *Huff* (Clozaril). There have even been story lines about psychiatric drug trials on *Law and Order*. On TV the downside of a medication's abuse is often minimized, and reversible, while the positive is promoted. But even if these drugs are portrayed in a negative context, just being seen in the media legitimizes their use. Like alcohol and cigarettes of popular culture's past, the use or abuse of psychotropic medication embedded in the dramatic TV or film narrative becomes a powerful message. Freud certainly was correct when he spoke of the way we do "thinking in pictures." Our unconscious operates in imagery, rather than in words; thus electronic images are a significant and influential force in everyday life.

While advertising in general psychiatric publications represents about 3 percent of total drug advertising budgets, the advertising revenues just from the 3 journals of The American Psychiatric Association have increased to 7.5 million dollars, a 22 percent increase from 2002 to 2003.[40] Ads pushing psychiatric drugs for children, of course, are a large source of revenue for the general medical journals as well. My favorite begins with the eye catching "From ABC to S.A.T." It draws attention to a full page picture of happy kids reading books, one younger, one older, next to a prescription pad whose face sheet has a prescription for a widely used psycho-stimulant. This is an effective ad, as your attention is first grabbed by the SAT phrase. The association of the pictures of the happy kids reading and the Rx pad with a script for a psycho-stimulant becomes a marketing slam-dunk. In the very same medical publication, a physician could view a similar ad that asks the reader to "Aim Higher," next to a picture of a father and son gazing into space with a telescope, as the logo for yet another psycho-stimulant is prominently displayed all over the glossy page. While the phrase "Aim Higher" is particularly offensive, given the possibility of abuse that these drugs are known for, the real shock is how vulnerable physicians are to marketing. Even with our graduate degrees and intellectual powers most of us do brush our teeth with Crest, because that's usually the only brand of toothpaste that we see advertised. Physicians are not immune to advertising, especially for the drugs we prescribe. In fact, the marketers know and target their medical audience well, with ads that offer symbols, like the SATs and telescopes, that are seductive and plug into the high regard we have for education. These ads promoting the medicating of kids do pay off for the drug companies, even in so-called peer reviewed medical journals, where apparently the articles are carefully scrutinized but not the advertisements.

In addition to professional organizations and journals, drug companies support advocate groups like the National Alliance for Research on Schizophrenia and Depression (NARSC) and Children and Adolescents with Attention Deficit Disorder (CHADD). They also "contribute" to grand rounds, newsletters, and research symposia for psychiatrists and primary care physicians. Richard Horton discusses this in his comprehensive article *The Dawn of McScience*[41]: "Even scientific journals, supposedly the neutral arbiters of quality by virtue of their much-vaunted process of critical peer review, are owned by publishers and scientific societies that derive and demand huge earnings from advertising drug companies." Mr. Horton exposes the ties of researchers to drug companies and the possibility of biased conclusions. He discusses the effects of introducing a "business culture into the university."

Pharmaceutical companies are also, not surprisingly, big boosters of the *DSM*, especially as it affects the diagnosis and medicalization of possible normal childhood states. Drugs now offer a solution to lack of focus, excessive energy, and angry feelings. One wonders what code number we would use to diagnose Huckleberry Finn, Tom Sawyer or even Peter Pan today. Would Oliver Twist need an antidepressant? Larry Rubin, a clinical psychologist, and creator of this very book, puts it best when he asks, "Which came first, the illness or the cure?"[42] He argues that a receptive market is needed for all these drugs. As a result, new illnesses have been created so that they may be treated.

Pharmaceuticals do pay for the various materials that fill physicians' mail boxes, inundating us almost daily with marketing literature, invitations to educational dinners, and paid-for surveys. *The Journal of Clinical Psychiatry's Supplement Preview* is usually the result of a teleconference developed by a "Continuing Medical Education Institute" pursuant to an unrestricted educational grant from a drug company. Most of the physicians writing the articles for these very professional looking supplements are consultants to the very drug companies whose pills are being evaluated in these so-called previews. Full disclosure lists of the researchers' relationships to pharmaceutical companies are long, and confusing.

In a comprehensive but disturbing article called "The Truth About the Drug Companies," Marcia Angell, a former editor in chief of *The New England Journal of Medicine*, considers these issues.[43] Angell discusses how the pharmaceutical industry's purposes have changed in the last two decades from research and innovation to marketing and profit. She demonstrates how the drug companies are now like "the Wizard of Oz ... now being exposed as something different from its image." In earning more than 200 billion a year, and outperforming the rest of the Fortune 500, the drug companies have become a powerful political lobby, with a self-serving agenda. This may have been the reason why it took so long for the government to finally pass the comprehensive Pediatric Research Equity Act of 2003, which insures the "effectiveness and safety of drugs by requiring clinical trails for use by children." Their political power also explains why Zoloft, the most widely prescribed antidepressant for children and adolescents, while failing to demonstrate better efficacy than a placebo in 1998, won a six month extension to continue marketing the drug by simply conducting two new clinical studies.[44] And while political efforts are costly, with over 650 lobbyists employed to fight for the pharmaceuticals, most profits still go to executives, and only a stingy 11 percent may go to research and development. Indeed, new biological breakthroughs are the products of academic and government money, not the pharmaceuticals' own labs.

Drug companies are far too busy promoting the blizzard of advertising we all now live in. Most of us are unaware, buried in a constant fog of marketing that makes us feel needy, inadequate, and desirous of the latest products. Advertising never tells us that we are okay. Its role is to create constant dissatisfaction with what we have and who we are. We are all caught up in wanting a younger look, a bigger TV, a status car and now even a better mood, and of course a smarter, well balanced, more talented child. Learning with phonics, academic centers, progressive nursery schools, musical-intelligent toys, and toddler computer software constantly scream out as glaring, shameful reminders to those parents who are allowing their kids to "fall behind," as parental guilt becomes an effective marketing tool not just for educational materials, but for the whole avalanche of junk marketed to parents via their kids, by the media.

Busy parents are easy prey to this realm of "junky kid commercialism," as they try to assuage their guilt in order to compensate for their unavailability. Parents succumb to the incessant nagging of their kids and buy the latest TV scripted fad toys advertised, with no batteries or parents included. These character toys, as well as the hypnotic video games kids compulsively operate, do little to promote play — play, which is so very important to child development, in using make believe and imagination to overcome grievances, in making the unfamiliar familiar and in rehearsing for adult roles. I remember my older son placing his baby doll over and over in a toy oven, or hanging it dangerously out the car window at the time of his baby brother's arrival. He also had a need to take his toy vacuum cleaner apart and then put it back together because the noise frightened him. This play was used to gain control and mastery over some difficult inner conflicts, such as rivalry and fear. Language and motor skills are also encouraged by play, as we observe the child giving a running verbal commentary as to what they are doing. Video games and fad TV toys do little to assist development or serve as a catalyst for the child's stories or concerns. They tell the media's stories, which are often violent, fragmented and often just hawking yet another product. But parents feel guilt and acquiesce all too easily to a child's demands. And if contaminating a child's inner life isn't bad enough, harried parents also feel the need to soothe their children with the fats, sugar and empty calories of fast food. Is it any wonder that both toys and fast food have come together in one of child marketing's greatest successes— Happy Meals?

The use of drugs for a kid's moods and behavior is just a further outgrowth of this guilty parent; it is a simple and quick solution, a phenomenon that sanctions the selling of childhood. Parents want their kids fixed quickly without doing the parental work of setting limits, being available, or demonstrating love.

The myth of a child-centered society becomes more and more exposed by the lack of a parental presence, a poor child health care system, poor quality education, foster-care abuses, unchecked commercialism, and now a possible over-utilization of unsafe child psychiatric medications. Talking the talk about child welfare seems easier for policy makers than walking the walk. A significant number of kids today are living in an updated version of a Grimm's fairytale with no happy ending in sight and magic only residing in a well- advertised pill.

Disguised with markers and signifiers, which are meant to confuse want with actual need, drugs are also promoted subliminally and placed in our culture's healers' very unconscious. Meds are certainly placed in the conscious and unconscious of the pediatricians, other primary care physicians and the mental health profession, where junk mail, faxes and reps claiming chemical and pharmaceutical quick cures, inundate medical and psychotherapy practices.

Dreams may have been the royal road to the unconscious in the psychiatry of yesteryear, but for the new psychiatry, the *DSM* and pills have not only provided a road to scientific legitimacy, but a golden freeway to financial success.

Discussion

It is easier and quicker to just give a pill, rather than doing the laborious work of understanding a child's dynamic psychology through play therapy sessions. It may also be less costly to dispense pills to a child, rather than pay for family psychotherapy or a special school. Pushing meds on kids, rather than psychotherapy, is certainly better financially for the HMOs, as it is for the drug industry. But is it as useful and safe? No! Children are not small adults. The positive results from adult studies cannot be extrapolated to children. Just as there are physical differences between adults and children, there are also metabolic differences between people of different ages. This is made quite clear in a recent *New Yorker* article, "The Pediatric Gap," which describes the inadequacy of our system of drug trials for children.[45]

Careful research with greater numbers of young subjects is needed, as are competent psychiatric examinations. This needs to be done before any intervention, psychotherapy or drugs, is ordered. There also must be closer continued monitoring once treatment begins.

We must have

- Better designed studies that follow ethical protocols with larger numbers of subjects in order to evaluate the usefulness and safety of psychoactive meds for kids.
- A public data bank of all pediatric psychopharmacology trials that includes negative (failure to show effect of drug over a placebo) as well as positive results.
- The FDA work in a less harried, more transparent, and apolitical manner.
- More parenting classes focusing on development, the importance of parental availability and the usefulness of psychiatric treatment.
- Child psychiatrists decide treatment needs of kids, rather than the irresponsible cost-cutting gate keepers of insurance companies.
- Recruitment of more child therapists.
- Limits on direct-to-consumer drug advertising.
- Hope that the "black box" warning will mean that kids get appropriate treatment and monitoring, rather than no treatment at all.
- Professional organizations of physicians, psychiatrists, psychologists, and social workers, as well as teachers and parents who cooperate with government agencies to advocate for safer and more effective methods of psychiatric treatment for children.

It is not just physicians that should abide by the Hippocratic Oath. Parents, mental health professionals, the pharmaceutical industry, managed care, and government agencies should be required to pledge (in relation to children), First, Do No Harm.

Afterword

The exhibit areas at the Child Meetings are now almost empty of those pharmaceutical companies that used to sell their antidepressants for children. There are no free pens or pads. At a relative small space, two drug reps speak authoritatively of their pills as part of a "whole package" of what depressed kids need. The size of the booths representing psycho-stimulants have grown since last year, hyperactively filling the antidepressant void. Media exposure and the FDA's "black box" decision about antidepressants have definitely affected shelf space. But the content of the scientific proceedings is still filled with "data driven" papers about drugs and molecules presented by physicians who offer long lists of financial and other ties to drug companies, while, remarkably, claiming that they have no conflicts of interest. Much work still has to be done.

Notes

1. Colby Stong, "FDA Black Box Warning on Antidepressants Creates Concerns for Clinicians," *NeuroPsychiatry Reviews,* December 2004, p. 1.

2. Editorial Staff, "Prescription for Confusion," *The New York Times,* December 28, 2004, sec. A, p. 22.

3. Marilyn Elias, "Strong Warnings Expected on Antidepressants for Kids," *USA Today,* September 9, 2004, sec. D, p. 10.

4. Shankar Vedantam, "Antidepressant Use in Children Soars Despite Efficacy Doubts," *Washington Post,* April 18, 2004, sec. A, p. 1.

5. Op. cit., p. 10.

6. Michelle Sullivan, "FDA Wants New Warnings on 10 Antidepresssants," *Clinical Psychiatry News,* April 2004, sec. 1, p. 8.

7. Deborah Shantin and Carol Drinkard, "Ambulatory Use of Psychotropics by Employer-Insured Children and Adolescents in a National Managed Care Organization," *Ambulatory Pediatrics* 2, no. 2 (2002), pp. 111–119.

8. Julie Zito, Albert Drivan, and Laurence Greenhill, "Trends in the Prescribing of Psychotropic Medications to Preschoolers," *Journal of the American Medical Association* 283 (2000), pp. 1025–1030.

9. Lawrence Diller, "Lessons from Three Year Olds," *Journal of Developmental and Behavioral Pediatrics* 23 (2002), pp. S10–S12.

10. Joan Arehart-Treichel, "Rapid Rise in Psychotropic Use Becomes Global Phenomenon," *Psychiatric News,* December 17, 2004, sec. 1, p. 33.

11. Thomas Delate, Alan Gelenberg, Valerie Simmons and Brenda Motherel, "Trends in the Use of Antidepressants in a National Sample of Commercially Insured Pediatric Patients," *Psychiatric Services* 55 (1998), pp. 387–391.

12. Benedetto Vitiello and Susan Swedo, "Antidepressant Medications in Children," *New England Journal of Medicine* 350 (2004), pp. 1489–1491.

13. Craig Whttington, Tim Kendall, Peter Fonagy, David Cottrell, Andrew Cotgrove and Ellen Boddington, "Selective Serotonin Reuptake Inhibitors in Childhood Depression: Systematic Review of Published Versus Unpublished Data," *Lancet* 363 (2004), pp. 1341–1345.

14. Barry Meier, "A Medical Journal Quandary: How to Report on Drug Trials," *New York Times,* June 21, 2004, sec. C, p. 1.

15. Tanya Albert, "Lawsuit Claims Glaxo Hid Paxil Findings," *American Medical News,* June 28, 2004, pp. 7–8.

16. Laura Landro, "How to Find the Latest on Results of Clinical Trials," *Wall Street Journal,* June 17, 2004, sec. D, p. 1.

17. Anna Matthews, "New Web Site to Offer Results of Drug Studies," *Wall Street Journal,* September 7, 2004, sec. B, p. 1.

18. Gardiner Harris, "F.D.A. Toughens Warning on Antidepressant Drugs," *New York Times,* October 16, 2004, sec. A, p. 9.

19. Heather Tesoriero, "New Drug Problem: Getting Antidepressants," *Wall Street Journal*, October 7, 2004, sec. D, p. 1.

20. Rita Rubin, "Can Americans trust their medicine?," *USA Today*, December 20, 2004, sec. A, p. 1.

21. Rosemary Frei, "Experts Warn of 'Chilling Effect' of Antidepressant Black Box Warning," *CNS News*, November 2004, sec. 1, p. 22.

22. Gardiner Harris, "Study Finds Less Youth Antidepressant Use," *New York Times*, September 21, 2004, sec. C, p. 1.

23. Ernest Sander, "Some Colleges Try Zero-Tolerance Toward Suicide Attempts," *The Wall Street Journal*, October 16, 2004, sec. B, p. 1.

24. Nicholas Zamiska, "Pressed to Do Well on Admissions Tests, Students Take Drugs," *The Wall Street Journal*, November 8, 2004, sec. A, p. 1.

25. Peter Gay, *Freud, A Life for Our Time* (New York: W.W. Norton and Company, 1998).

26. American Psychiatric Association, *Diagnostic and Statistical Manual of Mental Disorders* (Washington, D.C.: APA Press, 1952).

27. Sophia Dziegielewski, *DSM-IV-TR in Action* (New York: John Wiley and Sons, Inc., 2002).

28. American Psychiatric Association, *Diagnostic and Statistical Manual of Mental Disorders*, 3rd ed., revised (Washington, D.C.: APA Press, 1987).

29. American Psychiatric Association, *Diagnostic and Statistical Manual of Mental Disorders*, 4th ed. (Washington, D.C.: APA Press, 1994).

30. Alix Spiegel, "The Dictionary of Disorder," *The New Yorker*, January 3, 2005, p. 56.

31. Rober Pursell, communication with author, May 2004.

32. Dean Coddington, Elizabeth Fischler, Keith Moore and Richard Clarke, *Beyond Managed Care* (San Francisco: Jossy Bass, 2000).

33. Greg Bloche, "Back to the 90s: The Supreme Court Immunizes Managed Care," *New England Journal of Medicine* 351 (2000), pp. 1277–1279.

34. Leila Abboud, "Should Family Doctors Treat Serious Mental Illness?," *Wall Street Journal*, March 24, 2004, sec. D, p. 1.

35. Elliot Valenstein, *Blaming the Brain* (New York: The Free Press, 1988).

36. Richard Sherer, "Does DTC Advertising Benefit Patients?," *Psychiatric Times* 1 (2002), pp. 6–8.

37. Chris Adams, "FDA Inundated Trying to Assess Drug Ad Pitches," *Wall Street Journal*, March 14, 2002, sec. B, p. 1.

38. Vanessa Fuhrmans and Gautam Naik, "In Europe Prescription-Drug Ads Are Banned — and Health Costs Lower," *Wall Street Journal*, March 15, 2002, sec. B, p. 1.

39. Doug Brunk, "Direct-to-Consumer Advertising Set to Grow Exponentially," *Clinical Psychiatry News*, March 2004, p. 54.

40. James Scully, "Advertising Revenue Helps APA Meet Its Objective," *Psychiatric News*, April 16, 2004, p. 4.

41. Richard Horton, "The Dawn of McScience," *New York Review of Books*, 11 March 2004, sec. LI, p. 7.

42. Lawrence Rubin, communication with author, April 2004.

43. Marcia Angell, "The Truth About the Drug Companies," *New York Review of Books*, July 15, 2004, sec. LI, pp. 52–58.

44. Barbara Martinez and Christopher Windham, "Pfizer Finds Two Failed Trials Equal One Coup for Zoloft," *Wall Street Journal*, August 6, 2004, sec. B, p. 1.

45. Jerome Groupman, "The Pediatric Gap," *The New Yorker*, January 10, 2005, pp. 32–37.

8 False Advertising

Gender Stereotypes, Corporate Manipulation, and Consumer Resistance

C. RICHARD KING and MARCIE L. GILLILAND

[Psychotropics have tended] to keep women in their places, to make them comfortable in situations that have been uncomfortable, to encourage them to focus on tasks that did not matter.
— Peter Kramer[1]

In "How Prozac Saved My Marriage," Irene Duma offers the biting account of a woman trapped by cultural expectations who turns to psychotropic drugs to rescue herself, salvage her relationship, and end her "family's suffering."[2] Duma describes a life of disappointment and despair. She is caught in a marriage that is deeply unsatisfying and decidedly asymmetrical; her husband ignores her, preferring to watch TV, drink beer and polish his guns, sees her as little more than a domestic to raise his children and "to cook for him and clean his underwear," and blames her for the shortcomings of the relationship. When she thinks of leaving him, her mother reminds her that "at least he has not cheated on you" and "no man is going to want to a used woman.... Plus, I had the children to think about." While this painful story clearly highlights how gendered expectations, sex roles, and social privileges negatively affect women, Duma and those around her read her, and not society, as the problem. Consequently, she has repeatedly endeavored to fix herself and overcome her problems. She sought to be an ideal wife, getting implants and having what she hoped would be two "perfect children. On the advice of her priest, she tries to be "womanly and generous," volunteering at a nursing home. Most recently, she had hoped marital therapy would help, but her husband refused to go.

179

Stuck, isolated, and stigmatized, she made an appointment with a psychiatrist. Her doctor is little better than her spouse: "Dr. Thicke wasn't kind or nice, but his gruffness and lack of interest in me as a human only assured me of his competence as a scientist." After detailing her circumstances and the pain that they have caused her, "Dr. Thicke looked up from the TV guide he was reading and said that I shouldn't worry ... I was suffering from depression." He comforts her by noting "that depression is a disease suffered mostly by women, it makes us cranky and listless and a drag to be around. If I wanted to end my family's suffering, I should go on antidepressants." Duma finds great comfort in the diagnosis and even more in medication:

> Within weeks things had changed dramatically. I skipped gaily through my chores, I sang while I scrubbed the toilet, attended to all of my family's whims and fancies, and taught the old fogies at the home how to line dance.... The antidepressants had effectively prevented me from feeling any of the effects of life. I didn't have to hurt after all. The marriage was saved.

Duma finds in Prozac a way to be normal, to fit into stifling sexist stereotypes, to joyfully embrace the burdens of heterosexism, and to conform to the gendered expectation she and others have of her.

Like all satire, Duma uses humor and hyperbole to reveal fundamental truths. In her account, she calls attention to the misogyny of psychiatry and mainstream society, underscoring the ways that the family and other institutions combine with ideology to hurt women. In turn, she roundly critiques prevailing understandings of mental health, dismissing the logic of psychopharamacology with its easy, individualist solutions to persistent social ills. Moreover, in offering this story, which importantly lampoons the genre of personal success stories as well, she counters commercialized images and common sense ideas about mental health, gender, and normality.

While Duma makes it easy to laugh at notions of normality and how the practice of psychiatry has adversely affected women, her satirical account also poses a troubling question: "how is that forty years after the second wave of feminism, thirty-five years after the crystallization of the anti-psychiatry movement, and thirty years after the emergence of feminist therapy, psychology and psychiatry perpetuate gender stereotypes, reinforce cultural norms, and extend social control?" Indeed, even as feminist, humanist, and critical race theories have radically altered the practice of psychotherapy over the past half-century, the corporate marketing, professional dispension, and public discussion of psychotropic medications exhibit only superficial change. They continue to target women, rendering them inadequate, subordinate, and abnormal. Normality is prescribed and deeply desired, and being normal persistently pivots around gender. At the same time, Duma reminds us that consumers talk back, often in profoundly critical and powerfully creative ways. In her piece, she at once lampoons patriarchy, psychiatry, and simple solutions.

In this chapter, we probe these contradictions more deeply through an analysis of the marketing of psychotropic medications. Focusing on print media, we explore the content and context of corporate advertising and the ways in which consumers and artists have engaged them. On the one hand, we assert that the marketing of psychotropic medications reiterates the androcentric biases and sexist stereotypes central to psychiatry and mainstream society, manifesting itself both within the content of advertising campaigns and in its construction of the market. On the other hand, we map consumer resistance to corporate messages and cultural expectations in and through the domain of advertising, suggesting that while parodies and pastiche have proven effective for unsettling psychotropic advertising, when they fails to address gender, their critical force dissipates. Importantly, we argue, whereas the former actively seek to reconfigure gender in the present, the latter often fail to fully engage the gendered meanings of psychotropic advertising, a gap that has profound implications for their effectiveness.

Our discussion begins with an introduction to the social landscape structured by psychopharmacology and advertising. It then turns to the place of gender and misogyny in psychiatry and psychology. Against this background, we offer a critical reading of the marketing of psychotropic medications. Next, we detail the anti-advertisements produced by consumers.

Although deeply critical of the marketing of psychotropic medications, our argument does not question the utility of such drugs or the conditions they purport to alleviate. In fact, we accept that psychotropic medications serve an important role in the treatment of mental illness, especially when combined with therapy and administered in a context that understands the importance of environmental factors and questions social forces as well.

Entering Psychotropia

In 2005, nearly two decades after the release of Prozac, the American public has largely internalized cosmetic pharmacology and the conditions it purported to treat, including depression, anxiety, and shyness. They have become fixtures in the collective unconscious, accepted furnishings of consumer culture, informing common sense notions of the self, health, and the good life. We knew this from the outset of our study, anticipating a preponderance of print advertisements that would illuminate the place of gender in the commercialization of psychological problems and consumption of pharmaceutical solutions. We confidently set about to compare the quantity and content of advertisements in magazines most widely read by men, women, and people of color: *Maxim, GQ, Esquire, and Men's Health; Ladies' Home Journal, Good Housekeeping, Better Homes and Gardens, Glamour, Parents,* and *Parenting; Hispanic* and *Latina; Ebony, Essence,* and *Jet;* and even *Rolling Stone* and *Time.* We had speculated that such ads would be common in those periodicals read by white women, but absent from those read by men and people of color. To our surprise, such ads were not to be found in most mainstream magazines. In fact, a review of these magazines revealed only one ad in 2004 (for Zoloft in *Time*). Expanding our search to the last five years (2000–2004), out of the several hundred magazines reviewed, we found only one series of ads in *Ladies' Home Journal.* Initially, we were at a loss to explain this, until we reviewed journals aimed a psychiatrists. In the *Journal of American Psychiatry, Psychiatric Annals,* and the *Journal of Clinical Psychiatry,* ads for pharmaceuticals designed to treat conditions like depression and anxiety were fairly common.

This finding, which at the time felt more like a failure, held great insight. Indeed, it prompted us to think in more complex ways about psychotropic medications, particularly the social arrangements and cultural meanings that bring them to life. Perhaps most importantly, it pushed us to go beyond our preconceptions about advertising. Specific ads had to be understood as something more than texts offering up stories and stereotypes about gender, class, and the good life, while they encouraged doctors and patients to use particular drugs. Increasingly, as we probed the virtual absence of advertising for drugs designed to combat depression and anxiety in popular magazines, we began to glimpse a much more complicated social world. Not only do corporations encode messages reflecting and reinforcing dominant ideas about men, women, sexuality, the family, happiness and the like — in short normality, but corporate marketing strategies have encroached on the therapeutic process, reshaping its form and function in many cases. Interestingly, consumers have become quite savvy at decoding and even recoding this corporate-driven pharmaceutical advertising.

The evolving social world in which this corporate merchandising of mental illness and pharmacologic cure is understood might be best described as Psychotropia.[3] Psychotropia is not so much a place as a state of being, a social condition, and an historical conjucture. It refers to a set of social relations and cultural assumptions that pivot around the social subject and the good life and that begin to take shape in association with reconfigurations of work, home, and community variously talked about as post-industrialization, post-Fordism, postmodernity, and globalization. Psychotropia brings with it a faith in science, a desire for simple, individualistic solutions, and a language of naturalism that argues against cultural context. And while the dispensing and ingestion of chemical compounds animates this brave new world, there is nothing natural about it. It is a complex creation, emergent at the intersection of historical forces, political interests, and economic flows. Psychotropia feeds on a desire for normality, the orderly correspondence and introspective management of individuals, their longing to be the same, and the mass mediated images from which they fashion their identities and aspirations. It has seeped into every crevice and fold of modern society, knitting together disparate social domains, including health care, insurance, consumerism, work, and education. Consequently, Psychotropia unfolds as a restrictive regime of sorts, one that offers illusions of liberation and rebirth with assistance of a little pill — better living through chemistry to be sure.

Although it is a startling neologism, a number of social critics anticipated many of the core components of Psychotropia: social control, totality, normalization, cultural construction, and regulation. In *Brave New World*, Aldous Huxley spoke of a dystopian future in which drugs would be used to enforce social norms and tranquility.[4] Sociologist Erving Goffman turned his attention to the functional present, describing mental hospital and asylums as "total institutions" that enveloped and remade their wards. They dehumanized the mentally ill as they controlled them, managing all (or almost all) aspects of their daily lives.[5] At much the same time, Thomas Szasz began critiquing the psychiatric establishment. In contrast with many of his colleagues, Szasz asserted that mental illness was a myth, a social construct manufactured by psychiatry. Its manufacture of madness, he continued, hinged on the diagnosis, classification, and management of deviance, particularly transgressive behaviors that could be stigmatized and abnormal individuals who could be scapegoated. For Szasz, psychiatry had a politics and violence few noticed. Consequently, the discipline, and especially its reliance on opiates, had become fundamental to the regulation of mass society in twentieth century America, reinforcing prevailing preconceptions and preoccupations.[6] In Europe, Michel Foucault also struggled with questions of madness and incarceration, arriving at many of the same conclusions as well as many novel conceptions. Foucault highlighted the ways in which ideas and practices established conditions of possibility and animated specific kinds of people; the insane, the criminal, the student, or the homosexual, for instance. His studies of prisons, psychiatry, and sexuality shed light not simply on the production and regulation of deviance, but on normalization as well. That is, madness and other forms of deviance mattered for Foucault, precisely because of the ways in which they illuminated the underlying ideological and structural arrangements that secured and celebrated normality.[7] In these four scholars, concerned as they were with institutional psychiatry, we find inspiration for our explorations of psychotropic marketing, guided by their critical assessment of benevolence and progress, their attention to the politics of knowledge, their awareness of the constructed nature of normality and deviance, and their interrogation of the intersections of power, categorization, and humanness. We note, moreover, that much to our chagrin, they all failed to engage gender or the primacy of misogyny in psychiatry, and as a consequence shortly turn our attention to feminist readings of women and madness.

In memoirs, commentaries, and essays, journalists, pundits, and former users have offered less theoretically informed but equally penetrating visions of Psychotropia. Three works written across the past decade outline a broader public sentiment about the current psychosocial conjuncture. Elizabeth Wurtzel titles her personal account of life before and after being medicated, *Prozac Nation*.[8] Furthermore, she sardonically describes contemporary America as "the United States of Depression," capturing in part the pervasive sense of malady and anomie.[9] Similarly, Carla Spartos reports on the controversial release of Sarafem in article called "Sarafem Nation."[10] Finally, a former editor of *Vanity Fair*, Tina Brown, invokes "Paxil America" to render the current state of (psychic) affairs. Brown seizes on this phrase to encapsulate the essential place of psychotropic medication as enhancement, as savior, as register of fashion, linking the profitability of marketing anxiety in post–9/11 America with the popular disdain for dissent.[11] Together, these three authors point to a shared understanding of the ways that psychotropic drugs and the practices and preconceptions associated with them have come to saturate everyday life, threatening to dehumanize as they transform taken-for-granted freedoms, identities, and affiliations.

However it is named or theorized, social subjects enter psychotropia through a number of portals in seemingly countless roles for an array of reasons: as doctors or patients in a therapeutic process, as researchers, managers, or factory workers within big pharmaceuticals, as lawyers, litigants, and insurers involved in a wrongful death case. Significantly, consumer culture is perhaps the most invisible and pernicious gateway. Indeed, advertising campaigns aimed at doctors and consumers have made the assumptions and interventions associated with psychotropic medications ubiquitous, accepted and internalized. Marketing has reshaped the ways in which individuals and institutions approach questions of psychological well-being, means to improve it, and costs associated with and benefits derived cosmetic pharmacology, interpolating millions of unsuspecting consumers (even those without "problems") into Psychotropia.

On the one hand, advertising as one might expect has had an impact on consumers. It encourages them to reflect on their lives, to assess their moods and to evaluate whether what they are experiencing matches those portrayed as problematic, requiring them to seek counseling. Moreover, once at the doctor's office, the marketing of psychotropic medication continues to influence consumers, shaping their expectations and desires. Psychiatrist Jonathan Metzl reports patients come to see him with a definite sense of what they want: they want Prozac (or Celexa or Effexor and on) to reclaim themselves, to get healthy and happy again. Some even come to see him repeating the slogans from specific ads. One woman, whom he believed suffered from bipolar disorder, disputed his assessment: "You've got it all wrong — I came here for Paxil because I have chronic anxiety disorder." After viewing the ad in a women's magazine she "had decided it was me," asking, "Don't you think it will help me?" From these encounters, Metzl concludes that advertising increasingly plays an active role in therapy, structuring the interchange between patient and psychiatrist as much as it shapes desires and expectations.[12]

On the other hand, advertising for psychotropic medications has surely impacted clinicians as well. It not only "educates" them about specific drugs, but it places them within and increasingly commodified and branded landscape, as competing commercialized cures compete for attention, market share, and loyalty. A former user of Zoloft offers an intriguing reading of the ways in which branding is restructuring the clinical world. Benjamin Riley reports that he went to see a doctor because he felt "miserable, tired, and upset and frustrated to the point of tears." He was given a sample of Zoloft from his psychiatrist. Upon returning to her office for a follow up visit, he noticed to his horror something he initially had not: "Her office was full of Zoloft propoganda. A Zoloft clock hung on her wall. I wondered if I was going to get a free Zoloft t-shirt with my first visit." Riley's comments should give pause, encouraging reflection on how central consumer culture and commercial have become as gateways to Psychotropia.[13]

Women and Madness

Psychology and psychiatry have always had a problem with women, and they have always known (or so they have thought) how to fix them. A popular cartoon nicely encapsulates and playfully mocks the core presuppositions and basic structures at the heart of psychology and psychiatry's treatment of women. It features a princess quietly reclining on a consulting couch, while a psychoanalyst seated behind her pontificates. Arms folded across her abdomen, she stares politely at the castle ceiling, awaiting his diagnosis: "Since you are a damsel, I understand your natural predisposition to distress. Therefore, I'm going to prescribe a strong anti-depressant. Try to think of it as your little 'Knight-in-Shining-Armor-in-a-bottle.'"[14] The single-paneled comic highlights not only the primacy these fields have granted to feminine difference, which is routinely construed as biologically determined and abnormally expressed, but also the capacity of the male psychiatrist to diagnosis and prescribe, rescuing the damsel in distress through the male power to classify and dispense.

Historically, psychology and psychiatry have projected social problems and sexist stereotypes onto women, excluding their voices and experiences, while perpetuating male dominance.[15] Their uses and understandings of gender and sexuality have proven central to the fabrication of the normal and the deviant, the natural and the social, the sane and the insane, as well as what it means to be a man or a woman in the United States. Drawing on the dominant conception of gender roles, they have simultaneously reinforced misogynist conceptualization of women and pathologized them for conforming to and challenging normative definitions of femininity. Psychology and psychiatry have historically asserted that women are not only different from men, but lesser and in ways defective. In theory and in practice, these fields have insisted that women are less rational, less independent, less assertive and corollarily more emotional, childlike and needy. These foundational principles, according to Jessica Heriot, have long trapped women in a double-bind process, placing them in a paradoxical place: "To be a healthy woman by society's standards is to be a sick adult. On the other hand, for a women to aspire to a societal definition of adulthood is to do so at the cost of her womanhood."[16] Caught in this bind, women must choose between competing versions of deviance, all of which detrimentally impact them and their quality of life.

Accepted accounts of "psychological disorders" expose the shape and force of androcentric bias in these fields. Hysteria, for instance, once defined by the presence of fits and seizures, evolved over the course of the nineteenth century to characterize certain traits, moods, and personalities associated with women, making hysterical and feminine behaviors and attributes synonymous.[17] Even today, the expression of emotion and its connection to deviance is gendered. Women's emotional expressions are seen as "acting in" (e.g., depression, anxiety, eating disorders) whereas men's are characterized as "acting out" (e.g., violent behavior). Consequently, women are "treated" for their psychological "disorders" and men are punished for their behaviors within the criminal justice system. These practices reinforce the belief that women are crazy and need medication.[18] Similarly, personality disorders target and affect women differently than men. Paula Caplan notes that while women are stigmatized as suffering from Self Defeating Personality Disorder if they put others' needs before their own, men are considered normal if they cannot "identify and express a range of feelings."[19] Even the descriptions of men and women in case notes reveal striking differences. Based on a study of the *DSM-IV Casebook*, Jill Cermele and her colleagues found that while men and women were described in accordance with cultural expectations, women were more likely to be represented negatively and evaluated in light of their physical attractiveness, with women of color most likely to be sexualized.[20]

These patterns derive from a social context that has afforded unequal access to rights, representation, and resources to men and from a "science" of the mind that has routinely contributed to the maintenance of the status quo (read male dominance) and the extension of social control by pathologizing individuals and groups deemed deviant. Traditionally, psychiatry has reinforced male dominance, in its outcomes as well as in its processes. The psychiatrist (often male) has operated as a kind of hero, rescuing the vulnerable female patient, telling her what the truths are about her thoughts and feelings, pathologizing her experience. In locating problems in the feelings, reactions, and personality of individual women, moreover, it has disabled women, refusing to offer ways of listening and thinking that might validate their burdens and injuries or fight the powers that be. Psychology and psychiatry have failed women, precisely because their diagnoses and treatments all too often have ignored social structures and oppressive expectations of gender.

The emergence of the second wave of feminism initiated an interrogation of modern life on multiple fronts, pushing for social equality and cultural citizenship throughout society. Psychology and psychiatry crystallized as important spaces of struggles. A dissatisfaction with traditional, that is sexist, research methods, biased assessments and diagnostic tools, and a belief that the techniques of psychotherapy were extensions of patriarchy, motivated feminists, whether patients and professionals, to call for changes in how psychology and psychiatry functioned. While psychiatrists like

Thomas Szasz and Thomas Scheff were among the first to challenge these fields, arguing they were means of social control with a benevolent face, feminists such as Phyllis Chesler and Jean Baker Miller were among the first to expose psychology and psychiatry as misogynistic institutions that advanced patriarchy. Feminist critics also saw in psychiatry and psychology the workings of social control, but they were not content to limit their gaze to asylums and hospitals nor to call for deinstitutionalization or humanization. Instead, in questioning the methods and practices of psychology and psychiatry, they made connections between scientific diagnoses and cultural strereotypes, between roles in marriage, the workplace, and the counseling session, between the broader exclusion of women from professional and social life and their absence from these disciplines, between the general devaluation of women and their experiences and their stigmatization by doctors and therapists. In making these connections, feminists had a better understanding of the emerging shape of Psychotropia as the restructuring of self, psyche, science, and society through unthought practices, in silent yet oppressive assumptions, and in small, everyday forms than did their counterparts in the anti-psychiatry movement.

Phyllis Chesler's action at the 1970 annual meetings for the American Psychological Association offers a graphic illustration of the vision and challenge embodied by the then emergent feminist critique of psychology and psychiatry. Chesler initially had intended to present her research on what women really wanted from psychotherapy, but changed her mind. Instead, she asked for one million dollars in reparations for

> the women who had never been helped by the mental health professions but who had instead been further abused by them: punitively labeled, overly tranquilized, sexually seduced while in treatment, hospitalized against her will, given shock therapy, lobotomized, and above all, disliked as too "aggressive," "promiscuous," "depressed," "ugly," "old," "disgusting," or "incurable."[21]

These interventions and countless others laid the foundation for an array of impressive changes in research, teaching, and therapy. Nevertheless, despite the advances of feminism in psychiatry and psychology, men still dominate, and masculinity continues to center the notions of normality in accounts of deviance and treatment. Indeed, androcentric biases continue to shape the definitions of psychological health, the design of psychiatric drugs, and the implementation of treatment regimens. To contextualize our subsequent analysis of advertisements for psychotropic medications that fully substantiate this contention, two brief examples merit attention.

First, the diagnosis and treatment of depression remains terribly gendered, reflecting this older pattern. In the late 1970's, more than two-thirds of all psychotropic medications were dispensed to women.[22] Thirty-five years later, psychiatry and psychology have still not gotten it right. Depression remains overdiagnosed in women and underdiagnosed in men.[23] The interplays between gender and power differentials in hetero-sexual relationships and social control remain underappreciated or even ignored. Research conducted in the 1990's indicates that women are diag-nosed with depression two times more than men and that women account for approximately 70 percent of prescriptions for antidepressants.[24] At the same time, psychiatrists persist in locating women's problems in their moods, behaviors, and personalities, rather than a broader social context, searching for a cure in a bottle rather than through social change. Conse-quently, while abuse, poverty, marriage, children, and unequal pay all play a major role, too often women are blamed, stigmatized, and treated for "their" problems.[25] And medication turns attention away from the great need for fair and equal wages, equal status in society, and more responsive husbands.

Second, professional discourse about antidepressants, along with its underlying assumptions, appears to have had an impact on popular notions of women's mental status. Indeed, in a study of media reporting on psy-chotropic medications over a 15-year period, Jonathan Metzl and Joni Angel found not only a multitude of conditions attributed to women, including depressive disorders associated with menstruation and childbirth, but also that the focus, language, and images of the 261 articles was marked by gen-der differences. Women were more likely to be the subjects of the media accounts of depression and its treatment, appearing in such stories twice as often as men. Moreover, whereas women were depicted in emotional terms, including "feeling down," "never feeling happy," "crying," and "overwhelmed by sadness," men were presented in relation to their work or as suffering from a biochemical condition. Two concurrences are strik-ing here. First, media coverage connects depression with women, and importantly, does so at about the same rate as professional discourse does. Second, the popular accounts, like those found in more professional con-texts, rely on gendered expectations to describe individuals suffering from depression, reinforcing the rigid and sexist cultural categories. Together, these findings demonstrate the interplay of scientific or clinical interpre-tations, and mainstream or mundane understandings. In turn, they under-score the persistent and prominent force of sexism in both domains, a force that privileges men by celebrating their experiences and perspective, and pathologizes women by devaluing their experiences and marginalizing their perspectives.[26]

With these examples and this broader historical background in mind, we turn our attention to the marketing of psychotropic medication. Reading ads for drugs designed to improve mental functioning clarifies the articulations of gender and normality in Psychotropia.

Selling Gender

Advertising is arguably better suited than psychiatry to construct notions of normality and understandings of gender. Indeed, although it is often dismissed as trivial noise that consumers become adept at tuning out, advertising saturates daily life. Inescapable and invasive, corporate messages have come to play a key role in structuring who we are, what we desire, how we know and present our selves, how we regard and relate to others, and increasingly how we conceive of not simply the good life, but the shape of democracy and the contours of public life. Consequently, we cannot think of advertising, especially for psychotropic medications, as exclusively informational, unimportant, or instrumental; and only at our peril as social analysts and engaged citizens would we conceive of it as mere fantasy, somehow separable from "the a real" affairs of the world. Advertising, as countless studies have shown, reflects and reinforces cultural expectations and prevailing understandings of self and society.[27] Importantly, as a set of social texts, it simultaneously fosters desires (to smell good, look attractive, or be cool) and highlights deficiencies (bad breath, obesity, or awkwardness). It thrives on the production of insecurity, the persistent insinuation of inadequacy and imperfection. Not surprisingly, given the limited attention spans of consumers as well as economic and media constraints, advertising relies on cultural clichés and sexist stereotypes in order to package and sell "normality." It is a therapeutic discourse that promises to make consumers happy: buying a given product (whether it is deodorant, a diet supplement, a new car, or an anti-anxiety drug) will improve one's image, stature, health, comfort, relationships, and so on. Importantly, because, as our forgoing discussion noted, women are understood to be supplementary, lacking, and abnormal vis-à-vis the masculine norm, they more frequently become the targets of marketers. At its core, then, advertising pivots around normality and how to secure it, reminding consumers of what they lack or the ways in which they are abnormal.

As a consequence, advertising is perfectly positioned to construct psychological conditions in gendered terms meaningful to the broader public and to pitch medications as desirable remedies.[28] In this section, we offer an overview of the ways in which the marketing of drugs designed to alleviate depression and anxiety has enrolled gender for its own ends, unpacking the content of ads to highlight their reliance on sexist stereotypes.

For the past 50 years, advertisements for psychotropic drugs have pathologized women.[29] Importantly, as society has changed, so too have women been increasingly targeted as deviant and in need of medication.[30] Initially, marketers targeted married women, blaming them for the problems befalling men and mainstream society. Ads pictured them overwhelming and domineering; or, as one Valium ad suggests, hostile, enraged, and threatening before treatment, then calm and composed, back to normal as it were once medicated.[31] Later, in the wake of the second wave of feminism, as moral concerns and social debates shifted, single women became the focus of psychotropic advertising. Their difficulties and deviance were connected to their failure to conform and the absence of men.[32] More recently, a new era of psychopharmacology, inaugurated with the release of Prozac, joined with a number of social alterations, including a marked increase in dual career families, the multiplication of women's roles, a backlash against feminism, the myth of the superwoman, and upwardly mobile women who desired (or were told to desire) having it all (husband, kids, and career), to change the tone and themes of pharmaceutical marketing once again.[33] We analyze three representative ads, all of which appeared in the *American Journal of Psychiatry,* to illustrate the messages and myths used to sell psychotropic medications to and through women.[34]

First, an ad for Paxil centers on the face of a woman with eyes downcast, portrayed in a manner reminiscent of portrait photography. The accompanying text reads: "She's anxious. She's agitated. She can't sleep. She's depressed." The text works in two ways. First, it transforms moods into a clinical condition. Surely, being anxious or agitated need not lead to the inference that one suffers from depression, but the ad uses labeling to make this the logical conclusion. Second, the ad takes the woman out of context. She is little more than a face and four sentences. The reader has no knowledge of what makes her agitated or if that is unreasonable. Perhaps she cannot sleep because of stress at work or conflicts with a teenager, both of which would seem to be legitimate, if not healthy, feelings.

Another ad for Paxil focuses on the beaming face of a young and attractive woman, who smile over her shoulder at the reader. The text announces in big, bold letters, "I Can." The inset images running down the right side of the ad indicate the conditions the drug alleviates: it allows those who are depressed to have a successful and happy heterosexual relationship; those who suffer from social anxiety disorder can be excel at work; those beset by panic disorder can face life's challenges; and those with obsessive compulsive disorder can establish joyful, carefree friendships. Together, these images suggest women are lacking, unable, abnormal. Paxil enables them, granting them agency. It makes them competent. Much like Nike's "Just do it!" campaign, this ad suggests a false sense of power, which here is not only individualized and decontextualized, but also drug dependent. Finally, taking Paxil will allow women to resume their proper gender roles, tending to their interpersonal relationship and nurturing others as society expects of them.

Finally, consider an advertisement for Effexor. Amid graphs attesting to the drug's efficacy is a picture of woman in a business suit and groceries embracing a young boy. The accompanying caption, written to imitate the crayon scrawl of a preschooler, proclaims, "I got my mommy back!" Again, we have no context. We can surmise that the woman was for a time a bad mother and that Effexor made her better, that is allowed her to recommence caring for family. We can infer, moreover, that the drug has returned balance and order to a life thrown out of whack. Finally, we can take comfort in the fact that taking the medication restored the propriety of heterosexuality and middle class domesticity.

Significantly, these ads have much in common. They all focus on the problems of women, particularly career women. They postulate that it is something about the individual that is out of balance or abnormal, turning attention away from social context. And, they suggest that the pathological conditional afflicting these women can be treated with a specific medication which promises to restore normality to them.

Making a Market

Cultural expectations have not simply shaped the content of psychotropic advertising, they have imprinted the conception and construction of markets as well. Sarafem offers a clear illustration of this pattern. In 2001, Eli Lilly released Sarafem to treat Premenstrual Dysphoric Disorder (PMDD), a condition first included in the *Diagnostic Statistical Manual (DSM)*, the authoritative catalog of psychiatric disorders regularly criticized over the past 30 years as biased against women and furthering social control, in 1998. It refers to a set of symptoms occurring monthly, approximately a week before menstruation, including symptoms like fatigue, bloating, change of appetite, breast tenderness, anxiety, anger, irritability, and depression. By some estimates, three to ten percent of women suffer from PMDD.[35] Sarafem and its marketing were unique in at least two ways. First, to secure a hold among prescribing physicians, Eli Lilly pitched it almost exclusively to obstetricians and gynecologists, not psychiatrists, granting the former a novel specialization in women's mental health. Second, the pharmaceutical giant employed direct-to-consumer (DTC) ads, encouraging them to ask their doctor for a prescription, if it seemed right for them.

Sarfem was new and different in another way as well: to create Sarfem and treat the new condition PMDD, Eli Lilly repackaged Prozac, designing a pink and purple capsule to capture their new market. The use of traditionally feminine colors to hail women is noteworthy for the ways in which it enrolls gendered expectations. One cannot imagine the use of the color pink to market a medication for erectile dysfunction. In choosing the color scheme, Eli Lilly explicitly gendered Sarfem, playing off the very deep connection between color and gender that begins at birth and shapes the marking and making of acceptable identities, appropriate attire and self presentation, and inhabitable spaces. This choice, moreover, directs our attention to centrality of sexist ideologies and gendered inequalities to the meanings and marketing of Sarfem, and psychotropic medications more generally.

Sarfem proved controversial from the start, in part because linking women's mental health to their reproductive cycles historically has disenfranchised them.[36] Moreover, from the start, the new drug fostered radically different reactions among women — some of whom immediately and vocally criticized it, while others welcomed it as a recognition of their previously invisible suffering — because of how social (mis)conceptions and gender hierarchies encourage women to interpret how their menstrual cycles affect them.[37] Of equal importance, Sarfem sparked controversy for the manner in which it revealed the changing shape of Psychotropia. Not only had Eli Lilly opted to target consumers directly, no doubt in hopes of inciting consumer demand, but they unveiled Sarfem only months before its exclusive rights to the patent for fluoxetine (the active agent in Prozac) expired. In effect, the new drug was meant to extend the multinational corporation's place in a lucrative market, just as health management organizations, consumers, and physicians would opt for cheaper, unbranded drugs.

Marketing Sarfem hinged on the establishment of PMDD as a recognized condition. In 1993, the board of experts responsible for assembling the *DSM* opted not to place PMDD in the main body of the work, but relegated it to the appendix. Five years later, the same group conclude it was an organic condition, integrating it into the body of text. While changes in research findings, pressure from Eli Lilly, and economic factors arguably played a role in this process, we think two other factors are at work here. On the one hand, this entailed multiplication and division: it required "a market logic that splits, rather than groups, illness. This splitting complicates the idea that a person's relationship to a drug is really her/his body's relationship to a chemical compound."[38] Increasingly, social issues, especially identity construction and ideological constructs, such as gender, shape understanding of conditions and the creation of treatments for them. On the other hand, the long history of pathologizing women's bodies and feelings, particularly in connection to their reproductive cycles, surely contributed to this as well, precisely because women are always already suspect, understood as deviant and abnormal because they menstruate. Nash and Chrisler found that the use of the label Episodic Dysphoric Disorder, rather than Premenstrual Dysphoric Disorder, made it less likely that participants would deem changes associated with menstruation as problematic for women. Moreover,

> The premenstrual label did not influence women's perception of their own menstrual changes but made them more likely to attach a psychiatric label to women they knew who had the symptoms. Men had a more negative response to symptoms when they were associated with the menstrual cycle than with a more gender-neutral label.[39]

Clearly, gendering the condition as PMDD stigmatizes women, reflecting and reinforcing psychiatric conceptions and public understandings of them. Parallel questions and conditions for men are unthinkable in the current configuration of Psychotropia.

Advertisements for Sarafem suggest that women's biological cycles cause them to act irrationally, confirming widely held stereotypes about the emotionality of menstruating women. Television spots for the psychotropic medication depict an agitated woman struggling to button her pants, another struggling to take a shopping cart, a third snapping at her partner, and finally a woman sobbing uncontrollably on the couch. All closed with the tag phrase, "Sarafem — More like the woman you are." Pathologizing women, these ads perpetuate a broader set of ideological associations that deflect attention away from social hierarchies and their asymmetrical impacts on women. They delegitimate women's reasonable responses to the world around them, including work situations that often grant them little freedom or control, the burdens of working "the second shift," the responsibility to nurture familial relationships and affective networks. Worse, they imply that women are biologically inferior, subject to their hormonal and reproductive cycles.

Recoding Psychotropic Marketing

If advertising is the language of consumer culture, providing the grammar and vocabulary out of which individuals formulate self and society, then it should come as little surprise that many consumers express their discontent and distaste through the medium and its message. They actively create new ads, deface existing ads, and otherwise play around with marketing texts in an effort to unsettle their means and meanings. Advertisements for psychotropic drugs have proven to be an especially fecund resource for cultural critics. Consumers regularly responded to pharmaceutical marketing through spontaneous remarks, playful jokes and songs, organized movements to end psychiatry, while taking pride in "madness," and more formal commentaries in blogs and Internet forums. Importantly, they also do more than talk back to big pharmaceuticals, actively recoding advertising images and the broader cultural context which brings them to life. Two forms of consumer resistance merit detailed discussion: *symbolic goofing*, or the creation of artwork, often through the alteration or defacement of original corporate texts, to parody drug advertising, thus clarifying and contesting its meanings; and *culture jamming*, a more elaborate and arguably active critique of consumer culture that employs juxtaposition, pastiche, deconstruction, and reframing to illuminate dominant practices and precepts to theorize healthy relationships between self and society, and to make linkages between seemingly discrete registers of experience and significance.

Symbolic Goofing

For many consumers, corporate messages about psychological conditions, social problems, and biochemical solutions ring hollow. In psychotropic advertising, they find counterfeit images that misrepresent self and society. In response, some consumers playfully recode the marketing of drugs designed to combat depression and anxiety. They may write over ads for existing pharmaceuticals or invent novel products or fictional ads. These false advertisements subvert corporate intentions, endeavoring to make the truth of Psychotropia evident to a broader audience. Although it is impossible to know the prevalence of spoof ads, searches of the Internet revealed nearly a dozen examples of false advertising. Prozac, likely because of its prominence, is the most common target, but Xanax, Sarafem, and Zoloft receive critical treatment as well. These mock marketing texts range from self-contained creative commentaries to more elaborate marketing campaigns. Importantly, half of the spoofs activate gender to make plain the contours of Psychotropia as they make fun of the marketing animating it.

Although all parodies of psychotropic medications call them into question, some of them limit themselves to the conception and execution of pharmaceutical marketing. One such spoof promotes a fake drug, Fukitol. "The all-purpose lifestyle pharmaceutical," according to its Web site, would hit the market in May 2005, enjoying the success of products like Viagra. Given the invented scientific name "fukalthanol eutopiata," Fukitol was rendered as a blue and white capsule, emblazoned with a brand on one side and a series of three emoticons, progressing from a sad face to a happy face, on the other side. The new wonder drug is pitched in crass, if gender neutral, terms, marked by short sentences and profanity that refer to universal problems:

Depressed?	Family Problems?
Over Worked?	Money Worries?
Job Suck?	Well here is a pill for you!
Unappreciated?	When Life just Blows ... FUKITOL!

The parody derives its humor from the manner in which it mirrors and exaggerates ads for actual psychotropic medications. It outlines a series of commonplace problems, rather than psychological conditions, that can make life unbearable, proposing itself as the simple solution. In essence, the fabrication of Fukitol and the marketing scheme play with accepted conventions of pharmaceutical advertising to critique them, endeavoring to expose the absurdity of psychotropia through humor and hyperbole.[40]

Another creative critique invents Prozac-Pez. With a decidedly retro feel, a smiling woman in pillbox hat and smock akin to that worn by "cigarette girls" in the 1940's and 1950's extends a Pez container dispensing a pill. The caption below asks, "Ready to be happy?" The ad for the fictitious product works (to the extent that it does) because of how it highlights misgivings about the dispensing and consumption of psychotropic medication. Specifically, the comparison of Prozac and Pez suggest that such drugs have become like candy, a sweet, acceptable, and easily accessible, not to mention digestible, indulgence.[41]

In a similar fashion, the parody "Kellogg's Prozac Pills," juxtaposes two distinct brands (Kellogg's Frosted Flakes and Prozac) and two seemingly separate consumer worlds (breakfast cereal and pharmaceuticals). The recoded box features a bowl of Prozac, Tony the Tiger about to eat a big spoonful of Prozac pills, exclaiming "They're G-r-r-eat," and an inset promising an action figure of Courtney Love, former lead singer of the grunge band Hole, notorious for her drug abuse. The mock product subverts the codes of Psychotropia in at least three ways. First, the heaping bowl of pills questions the consumption of Prozac, critiquing its sheer size and ubiquity. Second, in common with the ad for Prozac-Pez, it connects psychotropic drugs with a product aimed at kids. Finally, the inclusion of Courtney Love links illicit and excessive drug use with more accepted forms.[42]

A more ambiguous spoof of Prozac centers on a domestic scene, a nuclear family in a kitchen cluttered with stuff. The son, in the foreground, searches for something in an overstocked refrigerator, while his sister opens a container of food. Behind her, but at the center of the image, the parents talk, perhaps even argue across the kitchen island. A simple catchphrase encapsulates the scene: "You'd kill them without it." Clearly, the celebrated medication brings stability to world out of balance, making life livable as it blunts destructive impulses. Unfortunately, this implied critique of the use of psychotropic drugs to contain socially unacceptable emotions fails to identify who needs medication, and thus limits its effectiveness.[43]

Whereas this reframing of Prozac offers a rather generic critique of the social construction of emotion, normality, and relationships, another take on the prominent drug renders a more focused and penetrating commentary. Referencing an era of domesticity before the second wave of feminism and the familiar look of the Tide laundry detergent box, this spoof presents a woman in a dress, apron and heels celebrating, if not embracing, "Prozac Mood Brightener." The bright orange box promises the consumer a "New Improved Life!" and to "wash your blues away!" The parody interrogates the logic underlying psychotropic medications, implying that they not only simplify self and society, but make an equation between mental health and sin, promising to cleanse one's soul and enhance quality of life. Moreover, it explicitly challenges the centrality of gender to Psychotropia as it links Prozac to domesticity, femininity, and (the alleviation of) deviance.[44]

Similarly, *The Onion*, a satirical newspaper, announced a new ad campaign for Zoloft, "Zoloft for everything." A mock ad accompanying the story centers on a woman, head in her hands, and asks, "Dishes piling up in the sink?" The spoof quotes a spokesperson for Pfizer, "Zoloft has always helped clinically depressed people ... now Zoloft can help anyone who needs their emotions leveled off. Do you find yourself feeling excited or sad? No one should have to suffer through those harrowing peaks and valleys." In response, the story continues, Eli Lilly was set to launch a new campaign of its own, "Pot roast burnt? Husband home with the flu? You're having one of those Prozac days." Importantly, while the absurdity of the ad questions Psychotropia generally, it offers a clear critique of the ways in which gender roles shape expectations of normality and the marketing of drugs to achieve it.[45]

Even more provocative is a parody of Sarafem. A false ad for the fictional Super Sarafem seeks to problematize the way in which its namesake targets women, questioning the legitimacy of Premenstrual Dysphoric Disorder and the associated abnormality it projects onto women. "Think it's PMS? Think again... It could be CBDD (Crazy Bitch Delusional Disorder)." In place of medical jargon, it invokes the profane encapsulations often employed to describe and dismiss behaviors deemed unfeminine and hence deviant. As forceful as this recoding of Sarafem is, the accompanying imagery complicates its critique, rendering it ambivalent. At the center of the spoof, below the tagline, is an image meant to convey euphoria, but which actually conjures a clichéd heterosexist fantasy: two beautiful women, tongues extended, kiss blissfully. Moreover, the noted side effects of Super Sarafem include "extreme euphoria that can result in lesbian behavior." At best, these references to lesbianism suggest that Super Sarafem so successfully restores normality that it transforms the women who take it into the ultimate male fantasy, hyper-feminine, conforming to all masculine desires socially and sexually. At worst, they completely undermine the parody's effort to critique the making and marketing of Sarafem as a patriarchal, heterosexist drug.[46]

Other artists link patriarchy and neo-conservativism. Three parodies enroll First Lady Laura Bush in their commentaries on Psychotropia. The first ad features a beaming Bush in a naval uniform congratulated by another, equally jubilant, older woman; it reads, "You're First Lady Now ... and XANAX helped you get there!"[47] The second ad again centers on a smiling Bush, accompanied by text: "Prozac gets me through a day with George. Stock up Today!"[48] And a third ad reworks an iconic World War II era poster to mock a Bush administration's statement that queried, If people are not happy with their jobs why don't they find new ones or go on Prozac? The original image features a woman (Rosie the Riveter) rolling up her sleeves and flexing her muscles under the banner, "We can do it!"[49] Literally defacing this familiar image, "Gregory" has pasted the Zoloft emoticon over the women's face and altered the call to arms, which now reads "We can't do it!" These spoofs all make explicit connections between particular politics and specific formulations of womanhood, insisting that the only way in which they are possible is if one is medicated.

False advertising affords consumers an opportunity to talk back to the seemingly impervious structures of Psychotropia. Its reliance on humor is a weapon to unsettle corporate messages and unveil hidden meanings.

Consequently, its fictions speak truths often inaudible in other forms or contexts. Finally, false advertising may give hope that in a moment of retrenchment and backlash, an understanding of gender hierarchies lives, perhaps even thrives, as a kind of popular feminism.

Culture Jamming

Consumer resistance to psychotropic marketing has not been limited to the charged humor that animates parody ads. It also has taken more fully theorized and overtly political forms. The creative and critical work associated with *Adbusters* exemplifies this emergent set of strategies.[50] Dubbing itself the "Journal of the Mental Environment" and the headquarters for "cultural revolution," *Adbusters* has undertaken an ambitious, informative, and often engaging project: subvert and transform the ideological and institutional foundation of modern society. The periodical has long taken active stands against consumer culture, especially the manner in which it destroys the environment and dehumanizes people through artificial desires, the management of the normal life, and distorted visions of the state of the world. More recently, in the wake of 9/11, it has vigorously sought to challenge American imperialism, the contradictions of "the war on terror," and the propaganda disguising the violence of the media, multinational conglomerates, and the military. It seeks to expose and undermine the workings of these semiotic and structural forces within its pages, on the World Wide Web, and through direct reader action, what it often calls "culture jamming."[51] The magazine employs commentaries and essays, photomontages, artwork, letters from readers, collage, news clippings, and juxtaposition to call into question taken-for-granted beliefs and behaviors. For instance, an image of a Nike swoosh at the bottom of toilet bowl might alert readers to the absurdity and ubiquity of branding; the juxtaposition of a Euro American girl and her American Girl doll wearing the same outfit with a young Palestinian boy in fatigues and a loaded AK-47 forces readers to think about the norms of childhood and the relativity of values; the counterposing of images of Josef Stalin and Bill Gates, bearing the captions "Big Brother" and "Little Brother" respectively, complicate accepted wisdom about freedom and social control; and an image of Vice President Dick Cheney retouched with a crude mustache and the phrase "Got Oil?" written in oil on his forehead raises unsettling questions about government-corporate relations no less than the future of oil reserves and the natural world more generally. At the same time, it has also created a number of creative ways for citizens to politicize consumption, such as "Buy Nothing Day" and "Turn off Your TV Week."

Importantly, for our purposes, *Adbusters* has also actively interrogated the pharmaceutical industry, especially its making and marketing of psychotropic drugs. To this end, it regularly runs commentaries and image montages and created a Web site to give consumers a voice.[52] One recent issue offers a nice encapsulation of how the periodical engages with and recodes psychotropic advertising. Specifically, issue 51 of *Adbusters*, titled "Systematically Distorted Information" and featuring hole at the center of each page, contains three "texts" that showcase the use of pastiche and juxtaposition to recode pharmaceutical ads.[53]

The first reprints a Lexapro ad, originally appearing in *Psychiatric Annals*. A slightly blurred image of woman's face, rendered in black and white, occupies the much of the page. She looks slightly downward, away from the reader, while the hole running through the center of the magazine becomes one her eyes. The original ad copy remains at the top of the image, a ruler marked with phrases conveying abnormality: "Too tired to exercise," "Feeling sad," and "Missed work again." A branch from a flowering tree has been overlayed in the bottom right corner. At the very top of the page, above the image, a phrase, highlighted and underlined in red, has been pasted in — "the world is under a great siege of hegemonic control in intellectual, political, and social thinking." At first blush, the collage seems to offer a critical reading of corporate psychopharmacology and its logic, namely that it is assaulting true and natural responses and emotions as encourages consumers to seek solace in chemical solutions. Complicating this reading is where the highlighted clipping takes the viewer's eye: it carries the reader to the facing page, to a highlighted passage in a longer commentary on George W. Bush, situated beneath the image of two United States soldiers whisking a suspect down the cereal aisle of a brightly lit grocery store. Where these texts meet is a more totalizing critique: big pharma and its marketing of antidepressants is connected up to more pervasive forms of violence, specifically the war in Iraq, the security and sensations demand by consumer capital, and the policing of transgression whether that be an unruly brown body over there or deviant emotions in middle class (female) minds.

Second, about 40 pages later, an equally startling use of collage and intertextuality appears. In this case, an ad for Paxil, from the *Journal of Clinical Psychiatry*, is introduced. It shows the devastating effects of social anxiety disorder on a young man, disabled in love and career — "I just can't." Paxil of course promises to alleviate his problem. This straightforward ad is complicated in two ways. On the one hand, it bears a passage from a reader's letter,

I awoke early one morning to a new doormat, mysteriously placed on the front porch. Good quality, thick weave, designed with a funky red circle and sharp, lower case letters reading "happy inside." Attached was a postcard from Target. Apparently, I could visit their store for many more wonderful items for my home. Everyone in the neighborhood woke up to the same doormat. Corporate America has announced that we are happy inside. It's official.

This experience makes an ironic comment on the hollowness of consumption, either of products or pharmaceutical: both promise to make one happy inside, but both are false promises made by corporations. Second, facing the reprinted and defaced Paxil ad are three letters from consumers. Each speaks from personal experience about the harms associated with taking psychotropics, including blunted personality, weight game, loss of true self, capitulation to commercial design, conformity, and the naturalness of discomfort. These voices destabilize the perfection and promise of the ad, subverting its capacity to control the message or heal the body.

Finally, a recent ad for Ritalin, showing two young students happily walking the school steps, expounds on how the drug improves attention and performance at school. It is strategically placed under an excerpt from *The Slow Poisoning of America*.[54] The passage describes the dangers of "industrial food additives":

kids take in toxins every time we thoughtlessly open a package of luncheon meat or serve up diet soda. Small daily doses add up, causing children's bodies to break down and succumb, in increasing numbers to attention deficit disorder, asthma, juvenile diabetes, gastric intestinal disease, obesity, allergies and cancer.

Clearly, the juxtaposition connects things many would prefer to keep separate—food additives, eating habits, and psychotropic medications that help people—to underscore the risk of using any of them.

These three ads share in common the use of juxtaposition and pastiche to reframe and problematize the product, its use, and the marketing of it. This kind of activist engagement with advertising clearly has great potential to unsettle their preferred readings, precisely because they make connections simultaneously to broader social forces (many of which have painful associations and consequences) and to the oppositional voices of consumers. Importantly, glaringly absent from *Adbusters'* interventions around psychotropic advertising—and culture, representation, consumption, and change generally—are questions of gender, race, and sexuality. Ads for antidepressant and anti-anxiety drugs do important work in constructing the normal, the good life, the consuming self detached from nature and society, the happy and healthy individual, all themes central to the magazine's political program; however, the marketing of these phar-maceuticals, as we have shown throughout this paper, pivots around tar-geting and pathologizing women. Consequently, for culture jamming with its very serious play and ironic subversions to make a difference, it must deploy and deconstruct the work of masculinity and femininity in these ads and their construction of normality. Otherwise, they just become one more phallocentric discourse that ignores women and their concerns, and hence, cannot include or benefit them.

Conclusions

We wish to close this paper with one final instance of satire. In the early 1990's, feminist therapist Paula Caplan proposed a new psychiatric diag-nosis, Delusional Dominating Personality Disorder (DDPD).[55] This perva-sive condition overwhelmingly afflicts men and is readily discernible to a trained professional:

> The presence of any one of the following delusions: (a) the delusion of per-sonal entitlement to the services of (1) any woman with whom one is person-ally associated, (2) females in general for males in general, (3) both of the above; (b) the delusion that women like to suffer and be ordered around; (c) the delusion that physical force is the best method for solving interpersonal problems; (d) the delusion of that sexual and aggressive impulses are uncon-trollable in (1) oneself, (2) males in general, (3) both of the above; (e) the delusion that pornography and erotica are identical...
> A distorted approach to sexuality, displaying itself in one or both of these ways: (a) a pathological need for flattery about one's sexual performance and/or the size of one's genitalia; (b) an infantile tendency to equate large breasts on women with their sexual attractiveness.
> A tendency to feel inordinately threatened by women who fail to disguise their intelligence.[56]

Caplan's ironic intervention underscores two fundamental features of Psy-chotropia: (1) gender animates the manufacture of madness and the means to alleviate it, no less than the marketing of conditions and their cures reviewed herein; and (2) any transformation of this complex, that wishes to be something other than a humorous aside or stylish trangression, must interrogate, unpack and unsettle the ways in which Psychotropia (ab)uses and (mis)understands women.

Marianne Marsh offers a helpful outline of an alternative, what she terms "feminist psychopharmacology," and how it might accomplish in its engagements and rearrangements with the symbolic and structural con-tours of Psychotropia.[57] Marsh calls for an approach to psychiatry that is attentive to context and history, aware of power, and interested in those it serves. Collaborative, empathetic, and transformative, her approach works against the prevailing model of psychiatry, refusing its commitments to hierarchy, pathology, and the status quo. Indeed, feminist psychopharmacology, according to Marsh, endeavors, at root, to empower and validate. Presently, both the corporate messages and professional discourse anchoring psychotropia disempower and invalidate women. If cultural critics and consumers, not to mention mainstream psychiatric professionals and advertising executives, were to embrace these principles, they could truly disrupt the marketing of psychotropic medications, revealing it to be a series of false advertisements harming women.

When we set out on this project, we were certain in finding a plethora of psychotropic ads in mainstream print media. To our surprise, this did not play out. Yet, what we discovered actually supports our premise. Psychopharmacolgy, psychiatry, and the psychology of advertising coexist in a dependent relationship within patriarchal processes.

Notes

1. Peter D. Kramer, *Listening to Prozac: A Psychiatrist Explores Antidepressant Drugs and the Remaking of the Self* (New York: Viking, 1993), p. 39.

2. Irene Duma, "How Prozac Saved My Marriage," *Happy Woman Magazine* (2000), <http://www.happywomanmagazine.com/Features/Prozac.htm> (viewed February 15, 2005).

3. Lawrence C. Rubin, communication with author, March 15, 2005.

4. Aldous Huxley, *Brave New World* (New York: Perennial Classics, 1998).

5. Erving Goffman, *Asylums* (New York: Anchor, 1961).

6. See for example, Thomas Szasz, *The Manufacture of Madness* (New York: Harper and Row, 1970); and Thomas Szasz, *The Myth of Mental Illness*, revised ed. (New York: Harper and Row, 1974).

7. See for example, Michel Foucault, *The History of Sexuality* (New York: Pantheon, 1977).

8. Elizabeth Wurtzel, *Prozac Nation: Young and Depressed in America* (New York: Houghton Mifflin, 1994).

9. Ibid., p. 297.

10. Carla Spartos, "Sarafem Nation: Renamed Prozac Targets Huge Market: Premenstrual Women," *Village Voice*, December 6–12, 2000.

11. Tina Brown, "Paxil Americana," *Salon Online Magazine*, May 15, 2003, <http://www.salon.com/opinion/brown/2003/05/15/pill> (viewed March 1, 2005). (archived)

12. Jonathan M. Metzl, "Introspections: Angela," *American Journal of Psychiatry* 159, no. 10 (2002), pp. 1665–1666.

13. Benjamin Riley, "Letter," *Adbusters*, July/August 2002, p. 42.

14. Found in Mary Crawford and Rhoda Unger, *Women and Gender: A Feminist Psychology*, 3rd ed. (New York: McGraw-Hill, 1997), p. 548.

15. Hope Landrine, "Revising the Framework of Abnormal Psychology," in Phyllis

Bronstein and Kathryn Quina, eds., *Teaching a Psychology of People* (Washington, D.C.: APA Press, 1988), pp. 37–44.

16. Jessica Heriot, "The Double Bind: Healing the Split," in *Women Changing Therapy: New Assessments, Values and Strategies in Feminist Therapy* (New York: Haworth Press, 1983).

17. Elaine Showalter, *The Female Malady: Women, Madness, and English Culture, 1830–1980* (New York: Pantheon Books, 1985).

18. Crawford and Under, op. cit.

19. Paula Caplan, *They Say You're Crazy: How the World's Most Power Psychiatrists Decide Who's Normal* (Reading, Massachusetts: Addison-Wesley, 1995), p. 169.

20. Jill A. Cermele, Sharon Daniels, and Kristin L. Anderson, "Defining Normal: Constructions of Race and Gender in the DSM-IV Casebook," *Feminism and Psychology* 11, no. 2 (2001), pp. 229–247.

21. Phyllis Chesler, *Women and Madness* (New York: Harcourt, Brace, and Jovanovich, 1989), p. xvii.

22. Cheryl B. Travis, *Women and Health: Mental Health Issue* (Hillsdale, New Jersey.: Erlbaum, 1988).

23. June Sprock and Carol Y. Yoder, "Women and Depression: An Update on the Report of the APA Task Force," *Sex Roles* 36 (1997), pp. 269–303.

24. E. McGrath, G.P. Keita, B.R. Strickland, and N.F. Russo, *Women and Depression: Risk Factors and Treatment Issues* (Washington, D.C.: American Psychological Association, 1990). See a summary of these findings here: <http://www.apa.org/ppo/issues/pwomenanddepress.html>.

25. See Mcgrath et al.; Frank D. Fincham, et al., "Marital Satisfaction and Depression: Different Causal Relationships for Men and Women?" *Psychological Science* 8 (1997), pp. 351–357.

26. Jonathan M. Metzl and Joni Angel, "Assessing the Impact of SSRI Anti-Depressants on Popular Notions of Women's Depressive Illness," *Social Science and Medicine* 58, no. 3 (2004), pp. 577–584.

27. See for example Anthony J. Cortese, *Provocateur: Images of Women and Minorities in Advertising* (Lanham, Maryland: Rowman and Littlefield, 2004).

28. Paula Gardner, "Distorted Packaging: Marketing Depression as Illness, Drugs as Cure," *Journal of Medical Humanities* 24, no. 1/2 (2003), pp. 105–130.

29. Jonathan M. Metzl, *Prozac on the Couch: Prescribing Gender in the Era of Wonder Drugs* (Durham: Duke University Press, 2003); see also Wanda Leppard, Shirley Matlie Ogletree, and Emily Wallen, "Gender Stereotyping in Medical Advertising: Much Ado About Something," *Sex Roles* 29, no. 11/12 (1993), pp. 829–838.

30. Metzl, op. cit.

31. Jonathan Metzl, "Mother's Little Helper: The Crisis of Psychoanalysis and the Miltown Revolution," *Gender and History* 15, no. 2 (2003), pp. 240–267.

32. Ibid.

33. Linda M. Blum and Nena F. Stracuzzi, "Gender in the Prozac Nation: Popular Discourse and Productive Feminism," *Gender and Society* 18, no. 3 (2004), pp. 269–283; Elizabeth Ettorre and Elianne Riska, *Gendered Moods: Psychotropics and Society* (New York: Routledge, 1995); Jonathan M. Metzl, "Selling Sanity Through Gender: The Psychodynamics of Psychotropics Advertising," *Journal of Medical Humanities* 24, no. 1/2 (2003), pp. 79–103; Sarah E.P. Munce, Emma K. Robertson, Stephanie N. Sansom, and Donna E. Stewart, "Who Is Portrayed in Psychotropic Drug Advertisements?" *The Journal of Nervous and Mental Disease* 192, no. 4 (2004), pp. 284–288; Jacquelyn Zita, *Prozac Feminism in Body Talk* (New York: Columbia University Press, 1998), pp. 61–79.

34. See Christina Hanganu-Bresh, "Advertising Depression: The Case of Paxil," for

examples discussed and for a sharp analysis that informs our own. Available online at <http://www.tc.umn.edu/~hana001/cccc.htm>.

35. Spartos, op. cit.

36. Emily Martin, *The Woman in the Body: A Cultural Analysis of Reproduction* (Boston: Beacon, 1987).

37. See Spartos, op. cit.

38. Nathan Greenslit, "Pharmaceutical Branding: Identity, Individuality, and Illness," *Molecular Interventions* 2 (2002), p. 343.

39. Quoted in Crawford and Unger, op. cit., p. 534.

40. Available online at <http://www.newhumanist.com.fukitol.html>. (archived)

41. Avaliable online at <http://www.sachsreport.com/>. (archived)

42. Available online at <http://parody.organique.com/images/zac.jpg>.

43. Available online at <http://adbusters.org/spoofads/prozac.jpg>. (archived)

44. Available online at <http://www.worth1000.com/entries/65500/65903pvXT_w.jpg>.

45. Available online at <http://open-eyes.org/cgi-bin/printableMessage.cgi?boardID=1&topicID=14&messageID=2474>.

46. Available online at <http://www.jokersupdates.com/archives/bb3ads/phin/phin_03_supersarafem.jpg>.

47. Available online at <http://www.newhumanist.com/xanax.html>. (archived)

48. Available online at <http://www.allhatnocattle.net/laura%20prozac.jpg>.

49. Available online at <http://www.leadpencil.net/blog/archives/2004_07.html>.

50. See Christine Harold, "Pranking Rhetoric: 'Culture Jamming' as Media Activism," *Critical Studies in Media Communication* 21, no. 3 (2004), pp. 189–211; Joseph D. Rumbo, "Consumer Resistance in a World of Advertising Clutter: The Case of Adbusters," *Psychology and Marketing* 19, no. 2 (2002), pp. 127–148.

51. <http://www.adbusters.org>.

52. See <http://www.prozacspotlight.org>.

53. *Adbusters* 51 (Jan./Feb. 2004). In standard *Adbuster* style, this issue lacks pagination.

54. John E. Erb and T. Michelle Erb, *The Slow Poisoning of America* (Palladin Press, 2003).

55. Paula Caplan, "Delusional Dominating Personality Disorder," *Feminism and Psychology* 1 (1991), pp. 171–174.

56. Ibid., p. 173.

57. Marianne Marsh, "Feminist Psychopharmacology: An Aspect of Feminist Psychiatry," *Women and Therapy* 16, no. 1 (1995), pp. 73–84.

Conclusion

Huxley's Prophecy

LAWRENCE C. RUBIN

> I wish there was a pill that would make everyone in my class be nice!
>
> — Zachary, age 11

Fifty years ago, Rod Serling beckoned us over the threshold tenuously separating reality from imagination into his Twilight Zone. It was a shadowy place where inner and outer realities melded imperceptibly into a menagerie of images sometimes beautiful, oftentimes frightening. Long before the advent of television and mass media, Plato beckoned us into his cave to ponder the very same distinction through an allegory that challenged our fundamental notion of reality. Now, over two thousand years later, at a crossroads that has been alternately dubbed hyperreality,[1] the postmodern era,[2] Pharmacracy[3] and the asylum that I refer to as Psychotropia, the ever-consuming public is consumed by media-based and socially constructed images of mental health and mental illness that are fueled by the machinery of free-market capitalism.

Psychotropia is not, as its name would suggest, a drug-based utopia. It is neither a place where the dialectic tension between mental health and mental illness is resolved, nor a futuristic medicalized landscape where there is a clearly labeled "pill for every ill." If anything, Pyschotropia is rather a dystopia, a shadow-opposite of an imaginary place where pills can bring inner and outer peace. As the essays in this volume have illustrated, the shadowy realities of Psychotropia, with its inherent and inescapable utopian-dystopian tension, are maintained by projections from virtually every form of modern media. Early in the twentieth century, Huxley's *Brave*

New World[4] introduced us to the miracle drug Soma, which tranquilized its citizenry into mindless conformity and equanimity. Fictional centuries later, the crew of the Federation Starship Enterprise would encounter neighboring planet-societies kept in seeming symbiotic balance by a drug called "Felicium," the so-called "cure."[5] In the present day, the pharmaceutical, media and advertising industries are seemingly driven by a perverse prime directive,[6] to seek out and discover mental (and physical) illnesses and then to develop medicinal treatments for them. Approaching food qua psychotropic substance, Phillip Vannini likened this process to "schizophrenic capitalism," or consumerism gone wild.

Psychotropia is now a place of uncertainty and illusion where the boundary between illness and well-being is fabricated, and where cure is relative rather than definitive. The potential consumers of these drugs— both adult and, as Mike Brody points out, children and their parents— are recruited from the legions of consumers of media: television, popular music, movies, print and the World Wide Web. Through explicit, implicit, and even perhaps subliminal promises of pharmacological well-being continually hailing us, we are led to question in a McLuhanian sense whether the message is in the medicine or whether the medicine is the message.

In the not-too-distant past as William Wingfield demonstrated, the brick-and mortar asylum system and biomedicine provided us with a certain sense of clarity about the causes and treatment of both physical and mental illness. Biomedically, disease and illness are synonymous; both are objective and objectifiable. In contrast, a biocultural perspective[7] invokes, and in turn relies on, the notion of social construction of illness. This is not to say that people are not afflicted with and overcome by coronary disease, strokes and cancer, or depression, anxiety and psychosis. Nor is it suggested that these afflictions are figments of the sufferer's imagination. Simply stated, but far from over-simplification, a biocultural model presumes that disease is objective and tangible, while illness is relative to the sufferer's perceptions and expectations, which are shaped by the cultural context. Bioculturally, illness reflects the disease process of the very culture in which it emerges. One does not ask, "what is the cause of or treatment for coronary disease or depression?" but rather "what does the prevalence of these ailments reveal about the culture in which they arise?"

David Morris, a proponent of bioculturalism, suggests that "the most common causes of sickness and death in every era are influenced by the prevailing conditions of life, and in the postmodern era, mass production, consumerism, the high cost of living relative to income, immediate fixes and frenetic pace are the prevailing conditions."[8] In this sense, the illnesses in Psychotropia, particularly the psychiatric ones that have been the focus of this book (depression, anxiety, psychosis, sexual dysfunctions, ADHD, etc.) may be better understood as manifestations of societal pathology. According to Morris, "depression might be imagined as the reversal of everything our culture admires; it cancels our romance with speed, reducing the sufferer to near comatose immobility, creating a pleasureless, profitless gloom that drags down anything lighthearted and joyous. It is as if in a single illness, the do-it-all, have-it-all lifestyle of postmodernism crashes to a halt."[9]

Enter psychotropic drugs, with their power to alleviate our societal ills, by creating internal, individualized utopias, decontextualized, deconstructed and immune from cultural and societal ravages. Unfortunately, as is the case with utopian visions, these chemically reconstituted better selves are themselves illusions waiting to be revealed. According to Metzl, who discusses the relationship between Prozac and gender in what he calls the "Prozac narrative" in literature, "the very escape that these texts celebrate, the sudden lifting of a miasma through chemical cure, is incompletely sustained."[10] For Metzl, the psychotropic enhancement of self is but a castle built on the shifting sands of postmodern selfhood. The fortress of self is replaced by a chemically gated community, as Gottschalk described earlier in this volume.

Earlier quoted statistics on the proliferation of psychotropic drug use, prescriptions, and money spent on both research, development, and advertising are testament to the ever-expanding bubble that, unlike its tech-equivalent, is unlikely to burst in the near future. We may be witnessing what Smith describes as phase one in the trajectory of euphoria,[11] which is characterized by wide embrace, wild enthusiasm and high hopes in the drug's ability to cure. For Smith, however, phases two and three are characterized by growing discomfort, eventual condemnation and return to a more judicious and rational level of drug use. While the power, efficacy and safety of psychotropic drugs to transform and, in essence, save our society from itself have come into question, the bubble has not yet burst, and the romance is far from over. As long as there is gold in them thar pills, this fall from grace is not likely in the near future, and the chemically reconstructed self appears to be the ideal, at least for now. Psychotropia appears safe.

Ironically, Psychotropia is a place of our own making, born from the fear of losing our collective grasp on reality and the corresponding need for security, safety and reassurance in a complex, over-stimulating and at times dangerous society. And this society moves at breakneck speed into a technological future without anything but these mass-produced and disseminated images of the present and their projections onto the cave walls of our future. In the absence of clarity of direction, we have empowered the pharmaceutical, advertising and media industries to interpret those images for us. We have re-created in virtual form Goffman's asylum, centering ourselves in its shadowy courtyards, readily tossing the keys to a self-serving triumvirate that we ourselves have empowered. We dutifully line up at the nursing stations of our lives, mouths open and palms up in eager gestures of psychiatric supplication. We sit in waiting rooms, thumbing through glossy panacea laden publications, and shuffle through corridors fed by electronic enticements of psychotropic well-being. In our free time, we tune in and turn on to one or another form of entertainment that deepens the message of the total institution through its direct and subliminal references to psychotropic drugs. Robert Keller offered striking examples of the insidious infusion of drug references, both psychotropic and street, into mainstream musical forms. Similarly, Meredith and Ann Knieval demonstrated how the silver screen has been transformed into a panoramic electronic billboard for the pharmaceutical industry. We work side by side, silently and collusively with the media, pharmaceutical and advertising industries—our Panoptic wardens, who with our collusive permission fortify the walls of Psychotropia around us. Aware perhaps that escape is unlikely and resistance futile, we nevertheless stand at the gate, waiting for Goffman.

Notes

1. The notion of "hyper-reality" implies that mass-produced and disseminated media images have come to replace reality. See Jean Beaudrillard, "The Masses: The Implosion of the Social in the Media," *New Literary History* 16 (1985), pp. 577–589.

2. See David Morris, *Illness and Culture in the Postmodern Age* (Los Angeles, Ca.: UCLA Press, 1998) for a complete discussion of postmodernism, as it applies to the social construction of illness and treatment.

3. Literally defined as "control through medicine," "pharmacracy" is used by the author to denote a society in which commerce drives the construction of disease and treatment (medication in our case). See Thomas Szasz, *Pharmacracy: Medicine and Politics in America* (Westport, Connecticutt: Greenwood Publishing Group, 2001).

4. Aldous Huxley, *Brave New World* (Garden City, N. Y.: Sun Dial Press, 1932).

5. "Symbiosis" was the television title of an episode of *Star Trek, The Next Generation*, Paramount Pictures, 1988.

6. "Prime Directive" is a term borrowed from the *Star Trek* television and movie series to denote the overarching imperative of non-interference with the culture and societies on alien worlds.

7. Morris, op. cit.

8. Ibid., p. 51.

9. Ibid., p. 62.

10. Jonathan Metzl, "Prozac and the Pharmacokinetics of Narrative Form," *Signs: The Journal of Women in Culture and Society* 27 (2001), pp. 347–380.

11. For Smith, there are three phases in the trajectory of euphoria: phase one (initial embrace, high hopes, and wild enthusiasm about the efficacy of drugs, phase two (condemnation, undervaluation and a falling from grace) and phase three (stability, rational re-appraisal and judicious use). See Mickey Smith, "*Small Comfort: A History of the Minor Tranquilizer* (New York: Praeger, 1985).

About the Contributors

Michael Brody, M.D., is a board certified child and adult psychiatrist in private practice. He is chairman of the Television and Media Committee of the American Academy of Child and Adolescent Psychiatry and professor of American studies at the University of Maryland, where he teaches a course on Children and Television. He has given testimony to Congress, the FTC, the FCC, the Department of Commerce and the White House on such topics as the Columbine High School shooting, educational TV, the TV ratings, the V Chip and children's privacy on the Internet.

Marcie L. Gilliland is a licensed mental health counselor in Washington, where she maintains a private practice while working part-time at Washington State University. Beginning with Take Back the Night marches in Lawrence, Kansas, in the mid–1980s, she has been advocating for the mental health needs of women. As a feminist therapist, she continues to find ways to work within a traditionally patriarchal field, requiring the analysis of how gender roles impact all of us.

Simon Gottschalk, Ph.D., is associate professor of sociology at the University of Nevada, Las Vegas. He has written on the sociology of mental illness, postmodernism, youth culture, mass media, cultural studies, qualitative research methods, environmental and social psychology, and terrorism, among others. He is currently the editor of *Symbolic Interaction*.

Robert Keller is currently a Ph.D. candidate in music theory at Louisiana State University, where he is a graduate instructor of music theory. Currently, his research interests include the study of popular music.

C. Richard King, who currently teaches comparative ethnic studies at Washington State University, received his Ph.D. in anthropology from the University of Illinois. He has written extensively on the racial and gender politics of American culture. He is the author or editor of numerous books, including most recently *Native Athletes in Sport and Society* (University of Nebraska Press, 2005).

Ann Kneavel earned a Ph.D. in British literature from the University of Ottawa. Currently she is head of Arts and Sciences at Goldey-Beacom College, Wilmington, Delaware, focusing her research on the interconnections of film and literature across various humanities disciplines.

Meredith Kneavel, Ph.D., is an assistant professor of psychology at Chestnut Hill College, where her scholarly interests include physiological effects of stress on the structure and function of the brain including neurotransmitter release, dendritic changes, and alterations in hormone release. She has also worked at Columbia University on determining the genetic causes of neurological disorders and the behavioral effects of known genetic alterations related to neurological disorders including ALS (Lou Gehrig's disease).

Lawrence C. Rubin, Ph.D., is professor of Counselor Education at St. Thomas University, in Miami, Florida, and a psychologist in private practice, where he works with children and families. His research interests are in the areas of popular culture, counseling ethics, medical sociology and play therapy.

Phillip Vannini, Ph.D., is a professorial research fellow in the School of Communication and Culture at Royal Roads University. He has published on theory and research dealing with popular culture, semiotics, and symbolic interactionism.

William Wingfield is a member of the graduate faculty for the Master of Arts in Liberal Studies at the University of Memphis. His research interests are trans-cultural comparisons, social philosophy and postmodern society.

Index